GUIDE TO ETHICAL PRACTICE
IN PSYCHOTHERAPY

Guide to Ethical Practice in Psychotherapy

ANDREW THOMPSON

University of Oregon

WILEY

A WILEY-INTERSCIENCE PUBLICATION

JOHN WILEY & SONS

New York • Chichester • Brisbane • Toronto • Singapore

This publication is designed to provide accurate and
authoritative information in regard to the subject
matter covered. It is sold with the understanding that
the publisher is not engaged in rendering legal, accounting,
or other professional service. If legal advice or other
expert assistance is required, the services of a competent
professional person should be sought. *From a Declaration
of Principles jointly adopted by a Committee of the
American Bar Association and a Committee of Publishers.*

Library of Congress Cataloging-in-Publication Data:

Thompson, Andrew, 1932–
    Guide to ethical practice in psychotherapy / by Andrew Thompson.
       p.   cm.
    Bibliography: p.
    ISBN 0-471-51347-4
    1. Psychotherapists—Ethics.   2. Psychotherapy—Moral and ethical
aspects.   I. Title.
RC455.2.E8T483   1989
174'.2—dc20   89-9136
                                                                          CIP

Printed in the United States of America

10   9   8   7   6   5   4   3   2   1

Preface

The purpose of this book is to provide an intellectual foundation for the ethical practice of psychotherapy. The proposed set of minimally overlapping, basic ethical principles is comprehensive, can support an infinite number of particular applications or derivations, and arguably underlies the extant guidelines. Current professional ethical codes are inadequate in two ways: one minor and one major. The minor shortcoming is that they are, to a certain extent, profession-bound, whereas the practice of psychotherapy and psychological counseling is not. More important, most of the codes are largely opaque in their basic underlying rationale. As a result practitioners can learn what to do or not to do in certain circumstances, but the reasons for such actions are only partially evident, and the sum total does not constitute an integrated, comprehensive, and coherent structure.

Consequently it is difficult to know how to extend any given principle or which, if any, principles to apply in an undepicted situation. Often one senses that a wrong was committed, that someone, for example, was misled or unfairly treated, but there is no apt way to address this within the code.

The search for a basic, readily understood and applicable, discrete, yet comprehensive, set of ethical principles (the ones that, in fact, already serve as the substratum of most ethical codes) led me to study those offered by philosophy. The following section of this book—Theoretical Background and Introduction—details this search and its results. The rest of the book is devoted to the application of these principles to the everyday practice of psychotherapy and psychological counseling. In the process I reference the relevant portions of extant professional codes. Thus the volume is both *descriptive* of current ethical injunctions and *prescriptive* with regard to classes of behavior that fall between the cracks of current codes.

LEGAL CONSIDERATIONS

The fear of legal reprisal has played an increasingly potent role in the practice of psychotherapy. The law is also often viewed, regrettably, as the arbiter of what is ethical or unethical. Because of this I have devoted a portion of almost all the chapters to the legal considerations that apply; some chapters are primarily concerned with these matters. Throughout the book, however, I stress that there is often a distinction between what is ethical and what is legal, and that it would be a mistake to supplant the one for the other. In some cases what is, or appears to be, legally proscribed or legally safe may not be ethical practice, and what is ethical practice may not be legal. In fact there are six different interactions between ethics and law:

1. *Ethical and Legal.* Following a just law
2. *Ethical and Illegal.* Disobeying an unjust law
3. *Ethical and Alegal.* Doing good where no law applies
4. *Unethical and Legal.* Following an unjust law
5. *Unethical and Illegal.* Breaking a just law
6. *Unethical and Alegal.* Doing harm that no law prohibits

The following are examples of these interactions:

1. *Ethical and Legal.* Keeping a client's confidences that are also protected by law from disclosure
2. *Ethical and Illegal.* Refusing to breach promised confidentiality even though commanded to by a court
3. *Ethical and Alegal.* Offering free service to impoverished clients
4. *Unethical and Legal.* Following the Federal Trade Commission's edict that professional ethics codes cannot prohibit the use of testimonials in advertising psychotherapy services
5. *Unethical and Illegal.* Disclosing confidential information protected by law from such disclosure
6. *Unethical and Alegal.* Promoting client dependency to enhance one's own feelings of power

Even the preceding lists do not adequately delineate the total interface between ethics and law. There are many gray areas in the law, sometimes caused, as described in Chapter 12 on the *Tarasoff* case, by variances in state laws. The professors of law and the attorneys I have consulted about gray areas have given me some advice that can be summed as follows:

"Consult your colleagues and then do what you decide is reasonable and right, and you will do what is legally defensible as well."

INTENDED AUDIENCE

This book is intended for all those who practice psychotherapy or psychological counseling, of whatever professional persuasion, as well as for those who plan to do so. Although framed theoretically, it is *applied* theory that reaches into every crevice of actual practice, or could do so. Readers should be able to determine, with some practice and discussion with colleagues, which principles to apply even in complex situations by acquainting themselves with the subject areas carved out under each principle in the book, and by the sample applications in each area and in the Appendix. Teachers will find that the Issues section at the end of each chapter can provide short essay exam questions.

TERMINOLOGY

I have freely interchanged the terms *psychotherapist, clinician,* and *practitioner* throughout the book. *Counselor* is equated with *psychological counselor,* and except in those few areas where the norm is to use the word *counselor* or *counseling* rather than *psychotherapist* or *psychotherapy,* these terms are also equivalent. I often mention both, as in "counselors and psychotherapists," simply to be sure some professionals won't feel excluded. I realize a case can be made for restricting the term *psychotherapist* to licensed PhD or MD practitioners, but I have chosen not to promote such a distinction in this book because the proposed ethical principles apply equally to all who engage in psychological counseling and/or psychotherapy.

ANDREW THOMPSON

Eugene, Oregon
October 1989

Acknowledgments

Thanks are due to a number of institutions and persons without whose help writing this book would have been a much more difficult, perhaps impossible, task. The University Press of America, publisher of my first book in this field, *Ethical Concerns in Psychotherapy and Their Legal Ramifications* (1983), generously allowed me to quote or adapt with modifications extensive portions from this book.

Both the American Psychiatric Association and the National Association of Social Workers responded promptly and fully to my inquiries for data relevant to the incidence of complaints they had received over the years about the ethical violations of their members.

The chapters on licensure and malpractice profited from the generosity of Dan Hogan (1979), author and copyright holder of several volumes on the regulation of psychotherapy, which works served, with his permission, as a rich source of apt quotations and proposals.

The American Association for Counseling and Development (AACD) and the American Psychological Association (APA)* granted me permission to adapt and reanalyze cases from their published casebooks. Situations 3, 4, 5, and 9 in the Appendix were taken from the AACD *Ethical Standards Casebook* (1982), copyright 1982 by the American Association for Counseling and Development; Situations 8, 10, and 11 are from the APA's *Casebook on Ethical Principles of Psychologists* (1987), copyright 1987 by the American Psychological Association (adapted by permission of the publisher). Thanks also are due to Ken Pope, chair of APA's Ethics Committee, who presented Situation 6 in a workshop in Portland, Oregon, in the summer of 1988.

In addition, the American Psychological Association has granted permission to quote passages from various ethical codes of that organization, including material from "Ethical Principles of Psychologists" (1981a), copyright 1981 by the American Psychological Association; "Specialty

---

*To avoid confusion of meaning, throughout this volume the acronym "APA" will refer only to the American Psychological Association. All references to the American Psychiatric Association will be spelled in full.

Guidelines for the Delivery of Services by Clinical Psychologists'' (1981b), copyright 1981 by the American Psychological Association; *Ethical Principles in the Conduct of Research with Human Participants* (1982), copyright 1982 by the American Psychological Association; and *General Guidelines for Providers of Psychological Services* (1987b), copyright 1987 by the American Psychological Association.

A number of law professors and attorneys were generous in their instructional time in response to my queries. These include Peter Swan of the University of Oregon Law School; Peter Ozanne, former professor of law at the same university; and Marc Hansen and Les Swanson, who are attorneys in Eugene, Oregon. Arnulf Zweig, professor of philosophy at the University of Oregon, assisted in the search for relevant references, especially with regard to the consideration of Self-Interest as an ethical principle.

Finally, I am grateful for the sustaining emotional support of my spouse, Marie-Anne.

A.T.

Contents

Theoretical Background and Introduction   1

PART ONE   AUTONOMY   13

1. Promotion of Autonomy   15

2. Autonomy and Dependency   31

3. Autonomy and Group Clients, Psychodiagnostic
   Testing, and Research   41

PART TWO   FIDELITY   53

4. The Nature of the Relationship   55

5. The Promise of Confidentiality   66

PART THREE   JUSTICE   87

6. The Principle of Justice   89

PART FOUR   BENEFICENCE   103

7. The Principle of Beneficence   105

PART FIVE   NONMALEFICENCE   119

8. Potential Harmful Effects of Psychotherapy on
   Individual and Group Clients   121

9. Regulation by Professional Associations 129

10. Licensure and Protection of the Public 139

11. Malpractice 153

12. The *Tarasoff* Case 168

13. Child Abuse 187

14. Suicide 194

PART SIX   SELF-INTEREST 205

15. The Principle of Self-Interest 207

Appendix: Sample Analyses of Cases 223

References 236

Author Index 249

Subject Index 252

GUIDE TO ETHICAL PRACTICE
IN PSYCHOTHERAPY

Theoretical Background and Introduction

In an ideal world there would be no need for ethics. In a less than ideal but harmonious world everyone would share a common view of ethics, of what is right and what is wrong. People would agree on what is good and what is bad, and they would establish mutual goals.

But in our Tower of Babel world there are multiple ethics, diverse formal and informal views of ethics, and thus differing, often irreconcilable rights and wrongs.

This state of affairs has been a boon to philosophers and others who thrive on intellectual confusion and relish the challenge of divining and hewing pristine principles that can turn chaos into order. Not a few of these thinkers have fashioned theories of right and wrong that have won followers and endured to this day.

Unfortunately, however, this theoretical diversity overwhelms the ordinary seeker for truth; one task for a book on ethics is to provide a structure for classifying and choosing among the various theories.

Fortunately this task has already been accomplished: Philosophers have recognized this problem and have sorted theories into various categories. A brief review of these dimensions will set the stage for choosing a particular orientation for this book.

NORMATIVE AND NONNORMATIVE ETHICAL THEORIES

Normative ethical theories are concerned, as the name implies, with setting ethical norms, or ideals for human behavior. Nonnormative theories are of two kinds: descriptive and metaethical. Descriptive ethics is used by anthropologists, historians, and sociologists when they explain *what is* or *what was* as opposed to *what should be*. For example, Margaret Mead (1932) discovered that premarital sex was considered quite appropriate and even encouraged in some island cultures, whereas it is considered a violation of divine will in other societies dominated by certain religions. These are facts and not statements of what should or should not be, albeit the facts arise from certain normative beliefs.

1

Metaethics is practiced by many modern philosophers and was part of the logical positivist movement in the first part of this century. It is devoted to analysis of cornerstone concepts of ethics and morality, such as "right," "obligation," "virtue," and "responsibility." These philosophers also analyze the logic of moral reasoning—how people arrive at what is right and wrong and justify their moral stands (Beauchamp & Childress, 1983; Braithwaite, 1950). Metaethics is further divided into two orientations: one toward formal, logical analysis of ethical terms; and the other toward informal, contextual, linguistic analysis of the ways those terms are used in ordinary language (Edel, 1973). A taste of formal, logical metaethics from Jan Narveson's book, *Morality and Utility* (1967) follows:

> What (if anything) are we saying about something when we call it good? By this time, philosophical analysis has reduced the area of reasonable disagreement to a rather narrow circle. It is agreed on all hands that to say that something is good is not, in the most obvious sense of the word "quality," to attribute a quality to it. It is, at least and in some way or other, to come out in favor of it, to recommend it. On the other hand, though goodness is not a quality, the man who calls something good is necessarily attributing some or other qualities (in the ordinary sense of "quality") to it. In calling something good, one is saying that there are reasons for preferring it, for being in favor of it, for using it, or whatever the appropriate attitude or activity may be. To say that there is a reason for preferring this particular thing is to say that it is of such a kind as to be preferred: to say, in short, that it is to be preferred because it is the sort of thing it is, or has the qualities it does. (pp. 266–267)

It is tempting to dismiss nonnormative ethics as being interesting but irrelevant to the present enterprise. However, descriptive ethics, by pointing out the range of various cultures' interpretations of right and wrong or good and bad, provides an indirect caution against quickly and wholeheartedly embracing any particular theory, set of principles, or perspective as being the final word in ethics. It also helps in the understanding of the moral views of others, such as clients and colleagues.

Metaethics also helps develop the realization that there is an underlying mesh in which people are apt to become entangled when reasoning ethically and arguing about right and wrong. Many disputes may be resolvable simply by analyzing the verbal context and the behaviors that accompany words and by discovering that the differences may be more stylistic than substantial. This approach also promises to enrich one's own moral perspective and enhance understanding of others.

Deontological and Consequential Approaches

Within the field of normative ethics there are two main divisions: deontological and consequential. The former is concerned with defining moral obligation or commitment. *Deon* is a Greek word meaning "that which is binding or needful" (Morris, 1981). Consequentialists also are concerned with this pursuit, but, as the name implies, the results of actions rather than the process are of prime importance.

Deontological theorists rely on a basic moral sensitivity or rational intuition to determine goodness and badness, right and wrong, whereas the consequentialists claim examination of the consequences of contemplated actions will determine their moral value. They separate means from ends in their analyses, whereas the deontologists see means and ends as part of the same unity.

The deontological approach is best exemplified by the theory of ethics developed by Immanuel Kant (1724–1804). Kant (1929) proposed a criterion for the goodness of acts, the Categorical Imperative: "Act only on that maxim whereby thou canst at the same time will that it should become universal law" (p. 302). Another criterion derived from this primary test is the Practical Imperative: "So act as to treat humanity, whether in thine own person or in that of any other, in every case as an end withal, never as a means only" (p. 309). This is akin to the Golden Rule: "Do unto others as you would have them do unto you."

In the Categorical Imperative the effect of generalizing of the act is the crucial issue; the Practical Imperative stresses the respect shown to others and to oneself and rejects the separation of means from ends in terms of their ethical significance.

One way Kant interpreted the Categorical Imperative was to establish certain absolute duties ("perfect duties," p. 302) that were to be observed on all relevant occasions *regardless* of apparent, anticipatable consequences of any particular act. These duties included the following: Never break a promise, never commit suicide, and never injure anyone else. He also established some "imperfect duties" (p. 302) that were to be observed, but not necessarily at every opportunity—for example, helping people in distress.

Consequentialism describes those theories that judge the goodness/badness of acts by virtue of their anticipated consequences. The definition of good consequences varies with the theoretician and includes such qualities as measurable physical pleasure, general pleasure, knowledge, friendship, health, courage, and happiness. David Hume (1711–1776), Jeremy Bentham (1748–1832), and John Stuart Mill (1806–1873) were among the most important founders of utilitarianism, the major branch of consequentialism. In their formulas for calculating goodness they emphasized both immediate and probable future consequences of an action. Maximum goodness is generally thought to be the greatest good for the greatest number.

To the consequentialists the nature of the act itself was considered morally irrelevant; it was only its consequences that mattered. However, this does not mean that immoral acts were likely to be considered as resulting in good consequences, as will be apparent in the next section, Rule and Act Utilitarianism (Beauchamp & Childress, 1983; Gelwick & Gelwick, 1986; Steininger, Newell, & Garcia, 1984). Jeremy Bentham (1970), whom Plamentatz (1958) described as "the most typical utilitarian of them all" (p. 38), wrote the following lines, which exemplify utilitarian thinking (italics are Bentham's emphasis):

1. Pleasures then, and the avoidance of pains, are the *ends* which the legislator has in view; it behoves [*sic*] him therefore to understand their *value*. Pleasures and pains are the *instruments* he has to work with: it behoves him therefore to understand their force, which is again, in another point of view, their value.

2. To a person considered *by himself* the value of a pleasure or pain considered *by itself*, will be greater or less, according to the four following circumstances:
   1. Its *intensity*.
   2. Its *duration*.
   3. Its *certainty* or *uncertainty*.
   4. Its *propinquity* or *remoteness*. (p. 59)

RULE AND ACT UTILITARIANISM

Should an act be judged only according to its particular anticipatable consequences within the given circumstance, or should it be judged according to general rules that define good acts? Is it all right, for example, to lie on a particular occasion because it seems likely that this would work out best for all concerned, or should one be concerned about establishing a bad precedent, of breaking the "tried and true" rule that "honesty is the best policy." Act utilitarians such as Bentham stress the importance of sticking to the observable and clearly foreseeable consequences in judging acts; rule utilitarians such as Mill stress the importance of possible future, general consequences of not following established rules for behavior.

Ironically, rule utilitarians seem close to Kant's position, despite their protestation to the contrary. Perhaps metaethics can determine the reality of these various conceptual distinctions. How great a difference is there, for example, between claiming that one should never be dishonest and that one should be dishonest only with great justification? Moreover, does absolute honesty really follow from Kant's Categorical Imperative? Isn't it possible that on occasion one would not only lie, but would will that others in similar or identical situations lie also?

Such considerations have led me to adopt for this book the theoretical approach described in the following section.

A COMPROMISE POSITION: W.D. ROSS'S MORAL INTUITIONISM

W.D. Ross (1877–1971) was a deontologist in that he considered rules to be primary and established separately from consequences. He differed from Kant in that he held that rules did not have to be invariably followed. He agreed with the consequentialists that anticipated consequences were relevant in judging which act was the best to perform in any given situation, although he differed from them in that consequences were not to be treated separately from, or considered of more value than, the preceding process.

His deontological approach was revealed in his claim that any mentally mature individual, upon sufficient reflection, would find certain ethical acts self-evident.

The categories of self-evident acts were referred to as *prima facie duties* to distinguish them from absolute, mandatory duties. Ross's list (1930), which he offered as probably incomplete, included:

Fidelity. Fulfilling promises, implicit or explicit

Reparation. Atoning for a previous wrongful act

Gratitude. Repaying services done by others

Justice. Preventing distribution of pleasure or happiness that is not in accordance with merit

Beneficence. Making the condition of others better with respect to virtue or intelligence

Self-Improvement. Improving one's own condition with respect to virtue or intelligence

Nonmaleficence. Not harming others, which is *prima facie* more binding than Beneficence

Ross recognized that in the actual world one's duty is seldom clear, even when one accepts the enumerated duties and is willing to act according to them. In fact, Ross speculated that in most situations several duties would apply and, to some extent, conflict with each other. These conflicts could be resolved only imperfectly by examination of the likely consequences of any given act. Ross considered consequences to be a natural expression of the act itself, rather than separable as the consequentialists treated them. "An act is not right because it, being one thing, produces good results different from itself; it is right because it is itself the production of a certain state of affairs" (pp. 46–47).

Ross also pointed out that the full set of consequences, present and future, was essentially unknowable, but this did not absolve anyone from trying to do the most right thing, given the circumstances with their inherent conflicts. He stated:

> The sense of our particular duty in particular circumstances, preceded by and informed by the fullest reflection we can bestow on the act in all its bearings, is highly fallible but it is the only guide we have to our duty. (p. 42)

This attitude or perspective is one that I hope will characterize the offerings in this book. Of the specific duties that I find most relevant to psychological care giving, Fidelity, Beneficence, Justice, and Nonmaleficence come from Ross's list; Autonomy is from the list proposed by Beauchamp and Childress in their forerunner to this book, *Principles of Biomedical Ethics* (1983). Contrary to Beauchamp and Childress, I have followed the lead of Karen Kitchener (1984) and have subsumed their complex of principles characterizing the professional–patient relationship (Veracity, Confidentiality, Privacy, and Fidelity) under Fidelity. Thus, the first five principles or *prima facie* duties are: Autonomy, Fidelity, Justice, Beneficence, and Nonmaleficence.

To these principles I have added a sixth—Self-Interest. This principle can be applied to individuals or, derivatively, to the organizations that represent their interests. The need for such a principle was recognized in Kant's writings. In his exposition of the Categorical Imperative, Kant (1929) noted that individuals have an "indirect" duty to secure their own happiness, "For discomfort with one's condition . . . might easily become *a great temptation to transgression of duty* [italics in original]" (pp. 277–278). In his *Metaphysic of Ethics* (1886), Kant pointed out that owing a duty to one's self is not a contradiction, rather just an extension of the imposition on ourselves of all ethical duties, whether to others or to ourselves. He specifies a number of self-duties including injunctions against self-murder and the unnatural use of self for sex. He also proposes that the primary commandment is "Know Thyself" (p. 257), in terms of being sensitive to one's conscience. One of the secondary commandments is "not to allow to go to rust and lay dormant the latent energies and native elements of his [Man's] system, whereof his reason might one day make use" (p. 261) This injunction to self-utilization is akin to Ross's duty of Self-Improvement.

More recently philosopher John Thomas (1987) notes: "In fact we do have moral duties to ourselves" (p. 20), among which is self-protection. The psychologist, Robert Perloff (1987), in his presidential address to the American Psychological Association introduced "the proposition that personal responsibility, in the service of self-interest, is an effective tool for enhancing personal well-being and, hence, for contributing to the public good" (p. 3).

It is obvious that self-interest affects ethical reasoning and behavior at every step of the way. Hence it is best to accord self-interest the place it usurps; otherwise our thinking in this arena will be obscured with unnecessarily hidden agendas. What is not let in the front door will seek entrance in the back. Acknowledging and legitimating the role of Self-Interest can improve our ethical analyses and promote ethical behavior.

I have followed the format of the other principles and divided Self-Interest into five components: Self-Autonomy, Self-Fidelity, Self-Justice, Self-Beneficence, and Self-Nonmaleficence. Throughout the book each of these will be applied, as relevant, in the discussions of the other principles.

ORGANIZATION OF THIS BOOK

Each of the six parts of this book is devoted to the particular decisions and practices that fit most appropriately under the aegis of one of the six principles. Some parts consist of several chapters, others contain only one. Every chapter ends with a list of the issues raised in that chapter.

Part One: Autonomy

There are three chapters in Part One. The first chapter points out that every clinician operates from a value-laden perspective, including views on what constitutes good and bad psychological functioning and what are appropriate treatments. It is shown that, by adhering to the principle of least intervention and providing meaningful informed consent, clinicians can *expose* their perspectives to clients rather than *impose* them. The role that advertising plays in informed consent and the current legal efforts to negate ethical guidelines for advertising are described in the concluding section.

Chapter 2 focuses on the interplay between promotion of clients' autonomy and the aspects of counseling and psychotherapy that inevitably promote dependency. Practices that promote autonomy or dependency are identified, including the use of deception in strategic therapy and in paradoxical techniques. The core issue in this chapter is how to minimize the creation of long-term dependency.

Chapter 3 examines how to preserve and promote autonomy in group counseling, psychodiagnostic assessment, and research. The impact and control of peer pressure and group norms are examined. Craddick's model for psychodiagnostic assessment is described. The chapter also highlights the role of informed consent in research, including research with minors and others who cannot give full consent.

Part Two: Fidelity

Chapter 4 identifies the major promises that frame the client–therapist relationship, many of which are implicit, rather than explicit. One major promise is that the therapist will work to help the client. I show how dual relationships, acceptance of gifts from clients, and implicit and explicit promises to third parties, including other therapists, relate to this basic promise.

Chapter 5 is devoted to the other major promise that characterizes traditional counseling and psychotherapy: confidentiality. This promise, although of secondary importance, demands a disproportionate amount of attention in view of its many complexities, including its regulation by law. When to release what information to whom under what circumstances is examined from both legal and ethical perspectives.

Part Three: Justice

Chapter 6 considers the principle of Justice. This principle is most relevant in making the initial decisions of what services to offer to whom. Justice is defined as a fair distribution of benefits, which is only of concern when the benefits are vital and are of limited availability. The claim of psychotherapy and psychological counseling to offer vital and scarce benefits, the criteria for fair distribution, the problems with applying the criteria, the impact of third-party reimbursement on the distribution system, and the problems of accommodating ethnic minorities and impoverished clients are examined in detail.

Part Four: Beneficence

Beneficence, also consisting of a single chapter, is portrayed as the ground in which the other principles figure, the bed in which they lie, because it is the core duty of help-giving professions. Its relationships to Nonmaleficence, to altruism, and to paternalism are examined. The beneficial aspects of record keeping, the issue of client access to records, continuing-education requirements for therapists, control of client–novice-counselor contacts, peer supervision for therapists, and methods of ensuring beneficial group counseling experiences are among the topics seen as most clearly related to this principle.

Part Five: Nonmaleficence

The seemingly disproportionate length of this part, comprising seven chapters, reflects society's concern with possible ill effects of counseling and therapy, as shown in the many applicable legal constraints and sanctions.

Chapter 8 sets the stage: It reviews the evidence that thoughtless, overenthusiastic, and incompetent practitioners have actually harmed their individual or group clients, largely because of the trust given them as "experts." Various kinds of psychological harm and ways of averting them are identified.

The role professional organizations play in regulating the various mental health professions is covered in Chapter 9. It asks whether a conflict exists between promoting the best interests of the profession and those of the consumer. The main factors that determine the effectiveness of professional regulation are identified, the available statistics on number and types of complaints and applied sanctions are reviewed, and trends are identified for each of the major mental health professions: psychiatry, psychology, and clinical social work. The issue of impaired therapists is raised, and the preliminary steps that are being taken in this area are described.

Chapter 10 describes the problematic role of licensure in determining who is qualified to practice psychotherapy and in protecting the public from incompetent and unethical practitioners. Are the established standards artificially high? Are they relevant? Do they unfairly discriminate against older applicants and against ethnic minorities? What does the present trend of licensing and certifying ever more groups, such as "Professional Mental Health Counselors," portend? Is Dan Hogan's registration system the solution? What modifications can or should be made in the present licensure system?

The role of malpractice suits as a way of regulating the practice of psychotherapy is reviewed in Chapter 11. It provides information to help in the understanding of this legal avenue and to undermine the crisis mentality regarding this area that seems to have taken over in some professional circles. The review includes a specification of the place of such suits in the legal system, a comprehensive explanation for the recent surge in malpractice suits, statistics regarding the more prevalent types of suits and trends in such statistics, an analysis of the four components that must be proven in such suits, and a set of recommendations for avoiding such legal actions.

Chapter 12 considers the precedent-setting *Tarasoff* case, its present status, and current and planned developments. It contains an analysis of such cases in terms of the ethical principles, showing how they dovetail, at times, with legal reasoning. The full analysis of the *Tarasoff* case includes the legal basis for the decision, the resultant pro and con arguments, the reasons for the variance in response to the decision in different states, and the case's current expansion in some states to the area of property damage and to counselors with master's degrees. The speculation as to whether *Tarasoff* should include AIDS victims and victims of sexual assault is reviewed. The chapter includes recommendations for dealing with potentially violent clients in an ethical manner that also provides some protection from legal liability.

Chapter 13 concentrates on the issue of disclosure of child abuse: What are the ethical and legal implications of reporting/not reporting? The harm that may result from either action is reviewed, and steps are suggested to help clinicians decide what to do if they suspect abuse.

The thorny issue of client suicide is the subject of Chapter 14. Is it ever justifiable to abet client suicide? How might clinicians inadvertently do so? Should clinicians always try to prevent it? What factors need to be weighed in making these decisions? How does the law treat suicide, and how can clinicians reduce risk of malpractice suits brought by relatives of the victim?

Part Six: Self-Interest

Chapter 15 presents the case for considering Self-Interest as an ethical duty of practitioners. A criterion for distinguishing Self-Interest from selfishness is proposed and applied to each of the component parts of Self-Interest: Self-Autonomy—promoting professional autonomy; Self-Fidelity—keeping one's promises to one's self; Self-Justice—getting one's due share of the benefits of being a professional psychotherapist, in the turf battle between the professions; Self-Beneficence—being nice to one's self, within reason, and engaging in self-improvement activities; and Self-Protection (Nonmaleficence to Self)—protecting the self from legal reprisals and also from burnout. There is a discussion of the possibility that fear of legal reprisals may lead to actions that substantially impair one's services to clients.

The Appendix poses sample situations, which are then analyzed according to the six principles.

PART ONE

Autonomy

If there is a single, overriding purpose of psychological counseling and psychotherapy, it is the promotion of Autonomy. Whether the client comes primarily for relief of emotional distress or for life enhancement, the intended treatment result is the maximization of the individual's ability to choose freely and competently how to conduct his or her life; that is, to be more goal directed and less controlled by fear or other emotions. Whereas members of other helping professions need only respect the autonomy of their clientele, psychological counselors and psychotherapists concern themselves with developing such autonomous functioning. Paradoxically, in order to do that, the client must often form a quite dependent relationship with the counselor or therapist, making it necessary to break off that dependency before the completion of treatment.

The following three chapters point out the many ways to promote autonomy and keep dependency in check. Chapter 1, after describing some general considerations and principles, focuses on specific pre- or early-onset variables of therapy that affect client autonomy. Chapter 2 reviews in-therapy variables. Chapter 3 examines Autonomy as it relates to the special concerns of group counseling and therapy, psychodiagnostic testing, and research.

CHAPTER 1

Promotion of Autonomy

THE THERAPIST AS A SECULAR MORAL AGENT

It is difficult to admit that the traditional view of psychological counselors and therapists as neutral third parties, objective observers, and change facilitators is a myth and, at most, an ideal that has never been and never will be reached. All individuals are captives of their perceptual system, which in turn is a result of individual genetic and environmental heritage. A small portion of that which influences every perception is conscious and malleable to self-control, but the major portion of what is perceived and conceived is inaccessible to therapists as well as to all other human beings.

This does not mean that we, as therapists, should not strive for objectivity, for neutrality; only that we should recognize the impossibility of obtaining it. It would be a disservice to our clients and a threat to their autonomy if we promoted the myth that we are completely unbiased, or nearly so, in our functioning as professionals.

However, that myth does exist, and it confers a special status upon counselors and psychotherapists. M.C. Lowe in his book, *Value Orientations in Counseling and Psychotherapy* (1969) notes:

> It is unlikely that our society will experience the complete moral breakdown that some alarmists foresee. Many still find direction in traditional morality, while others with sufficient self-possession are secure in a world which some find disordered and turbulent. The morally dispossesed commonly seek the help of a counselor or psychotherapist as a source of moral direction—often the only available human resource for those outside of the social order. Although the therapist does not usually consider himself a moralist, he is, however, one of the few whose moral authority the typical modern man can still accept. (p. 9)

Upon reflection it is clear that not only do some "morally dispossessed" seek the help of therapists, they are referred to such helpers by others in society. Those who seem to have lost their direction or appear unable to face or effectively cope with the stress of their existences are often placed in settings where they receive psychological care. Although these professionals do not purport to give "moral guidance" in the traditional sense of the term, they are expected to know what is psychologically good or bad and to direct or assist people to strive for and achieve "healthy" ways of thinking, feeling, and behaving. Not surprisingly, people who act in psychologically healthy ways also are more apt to act in societally approved ways—that is, morally good ways.

Diagnoses as Moral Judgments

One important component of the therapist's role as a moral agent, although, again, it is not usually thought of in this way, is the act of conferring a diagnosis on a person. Whether formal or informal, whether recorded or only in the therapist's mind, the diagnosis leads to a course of treatment that is peculiar to the diagnosed condition and that may impinge on the client's autonomy in a number of different ways. Perry London was perhaps the first to recognize these implications in his seminal book, *The Modes and Morals of Psychotherapy* (1964):

> Moral considerations may dictate, in large part, how the therapist defines his client's needs, how he operates in the therapeutic situation, how he defines "treatment," and "cure," and even "reality." . . . Students of mental health find that it is difficult to *define* such terms as "health," "illness," and "normality" without some reference to morals; and worse still, they cannot discuss the proper treatment of what they have defined without recognizing and involving their own moral commitments.

> The issue is the same whether the problem is a social one like prostitution or an apparently individual one like obsessional neuroses. Neither can be called an illness on the grounds of invasion by a foreign body or of the malfunctioning of specific organs. Nor do people die directly from them. They may be abnormal in a statistical sense, but this is hardly a basis for worry. Living one hundred years or making a million dollars is also deviant in that sense. The objectionable feature of these problems concerns the violation of the public moral code, in the one case, and the experience of apparently unnecessary personal anguish—in the other. In both, the assumption of a moral desideratum underlies the definition. (p. 5)

In truth, even the distinction between "violation of the public moral code" and "unnecessary personal anguish" is not as firm as Perry London portrays it. Charles Silverstein points out this problem in his monograph on psychiatric diagnoses (1984). He recounts, for example, the various disorders created by Benjamin Rush, the leader of the development of psychiatry during the American Revolution. Rush identified as medical problems such acts as lying, drunkenness, and crime. He also, being himself an avid advocate of the Revolution, referred to those who opposed the Revolution as suffering from the mental disorder of "revolutiona."

Silverstein claims that this tendency to ascribe psychiatric diagnoses to societally disapproved behavior is alive and well, especially in the area of sex. He notes that it wasn't until 1973 that the American Psychiatric Association declassified homosexuality as a mental disorder and that the American Psychological Association (APA) followed suit in 1975. Silverstein proposes that a similar fate should occur to all the paraphilias: zoophilia, pedophilia, exhibitionism, voyeurism, masochism, sadism, and the residual category of atypical paraphilia, which includes coprophilia (love of feces) and telephone scatologia (lewdness on the telephone).

There is no question that the behavior patterns characterizing the paraphilias arouse disgust and moral reprehension in most people and the "syndromes" that are not acts between consenting adults obviously have criminal aspects, but Silverstein claims that is insufficient basis for making them "mental disorders" with all that implies regarding the necessity and appropriateness of psychological treatment, perhaps even coercively applied. Just because these behaviors are morally reprehensible in our society does not mean there is something psychologically dysfunctional with everyone who engages in them. At the same time those individuals who are distressed about their own functioning in these (or any other) areas may have a mental disorder and can profit from treatment for it.

Thomas Szasz (1960) goes one step further—he sees *all* psychiatric diagnosis as supporting "the myth of mental illness" and argues that the patient should be charged with both the responsibility for and the authority for undertaking any treatment. Diagnoses are seen as ways of wrongfully transferring the authority and responsibility from the patient to the treating professional.

Martin Gross in his best seller, *The Psychological Society* (1978), takes a similar stance. He claims that psychiatrists and psychologists, by and large, create the illnesses they then set out to cure.

Silverstein, Szasz, and Gross may be radical in the totality of their respective positions but each of them has touched upon a moral issue of some consequence. Where there is insufficient basis to declare as a crime behavior that is morally repugnant to the dominant society or to the dominant members of society, there may well be a tendency to declare it an "illness." Thus people who practice or who relish imagining the practice of such behavior are identified as "sick" and "in need of care."

This identity in turn gives impetus to persuading, and perhaps even in some ways coercing, these people to get "treatment"—that is, it impinges on their autonomy.

Szasz has also put his finger on one of the important side effects of diagnoses, especially formal ones. The recipients are categorized in a way that is often conceptually foreign to them and thus are immediately at a disadvantage in knowing the appropriate response—that is, they lose some control over what happens to them. They cannot even cooperate without being taught how to cooperate in the treatment for their ascribed disorders. Ordinary, nonpsychiatric means for implementing change, which they could apply themselves without direction or assistance, are to some extent proscribed or replaced. Thus there is a real shift of responsibility from the diagnosed to the diagnoser, with a corresponding threat to the autonomy of the former.

Gross is also correct in his perception that it is all too easy to convince some people that their difficulties are unusual in the sense that they cannot be resolved as well by any means other than psychotherapy or psychotropic drugs. As compared with other cultures, psychiatry and psychology in our culture have been enormously successful at convincing people that a whole host of psychological disorders, ranging from "mental blocks" to psychoses, can only be accurately identified and treated by professional mental health practitioners. This attitude provides such professionals with considerable power to influence suffering inquirers that they indeed have something seriously wrong and need to be treated, perhaps for a long time.

Granting the truth of these observations how can one ethically proceed with diagnosis? The counselor or psychotherapist cannot operate outside of a societal context nor function at all without using his or her own ways of classification and models of human functioning, in order to understand clients. The very process of counseling or therapy requires a minimum conceptualization of clients' predicaments before beginning to help them, and the therapist cannot avoid conveying this understanding to clients. In fact, "insight" therapies involve implicit or explicit offering of alternative ways of self-conceptualization to clients, and therapy is often only considered to be successful to the extent that clients accept these concepts as their own and act on them.

Abuse of client autonomy occurs, then, whenever this process of diagnosis and communication results in the *imposition* of the therapist's values, moral outlook, or point of view upon the client, as opposed to their *exposition*, in which the therapist freely allows the client to make an informed, selective acceptance among useful perspectives.

PROMOTING AUTONOMY

Perhaps the best way to approach the task of granting the client maximum autonomy, given the nature of the client and the situation, is to analyze what the therapist can truly claim to be expert at and how this compares to clients' expertise about themselves.

Who is the expert—therapist or client?

On how the client feels
On what has happened to the client
On what is happening to the client
On what has worked and what hasn't worked in the past for the client
On the interests, values, and goals of the client

Although counselors and psychotherapists, as trained observers, may have good ideas about some of these items as well as some information for clients regarding their external behavior and its relation to their feelings or other experiences they may not be willing or able to look at, therapists, no matter how long they may have worked with various clients, will always have but an external, very limited, knowledge of their clients' day-in and day-out, year-in and year-out experiences.

What, then, does the therapist's expertise consist of?

Observations of the client's behavior during the therapy sessions and interpretations of such behavior
Notation of reactions to the client and interpretation of these reactions
Knowledge of ways in which thoughts, feelings, and actions may be distorted and dysfunctional
Knowledge of ways in which such difficulties can be overcome

This cursory analysis makes it obvious that for therapeutic change to occur, the two sets of expertises need to get together. It would seem that one way in which that can occur, which stresses protection of autonomy on both sides, is *cooperation*. This is opposed to an authoritarian model in which the therapist is the only expert. Public Citizen's consumer's guide on finding a psychotherapist succinctly states this viewpoint (Adams & Orgel, 1975):

A mental health professional has a specialized body of knowledge about the field which most consumers do not have. On the other hand, the consumer has a specialized body of personal knowledge without which the therapist's expert knowledge is useless. In that sense the consumer is an equal, and by entering into a negotiation as an equal party with the therapist, you set an important precedent which could have lasting effect on the progress and effectiveness of your therapy. (p. 37)

Principle of Least Intervention

With the mental stage set for promotion of autonomy, it is now possible to consider taking more specific strategies to accomplish this goal. The following passage describes one such strategy (Kanfer & Goldstein, 1980):

> While it is obvious that almost any person might benefit from psychological counseling or a helping relationship, it is essentially the task of the helper to intervene in the client's everyday life only to the extent the client desires a change. Once the jointly agreed upon objective is reached, the helper should either terminate the relationship or discuss in detail with the client the possibility of future change programs. Only if the client agrees to additional programs should they be undertaken. A prior problem concerns the question of whether any treatment should take place at all. In some instances, clients will seek assistance for problems that actually turn out to be common difficulties in everyday life. In such cases, for example, when a client is experiencing a grief reaction after the death of a close relative, information and reassurance may be sufficient. Similarly, parents may refer their children for assistance when, in fact, the child's behavior is not unusual for his age group. In such instances, behavior change programs would not be undertaken and it may be possible to terminate the interaction when reassurance and information are given to the client. (p. 15)

Those therapists who are not behaviorally oriented may find the language not to their liking, but the general principle of intervening only to the extent of the client's explicit agreement, and only when a genuine need exists, could apply to all psychological care givers.

Informed Consent

A complimentary strategy is for the therapist to provide potential clients with sufficient information about his or her initial evaluation, the treatment plan, possible length of therapy, and so on, in order that they will be in a position to make an informed judgment whether to be clients at all, and, if so, to what degree they will go along with the proposals for treatment. This approach is referred to as "informed consent."

Informed consent is traditionally conceptualized as consisting of three factors:

1. Fullness, adequateness of the information
2. Competency of the potential client to comprehend the information
3. Coercive elements

Fullness of Information

Any experienced communicator knows there is seldom, if ever, simple, easy transmission of information with any complexity from one party to another. Knowing what to transmit, how to transmit it, and when is a real art. The objective is clear—transmission of the essential elements of the proposed treatment—but determining what is essential and what is nonessential is no easy task. Compounding the difficulty is the necessity of accurately judging the degree of complexity the client can handle, the appropriate kind or level of language, and the client's readiness for the information.

A definition for *essential* is "that which is most apt to be important to clients in making their decisions." Ideally this means tailoring the communication to individual clients, which is not possible in any standard consent form. This definition has been referred to by Beauchamp and Childress (1983) as the "subjective standard" as opposed to the "professional practice standard" and the "reasonable person standard" (p. 74). It also requires the communicator to have a good idea of what individual clients would judge important, which is unrealistic because consent is obtained at the outset of treatment before the counselor has much knowledge of the client. Therefore, it is more pragmatic to communicate that which one would presume most clients would want to know and which they might well use in making their decisions.

The court, dealing mostly with medical malpractice suits, has alternated primarily between the two other standards decribed by Beauchamp and Childress: the "reasonable person" standard and the "professional practice standard." The latter standard refers to what is normal disclosure by professionals in the field, however adequate or inadequate that may be, and can only be determined by experts—that is, fellow professionals. The "reasonable person" standard allows jurors to decide what a reasonable person would consider significant to know about any given treatment in order to be informed about it.

As to the actual content of the communications there have been several proposals. Hare-Mustin, Marecek, Kaplan, and Liss-Levinson (1979) state:

Most therapy contracts specify some or all of the following: the methods of therapy, its goals, the length and frequency of sessions, the duration of treatment, the cost and the method of payment, provisions for cancellation and renegotiation of the contract, the extent of each person's responsibility, and the degree of confidentiality. (pp. 8–9)

Hare-Mustin et al. also recommend including a description of aversive techniques and techniques that might be at odds with the client's values, as well as a statement of whether family or other third parties are also going to be involved. Others have argued for inclusion of information on likely side effects of counseling, such as the disturbance of close relationships that might be expected if one member of a pair were to change significantly, or diminution of one's religious faith because most therapists are secularly oriented and most clients are religiously oriented (Bergin, 1980; Jensen & Bergin, 1988).

One additional item that the APA judges essential to communicate to prospective clients applies to counselors-in-training, and thus to their supervisors. In 1984 the Ethics Committee of the APA issued a ruling ("Ethics Statement Issued," 1984) to the effect that such counselors "should inform their clients at the beginning of a professional relationship if they intend to share information about their case with a supervisor or consultant" (p. 36). Otherwise sharing of such information would violate the confidentiality of the client.

Consumer protection groups such as Ralph Nader's Public Citizen advocate contractual relationships between clients and therapists. The proposed "Elements of a Contract" (Adams & Orgel, 1975) emphasize the establishment of mutually agreed-upon goals and a clear description of the services to be rendered, as well as "establishment of access by patient and Dr. to document which becomes part of medical record ... and control by patient over medical record and its contents and use of any information therein" (p. 39). Adams and Orgel predict that such contracts could be negotiated within one to three sessions, but they allow that some therapists, particularly those who "have traditionally enjoyed superior roles" (p. 38) and those who practice a method of therapy "where the dependent role of the patient is stressed" (p. 38), may not agree to such stipulations.

One major problem with including everything in the contract that the client and therapist "should" discuss and agree on before beginning counseling or therapy is that there is simply too much to communicate meaningfully, much less negotiate at that point. With many clients who are seeking immediate relief, such negotiations might only add to their distress. To some extent this can be ameliorated by carefully choosing the amount of communication presented to clients for immediate oral discussion and the amount given in written form to be taken home and read at their leisure. But the hazard remains that in the therapist's attempt to be "ethical" or to avoid legal reprisal for providing inadequate information, the client suffers rather than benefits.

Handelsman and Galvin (1988) point out that most modes of transmission of data to clients do not adequately protect the right of clients to *refuse* information that they are not interested in knowing or even desire *not* to be exposed to. This obviously takes place in a medical setting where many patients do not want to know any of the details of their treatment, being content to leave everything in the hands of the experts. Handelsman and Galvin have developed a written list of questions that clients can choose to ask or not to ask their therapists such as, "How does your kind of therapy work?" "What other types of therapy or help are there?" "How are appointments scheduled?" "What kind of records do you keep?" "What is your fee?" and "What is your training and experience?" (p. 225). Another advantage of this format is that the answers are given orally, although written information may also be available, thus making it more of a personal encounter.

This format may well have been inspired by an earlier survey that Handelsman participated in, assessing the practices of 196 psychologists in private practice (Handelsman, Kemper, Kesson-Craig, McLain, & Johnsrud, 1986). Most of the 104 respondents preferred to use only oral agreements; less than 30% had their clients read and sign written consent forms. The authors judged the average readability of the forms that were sent in as being "in the 'difficult' range, equivalent to an academically oriented magazine" (p. 514). Also the content was primarily limited to financial issues such as the method of payment and the policy concerning fees for missed appointments. A majority of the forms also described the limits of confidentiality such as potential danger to self or others and child abuse. No form covered all the limits. The authors concluded that the clinicians were probably attempting to avoid malpractice suits with written forms but were not satisfying the ethical requirements of informed consent. They further speculated that such difficult, incomplete forms may actually serve more to incriminate than to protect the clinician.

Competency of Potential Clients

With some clients, minors and those who are obviously mentally incapacitated, the issue of competency to give informed consent can sometimes be resolved by finding or appointing a representative of the client who would be likely to have the client's best interest at heart. This personal representative can then consent or not consent on the behalf of the client.

Recent studies indicate that adolescents aged 15 years and older should be afforded the same informed consent as adults. Belter and Grisso (1984) presented videotapes of counselors explaining first the various rights of clients and then the nature of counseling. The subjects, all males aged 9, 15, or 21 years, were tested 1 and 2 weeks later in various ways to determine if they understood what rights they had. The experimenters concluded "that by age 15, the average adolescent is fully capable of comprehending and exercising his or her rights" (p. 899).

Melton (1983) reviewed developmental literature and the recent tradition of the law on juvenile rights. He states: "In terms of competence to consent to psychotherapy ... there is evidence that adolescents have adult-like concepts of psychotherapy, mental health professionals, and mental disorder itself" (p. 101).

Nevertheless, whether child, adolescent, or adult, clients often enter psychotherapy at times of crisis when they are irrational to a significant degree. It is questionable that such clients are competent to give their informed consent until such time as they have had a chance to calm down and, in their initial contact with a counselor, receive some reassurance that things will be better. Also the most important issue, that of whether a counselor and a client can work together, is not discovered through pretherapy informed consent agreements, but requires one or more sessions to form an initial judgment. No written description of what to expect can substitute for direct interaction.

For these reasons informed consent that protects the autonomy of clients needs to be approached in a variety of ways and over a period of time. Some matters such as the financial arrangements, provisions for cancellation, usual length of sessions, and general confidentiality limits are probably best stated in writing and given to clients to take home and review at their leisure. Other things can be handled orally when appropriate, perhaps by the method proposed by Handelsman and Galvin (1988). Negotiating the goals of counseling or therapy may or may not need to be formally done and committed to paper, depending on the client, the therapist, and the therapeutic bent of the therapist; but in any case it should be recognized that establishing even preliminary goals may take several sessions, and that they may well need refinement or even renegotiation at later points. All this implies that the arrangement should make it easy for the client and the therapist to back out of the relationship until such point as preliminary agreements are firmly in place. There are other items that often can be meaningfully conveyed and agreed upon only after therapy has begun. These will be reviewed in the following chapters.

Coercive Elements

The third consideration in determining informed consent is the presence or absence of coercive elements in the proposal to initiate counseling or therapy. Some clients, whether they actually cooperate in any treatment, are clearly coerced to go to a counselor or therapist. These include court-mandated clients. Others are coerced indirectly because they know that they are more apt to be released from the institution in which they are involuntarily staying, or will receive more prerogatives in the institution, if they seek out and apparently profit from counseling. Considerable coercion can also exist for people who are out in society, free to come and go where they will. Spouses or other family members, employers, lovers, and even friends may threaten some sort of reprisal if the individual doesn't get counseling for problems perceived by these others.

One can, of course, argue that coercion does not negate informed consent, as long as the conditions under which the counseling will take place are made explicit, and the client understands them and has alternatives. Generally, however, the ethical solution is to reduce the coercive element as much as possible. Some therapists, claiming that therapy cannot take place if the clients believe they were forced to participate, will refuse to take mandated clients. Others prefer mandated clients but claim that they are able to find a common ground with the clients, thus facilitating true, freely cooperative treatment.

Client Referral: Potential for Abuse

It can adversely impact client autonomy when the referral procedure for psychological services limits information about the full range of possibilities and pressures clients to seek out help from particular providers. These are recognized as ethical problems in professional codes in several ways. It is considered a misuse of one's position as a teacher, employer, supervisor, or some authoritative role to offer therapy or counseling to one's own students, employees, and so forth, because they may fear that refusing such suggestions will adversely affect the already established relationship (APA, 1981a, Section 6a).

Receiving money from persons to whom one refers potential clients is also considered unethical because that will dispose the referrer to restrict referrals to those who pay for such referrals or who pay the most (APA, 1981a, Section 6d).

Often agencies or agency employees who are unable to offer required services are in the position of referring to private practitioners. In such cases knowledge of appropriate services and service providers may be restricted if agencies typically refer to their employees who are also in private practice (Kelley & Alexander, 1985).

THE ROLE OF ADVERTISING IN SETTING EXPECTATIONS AND IN CREATING NEEDS

Advertising, unethically done, can threaten client autonomy in two ways: It can deceive the prospective client-consumer into believing, unrealistically, that certain benefits are likely to, or sure to, accrue from participating in a particular treatment program; or, it can scare or otherwise persuade the consumer into seeking treatment for a condition that is not really serious or may not even properly constitute a psychological problem. Because such advertising misinforms, rather than informs, it is impossible for the consumer to make an informed choice whether to enroll in the described program.

Deception in advertising can take many forms. As outlined in the Public Statements section (Principle 4) of the APA "Ethical Principles" (1981a), one can misinform by inaccurately stating qualifications of the treatment providers, by misrepresenting the nature of the treatment, by selectively portraying the anticipated results (as by using testimonials from satisfied former participants), by leading consumers to believe that certain prestigious organizations or people are sponsoring the program when in fact they are not, and by distorting facts in other ways such as with omission and deliberate misstatements.

One can also lure consumers into seeking unnecessary treatment in a number of ways, ranging from "Everyone else is doing it, and you don't want to be left behind," to "If you [or your children] don't avail yourself of this opportunity you are likely to experience disastrous personal consequences in the future." An example of the latter type of advertising is reported in the *APA Monitor*. Carol Turkington (1986, May) recounts this true story:

> A busload of children kidnapped by terrorists were released at a shopping center, where their parents had gathered to meet them. A psychologist was there, too, passing out business cards that identified him as an expert on hostages. His material warned: "It is a well-known fact that hostages can suffer serious emotional delayed reactions. Preventative psychotherapy for your child is a must." (p. 32)

According to the same *APA Monitor* article, tacky and bizarre advertising is also unethical, not because of potentially deleterious effects on the client, but because it would reflect badly on the profession. One example given was the advertising of a newly licensed psychologist:

> [She] was looking for a novel way to advertise her new private practice. Her answer: a full-page ad in the local paper announcing an open house with "Psycho, the Crazy Clown," free balloons printed with her address and phone number, a "First Session Free" coupon and a door prize of 20 free sessions. (p. 32)

Another type of advertising that could threaten the autonomy of potential clients is direct solicitation, which is also forbidden by the "Ethical Principles." The example given in the *APA Monitor* is the soliciting by a well-known psychiatrist who gave a lecture on stress and tension at a state university. Several student assistants, while distributing brochures about his private clinic and other workshops he offered, approached some members of the audience and told them, "You look troubled. Perhaps some of this material will be helpful to you." (Turkington, 1986, p. 32). (This could also serve as an example of using threats.)

Dos and Don'ts of Advertising

One way of summarizing the ethical injunctions that apply to respecting and promoting client autonomy is to put them in terms of "dos" and "don'ts." Following is such a list:

Don't make promises regarding results of the treatment.

Do describe the objectives and goals of the treatment.

Don't make threats as to what might happen if the person doesn't receive treatment.

Do describe the objectives and goals of the treatment.

Don't claim unique qualifications for helping others (thus implicitly promising especially good results as well as making highly questionable claims about your qualifications).

Do describe accurately your relevant qualifications (training, experience, credentials).

Don't use testimonials or other highly selective evidence as "proof" of the value of your program.

Do refer to replicated, scientific studies that bear upon your program.

Finally, *do* describe accurately the main features of the procedures and methods that characterize your treatment program and services.

Legal Developments: Is Ethical Advertising Illegal?

An interesting twist has arisen in recent years: In the interest of consumer protection, legal cases have been fought and won that strike down the restrictions on advertising placed by various professions on their practitioners. For example, lawyers are now free to advertise their fees for performing standard services, such as the drafting of wills and uncontested divorces. This allows consumers to shop and save.

The focus has now changed to our backyard. The Attorney General of Arizona has successfully challenged the advertising restrictions in the codes of physicians, chiropractors, and podiatrists, and is currently engaged in challenging the advertising guidelines of the state's psychological association. The national APA Psychology Defense Fund is helping to fight this challenge. The suit charged that the psychological association was practicing restraint of trade by "unreasonably restricting advertising and solicitation of clients" (Turkington, 1986, June, p. 36). It is specifically alleged that psychologists are prohibited from "disseminating certain types of truthful and useful information" including data "on the comparative desirability of services and psychologists' abilities" (p. 36).

It appears that Arizona's Attorney General believes that psychologists know facts about each other's services that are meaningful and could be shared to the benefit of the consumer. But reliable and significantly comprehensive data on the desirability of services and practitioner abilities are simply not available and may never be available in view of the difficulties of collecting such information. There is no systematic evaluation of the abilities of various psychologists; even the national qualifying exams for psychologists, for example, sample the knowledge the candidates have in various areas, but this knowledge is often only tangentially related to their actual competencies and practices. Some therapists may gain a reputation based on certain exceptionally successful or unsuccessful cases, or on how impressive they are in their contacts with each other, but their day-in, day-out functioning with clients and the "desirability" of their services are other considerations altogether.

Texas has already enacted a law that allows for direct advertising and permits competitive bidding by licensed practitioners as long as it is not false, misleading, or deceptive (Licensed Professional Act of 1981, cited in Mappes, Robb, & Engels, 1985). Whether this law poses an ethical problem will depend on how it is interpreted. On the surface mentioning prices for services would not seem to be unethical, and certainly prohibiting misleading and erroneous ads is in the spirit of ethical limitations as well.

Much more threatening to ethical advertising is the stance taken by the Federal Trade Commission (FTC). This commission has demanded that professional health organizations remove certain sections of their ethical codes, contending that these sections illegally restrain competition in delivery of services and the sale of products and publications (Bales, 1988, March). With respect to the "Ethical Principles" of the APA (1981a), the FTC takes exception to the prohibitions against using testimonials from clients, advertising of unique abilities, advertising that appeals to client fears or anxieties, comparison of relative desirability of services, direct solicitation of clients, receiving compensation for referrals of clients, and offering competitive services to clients of other professionals. Removing these limitations would gut the code of many of its essential sections, yet the APA apparently has already acceded to these requests: "APA counsel Donald Bersoff pointed out that the association 'in effect has already done most of what the FTC wants; it just hasn't formalized it'" (Bales, 1988, March, p. 19). This is in spite of the opinion of the APA Ethics Committee: "The Federal Trade Commission can be interpreted as taking the stance that anything short of fraud is appropriate and legal" (Ethics Committee of the American Psychological Association, 1985, p. 696).

ISSUES

Can therapists and counselors be morally objective?
What moral judgments do they have to make to function in their profession?

Psychodiagnosis

Is diagnosis a value-laden process?
Are diagnoses of sexual deviations disguised vehicles for imposing society's disapproval of certain behaviors?
Do diagnoses take the responsibility for the treatment away from the patient?
Do therapists create the illnesses they then set out to cure?
What expertise do clients possess? Does their expertise necessitate that they be equal partners in a cooperative enterprise?
Who should decide how much treatment or intervention is necessary?

Informed Consent

What information should clients receive prior to and early in treatment?
How and when can such information best be transmitted?

How should information be transmitted when clients are too young or otherwise unable to comprehend fully the proposed treatment?

What role does coercion play in informed consent?

In what ways can referral of clients for counseling or therapy impose on client autonomy?

What are the ethical guidelines for advertising? The legal guidelines? Do they conflict?

CHAPTER 2

Autonomy and Dependency

DEPENDENCY IN THE THERAPIST–CLIENT RELATIONSHIP

Once the consumer becomes a client the major threat to his or her autonomy is that of becoming overly dependent on the therapist. Any collaborative relationship involves some dependence on the other party to fulfill his or her part of the bargain. Thus clients, provisionally at least, trust therapists to apply their skills and knowledge to help them, and therapists trust clients to provide sufficient information about themselves and their situation so they will know how to proceed. They also expect clients to pay whatever fees may be agreed upon. These factors alone ensure that there is a built-in mutual dependency.

However, because the personal disclosure is one-sided, and because the therapists are presumed to be experts in psychological functioning, the personal relationship between therapists and their clients soon develops a power differential that makes the clients more vulnerable to reactions of their therapists. Should, for example, a therapist appear quite troubled and concerned about some revelation, classifying it as a major problem that the client must overcome, then it would be difficult for even the most hardy client not to accept that judgment, albeit he or she was not previously of that opinion. Often only a counterjudgment by another therapist would be likely to free the client to form an independent opinion in the matter. Furthermore, the more time spent in therapy, and the more client effort expended to overcome the alleged difficulty, the more investment both the client and the therapist would have in continuing to treat this area as a serious problem.

To go one step farther, the more "psychological problems" that are discovered, and the more therapists treat them as needing the specific treatment that therapy provides, the more likely clients are to believe that they need therapy, perhaps indefinitely. Martin Gross (1978) has referred to such clients as "therapy addicts," people who have become convinced that they cannot function without therapy. The presence of such a phenomenon in our society is attested to by the many jokes about people who must check out trivial decisions with "their shrink" before proceeding.

If, then, therapists wish to preserve and promote the autonomy of their clients as much as possible, it behooves them to become alert to those practices that promote dependency and to try to minimize or avoid them. It is also important to identify practices that promote autonomy and to invoke them whenever possible, although not at the risk of jeopardizing the therapy.

I am *not* saying that dependency-promoting practices are unethical per se and autonomy-promoting ones are ethical; rather simply that given the overreaching goal of promoting autonomy, clinicians should sensitize themselves to which practices promote which tendency. It may well be that dependency needs to be deliberately cultivated and structured by the therapist at certain points in the therapy as an interim step to promoting the client's autonomy.

The following sections describe some of the more prevalent examples of both types of practices.

DEPENDENCY-PROMOTING PRACTICES

The single most pervasive way of promoting dependency is also the most subtle and probably the most powerful: It is the assumption by the therapist of all the little decisions regarding the minute-to-minute course of therapy, such as when to introduce, when to break off, and when to pursue a topic. Making such decisions is the therapist's job; yet to some degree this responsibility can and probably should be referred to the client. For example: A client suddenly tenses and becomes tight-lipped at the mention of his father. Should the therapist gently prod the client to talk more about this relationship or should he or she drop it for now, as it would seem the client would prefer? A third choice would be to defer this issue to the client: "It seems to me that your relationship with your father is a sensitive area for you—would you want to talk about it now, or come back to it later?" Frequent posing of such questions draws the client into the therapy relationship as more of an equal partner, and, in this way, is consistent with promotion of client autonomy.

Other specific practices that promote dependency include mystification, ambiguity, highly structured techniques, "hard sell" approaches, reassurance, friendship, client advocacy, and deception. The following sections contain slightly edited descriptions of these practices and the ways they can promote dependency; they are taken from my earlier book on ethics (Thompson, 1983, pp. 38–41).

Mystification

As a general rule, the less clients understand of what is going on and why, the less capable they are of exercising their own judgment about what happens to them. Thus dependency is enhanced by any technique or approach that incorporates mystification (Hare-Mustin et al., 1979). For many clients or potential clients there is a certain attractiveness about little-understood techniques or therapies, especially if they promise to release untapped powers or break through to long-repressed parts of themselves. There is a corresponding temptation for the therapist who is seeking fame or fortune to "cash in" on such tendencies, and it is hard for even the most ethical therapist to resist the shamanlike role enjoyed by persons who administer such techniques.

A case in point is hypnotism. Since its origin as "animal magnetism," hypnotism has often been considered a sort of magical cure by laypeople and sometimes professionals as well. Freud experimented with its use and discarded it as being too inconsistent and sometimes counterproductive in its effectiveness. Today it has made a comeback, albeit the emphasis has changed from achieving deep trance states, which many people are unwilling or unable to achieve, to relaxed passivity and receptivity. Regardless of its depth, the desired state is one of increased suggestibility to whatever doctrine or instructions the therapist wishes to convey—that is, a state of high dependency. This is not to say that the subject completely relinquishes self-control, only that the control of the therapist relative to the client is enhanced.

There are a number of ways of augmenting client control and reducing mystification in hypnosis. One way is to thoroughly explain what the client can expect and correct misapprehensions. It can be pointed out, for example, that hypnosis can be self-initiated and utilized in learning self-control (Katz, 1979; Redd, Andresen, & Minagawa, 1982). Clients can preapprove the basic hypnotic suggestions and can learn to self-induce hypnosis via audiotape recordings that they take home with them. Finally each session can be debriefed to clarify exactly what happened and why and to give the client the opportunity to choose whether to repeat the experience. Similar precautions can be taken with any other technique that has special potential for misuse.

Ambiguity

Both ends of the structured-unstructured dimension are antithetical to autonomous functioning. Any method characterized by a deliberately induced, high degree of ambiguity can promote dependency because clients, in their anxious search for the "right" thing to say or do, will be disposed to look for subtle cues from the therapist and thus will be highly susceptible to such cues. The psychoanalytic techniques of free association and dream interpretation, in conjunction with the relatively unresponsive and perhaps out-of-sight therapist clearly utilize ambiguity. The frequency of sessions and the length of the overall therapy in classical psychoanalysis also contribute to the possibility that the client will become highly dependent on the therapist during the course of therapy.

Highly Structured Techniques

Any step-by-step, therapist-guided approach, whether it be part of behavior modification, Gestalt therapy, neurolinguistic programming, or any other approach or therapy, is dependency-promoting insofar as it inhibits clients from exercising their own judgment once the procedure has been initiated. This can be somewhat attenuated if the proposed procedure is accompanied by a full description, explanation of purpose, and provision of alternatives. Advice-giving or "homework" assignments are also conducive to dependency, especially when the supporting rationale is omitted.

"Hard Sell"

Cognitive restructuring therapies such as Ellis's Rational Emotive Therapy (RET) can also be practiced so as to promote dependence on the therapist's judgment as to what is "rational" and thus "right" as opposed to what is "irrational." This occurs when therapists, secure in their beliefs that they know what is best for their clients to believe, engage in forceful "hard sell" approaches designed to correct the allegedly faulty beliefs of their clients. For example, as Mahoney points out (1974), RET implicitly assumes that it is always irrational to be extremely upset, yet there is nothing self-evident about this premise.

Reassurance

Offering of evaluative comments, whether in the form of reassurance or of criticism, also tends to promote dependency in established relationships. For example, reassurances to clients such as "It will be all right" or "Things will get better" put therapists in the role of knowing what the future holds for their clients, thus diminishing clients' own judgments about the matter in focus. Even such congratulatory statements as "You handled that much better this time" and "You have really made progress" tend to accentuate therapists' expertise and to threaten the substitution of their perspective for that of their clients.

Friendship

It also promotes dependency to incorporate elements of friendship, such as therapist self-disclosure and physical expressions of affection and comfort, into the client-therapist relationship. The discussion of Fidelity (Part Two) explores the ramifications of establishing full dual relationships; for now, insofar as client relationships with their therapists become substitutes for other relationships, rather than providing support in establishing new ones, clients are made dependent on their therapists.

Client Advocacy

Intercession by third parties on behalf of individual clients, when it may be presumed that they could have accomplished much the same thing by themselves, albeit with some skills training and support, is also obviously dependency-building. This should be separated from intercession or political activity on behalf of clients as a group or as an unfairly treated class. Such activity is advocated by many practitioners as being a social and ethical responsibility of their professions.

Deception

The final collection of practices that promote dependency are those that involve the therapist's deliberate deception of the client. "Strategic" therapists, for example, who operate on the ethical theory that the means justify the end, freely admit to fooling or tricking their clients into actions that will break the vicious cycles of thoughts, actions, and emotions constituting their problems in living. Insight is irrelevant; what is important is that the therapist-chosen strategically selected intervention works. Haley (1970) describes an intervention by the late Milton Erikson in which he, unbeknown to his clients, arranged for an encounter between a very shy, isolated client and two other clients, a man and a wife who were very sociable. As the story goes, a friendship began, flourished, and contributed greatly to the socialization of the shy client. Although the clients later discovered that they all had the same therapist, Haley's description did not disclose whether they ever realized that their meeting was anything but a chance encounter; certainly Erikson set it up so that they would initially perceive it as accidental.

Other deceptive techniques include the armamentarium of paradoxical intentions, commands, and other techniques that have recently been disseminated in a spate of books for professional therapists. When a client, for example, receives a command to perform a particular action, and the rationale for doing so is designed to be effective, but not truthful, the client is being deceived. Deceived clients lack the information to make autonomous decisions. It has been argued that such techniques are not substantially different in kind or in ethicality from most other therapeutic interentions; and, in fact, not using them with certain types of resistant clients may actually be a form of malpractice. (Brown & Slee, 1986). Haley (cited in Wendorf & Wendorf, 1985) has also argued that many indirect manipulations, such as "paradoxes" are harmless, helpful, and often transparent to the clients. One concern, however, that has received less attention is the effect upon the therapists themselves. Wendorf and Wendorf argue that the therapists risk thinking of themselves as "benevolent societal decision makers, culturally sanctioned parents for the problematic," and even "all-knowing and all-powerful healers" (p. 449). They also claim that deceptive paradoxes are unnecessary, because literal truth is just as efficacious.

Illegal Dependency

In certain unusual circumstances client dependency on his or her therapist will be found illegal. This is most apt to occur if the therapist is named as a beneficiary in the will of a deceased client and relatives contest this on the grounds that the therapist exercised "undue influence" to obtain this bequest. Also parents who have lost substantial control over their children who are or have been in therapy may charge undue influence or child enticement. There may even be charges of alienation of affection by spouses who perceive the therapist as replacing them. (Schwitzgebel & Schwitzgebel, 1980).

AUTONOMY-PROMOTING PRACTICES

The most general way of promoting client autonomy throughout the course of counseling is to avoid doing for clients what they can do for themselves. This extends to actively soliciting client input on decisions affecting the choice of focus, treatment procedures, and any other aspect that may affect what happens to them during counseling. Some more specific techniques follow.

Introduction of New Techniques

It has been proposed that counselors ought to solicit their client's consent before engaging in new techniques, especially experimental ones (American Association for Counseling and Development, 1988, Section B: 15) or ones that might be at odds with the client's values (Hare-Mustin et al., 1979).

Some techniques, however, such as deliberate provocation of clients' anger in order to access the true emotions and beliefs of involuntary clients (Farrely & Brandsma, 1974), would have their value destroyed by asking clients beforehand to provide their informed consent to the technique. Even getting the general permission of such clients to use various procedures without first explaining them would be unrealistic. Such deceptive techniques are justified by appeal to other, presumably overriding principles, such as Beneficence or Nonmaleficence.

The Client as a Personal Scientist

Mahoney (1974) has described a whole cluster of various autonomy-promoting techniques and procedures that fit into his theoretical approach but can also be incorporated either singly or in combination with many other approaches. He refers to his cognitive-behavioral model as making clients into their own personal scientists; that is, clients are taught to view themselves objectively and to try out in an scientifically experimental manner various ways of changing their lives.

This model portrays the therapist as a "technical consultant" who instructs clients how to delineate and analyze representative problems of personal adjustment, thus making them independent of the therapist in dealing with future situations. The therapist typically elicits the faulty beliefs of clients through a process akin to the one Socrates reportedly used in his search for truth. An example of a Socratic Dialogue follows (adapted from Thompson, 1983, pp. 43–44):

CLIENT: Well, I got rejected again.

THERAPIST: What do you mean, "rejected"?

CLIENT: I asked a girl out, and she said no.

THERAPIST: Did you ask her to someplace in particular?

CLIENT: Not exactly, I just asked if she liked to ski.

THERAPIST: Did you tell her you wanted to take her skiing?

CLIENT: No, I thought she would know that without my having to ask.

THERAPIST: So you neither clearly stated your interest in doing anything with her nor did you ask her to do anything in particular?

CLIENT: Yeah, you're right. I never thought of it that way. I guess I didn't put myself on the line in any way.

Mahoney also recommends that therapists, as consultants, do not offer *interpretations* of client data, but rather *hypotheses*, which they encourage their clients to try on for size, perhaps by engaging in experimental behavior that confirms or disproves the value and accuracy of a particular way of thinking and acting. This is in contrast to the therapists' conveying "truths" that they are privy to and that their clients will accept if the timing is right.

In Mahoney's model solutions or resolutions to various problem situations are multiple, rather than singular, and are reached by brainstorming and experimentation.

Finally, the model recommends that the termination of the therapy process be a fading out, rather than an abrupt cessation of regular sessions. Thus, a client may change from once weekly, to once every 2 weeks, to once a month, and then finally to 6-month or 1-year follow-ups. This policy allows clients the necessary time to try out their new insights and behaviors, and to work out any kinks or unforeseen interferences.

Timely Termination

Regardless of whether the termination is a fading out or a more abrupt cessation, it is important that it take place as soon as it is clear that further counseling or therapy is of dubious value, in accordance with the principle of least intervention. This is recognized in the *Ethical Standards* of the American Association for Counseling and Development (1988, Section B: 12). It is also stated in Principle 6e of "Ethical Principles of Psychologists" (APA, 1981a):

> Psychologists terminate a clinical or counseling relationship when it is reasonably clear that the consumer is not benefiting from it. They offer to help the consumer locate alternative sources of assistance.

CULTS FOR PSYCHOTHERAPISTS

Ironically, therapists themselves are not immune from forming overly dependent relationships with their clients when they need reassurance that they are doing a good job in order to feel good about themselves. Therapists may also develop overly dependent relationships by being members of close-knit therapy groups headed by a "master" therapist. Temerlin and Temerlin (1982) investigated five different therapy cults and treated 17 therapists who were members of these cults, including 13 clinical psychologists, 2 social workers, and 2 psychiatrists. The cult leaders, described as "charismatic" and very self-assured, were able to gain such ascendacy that they freely commanded members to perform household chores and dictated members' choice of friends and associates, even of marriage partners. At first it may be difficult to conceive this happening to professional psychotherapists, but it becomes more understandable when one considers the lack of tangible success in such work, the bewildering choice of theoretical models and techniques, the overwhelming amount of potentially relevant professional literature, and the need for referrals from other therapists to start and perhaps even to survive in private practice.

INFORMED CONSENT DURING THERAPY: CLIENT EXPECTATIONS

One way to provide clients with accurate information about the role of the therapist and their respective counterroles, is to disabuse them of inaccurate expectations regarding these roles and therapy itself. Some clients, having been seen before by other counselors in other institutions or settings, will expect much the same type of service. Others will have been influenced by what friends or family have said about the counseling they received or by movies they have seen or books they have read, and so forth. Still others will project onto the counselor and the counseling what they want to be true or, perhaps, what they fear will be true. All these expectations are bound to be inaccurate, the only question is, to what degree.

There are several methods for correcting such expectations. First, they can be anticipated in some cases. For example, the therapist can anticipate that clients who know they are going to see counselors-in-training may expect that these counselors will be less apt to be "professional," less competent, more vulnerable to criticism, more manipulable, more like peers, and therefore more easily persuaded to be friends as well as or instead of counselors. Not all such expectations are erroneous in general, but they may be in particular cases, and certainly counselors can be alert to the subtle cues that clients are looking for a friend or a lover, rather than a professional relationship, and act quickly to dispel such notions.

Clients who were previously seen for long-term therapy but are now in a setting that emphasizes short-term therapy need to learn this fact as soon as possible. Or perhaps the therapist makes the judgment that a client could profit more from short-term therapy this time round, even though long-term is available; the client would need for this to be explained early on in order to adjust to the different pace gracefully and quickly.

Most expectations cannot be anticipated. The sharp observer can detect them though. For example, in doing marital counseling, you notice that the two spouses look to you, the counselor, when talking about each other, as if the partner weren't present. From this and other cues, you hypothesize that they expect your role to be that of a go-between and a referee. What you do with this hypothesis is up to you and your judgment of the most effective intervention. You might simply express it as a hypothesis and ask the clients if it is true. You could ask them to look at each other instead of you when talking about each other, and to avoid the third person pronouns of "she" and "he." You could decide to accept the role they have assigned you for now and comment on it at a later time. Or you could do some combination of these things and several others. The approach that, ostensibly at least, offers most autonomy to your clients is checking out your hypothesis before proceeding. If they agree with your interpretation, then you can jointly and explicitly establish your reciprocal roles in counseling.

ISSUES

What feature(s) of psychotherapy create a power differential in the client–therapist relationship?

Are dependency-promoting practices unethical?

What are some common dependency-promoting practices?

What effect may use of dependency-promoting practices such as deception have on the therapists who employ them?

When is client dependency apt to be legally challenged?

What are some common autonomy-promoting practices?

Is there any proof that therapists themselves are far from immune from becoming highly dependent on certain others?

How does informed consent play a major role during counseling and therapy?

CHAPTER 3

Autonomy and Group Clients, Psychodiagnostic Testing, and Research

AUTONOMY AND GROUP CLIENTS

There are a number of important distinctions between individual counseling and psychotherapy and group counseling and psychotherapy. Some of these lead to different procedures or different emphases with respect to the promotion of the autonomy of the clients involved, as described in the following sections.

The dos and don'ts of advertising are essentially the same for individual and group services. The only difference is that group programs are far more likely to be described in some form of advertising, whether it is an actual ad, a poster, a notice, and/or a written description for distribution to people who inquire about the availability of certain groups. No written description, however complete, will suffice to provide adequate information about the nature of the group or its leaders, just as such a description cannot give individual clients the "flavor" of interacting with the therapist or all essential information about their role *vis à vis* the therapist.

Thus it is that professional ethics codes recommend screening interviews as a means of obtaining informed consent, and, as elaborated under Beneficence, as a means of selecting out inappropriate applicants (American Association for Counseling and Development, 1988; APA, 1973; Association for Specialists in Group Work [ASGW], *Guidelines for Group Leaders*, 1980, cited in Roberts, 1982). Sometimes the first session of the group is set aside for explaining the objectives and procedures of the group and acquainting prospective group members with each other. Those who don't wish to continue are then free to terminate at the end of the session without any sort of coercion. This, of course, can also be done in addition to screening interviews with the leaders.

In institutions such as psychiatric hospitals the patients have little choice whether they are members of therapy groups. The screening is done prior to assignment to a particular ward with its ward treatment program, or at some time after initial admission to the ward as a prescribed part of their particular therapy. This, however, does not obviate responsibility to describe the group's goals and procedures to such patients, thus enabling them, if they choose, to participate meaningfully in the group experience.

Once the group has started, another issue becomes salient—the allowable degree of pressure on individual members for conformance to group norms. In individual therapy only the therapist exerts pressure on the client to focus on certain subjects or to react in certain ways. But a group can multiply this type of pressure manyfold, especially for clients especially sensitive to peer pressure. To protect individual autonomy, the group leaders must intervene as necessary (ASGW *Guidelines*, cited in Roberts, 1982):

> Group leaders shall protect member rights against physical threats, intimidation, coercion, and undue peer pressure insofar as is reasonably possible. (Section B-1)

As explained in Chapter 8, unless the therapist provides this protection, some members may incur serious psychological harm.

It also protects autonomy to make clear that members can voluntarily discontinue participation in the group at any time, even as they freely choose whether to enter the group experience. Stressing this option, however, threatens the cohesiveness, the sense of working together, the sense of community that is essential to successful groups—that is, Beneficence is threatened for all group members. For this reason most group leaders ask that the members make some sort of definite commitment to the group, such as promising to voice any ongoing dissatisfaction with group functioning, and promising not to quit without first explaining why and allowing the other members to respond. It is an almost palpable experience when members are absent, if only late for a few minutes, much less leaving altogether, and the disruptive effect must be worked through before a group can again function. Different writers take somewhat different positions on this. Corey and Corey (1987), for example, although stating that individuals have the right to leave groups, also propose that such members agree to explain their reasons to the other group members before departure. Lakin (1986) points out that this ignores the likelihood that the group will be reluctant to allow a member's leaving.

Sometimes groups, especially "growth" groups, make decisions about their own activities based on the enthusiasm of the moment voiced by some of the more potent members—such as deciding to hold a marathon session, or throw a party, or try out some experimental procedure one of the members has gone through in another group or has heard about. What is the leaders' role when such proposals are thrown out and apparently accepted? From the standpoint of Autonomy the leaders should make sure that this, indeed, is the decision of each and every member of the group and that some members are not being stampeded into acquiescence. Also, to protect their own autonomy, leaders must individually decide what they think about the proposal and voice their objections, if any. If, in the leaders' considered opinion, it would be unwise for the group to proceed in the proposed fashion, then it is their responsibility to refuse to participate in, endorse, or enable such an activity in any way. Sometimes a cooling-off period is appropriate before making a final decision.

Lakin also points out ethical problems that arise when therapists form groups consisting of their own individual clients. Confidentiality is an issue insofar as such therapists may not be able to separate what they have heard in individual sessions from that brought out in group and inadvertently share the private material with the group. Also the participants will not be sure whether therapist-offered observations or interpretations originate from one or both sources. More important from the point of view of client autonomy is the danger that when the therapist fills the role of both group leader and of individual therapist, the client might adopt an attitude of "unqualified faith" (p. 460) in the therapist. Indeed that seems to have happened even with therapists who are themselves clients in the psychotherapist cults referred to earlier (Temerlin & Temerlin, 1982).

CLINICAL PSYCHODIAGNOSTIC TESTING AND AUTONOMY

One aspect of psychological testing particularly relevant to the practice of psychotherapy and counseling is the testing clients undergo to help guide subsequent therapy or counseling. Often psychologists and psychotherapists are also asked to assist in the determination of other decisions, such as eligibility for certain programs or benefits, the legal sanity or insanity of a person, child custody, and degree and type of brain damage. In most such cases the client is multiple, including both the person being tested and the referring source. How the two parties are treated—who gets what information and for what purposes and with what safeguards—is of ethical import, involving all the ethical principles.

Fidelity is involved in that the test taker receives promises regarding the use and confidentiality of the test results as well as the accuracy and value of the tests for both the test taker and the referrer.

Beneficence is an issue because it is often questionable whether the test taker is benefiting from the testing or only the referral source.

Nonmaleficence is a concern because inaccurate results, overinterpreted and otherwise misinterpreted tests, and misuse of tests can adversely impact both the test takers and society.

Justice is particularly relevant when test results are interpreted or used in such a way as to deny test takers benefits received by others who are actually no better qualified, or qualifiable (in the case where specific training can easily make up for test-detected deficits).

Autonomy is especially relevant to the test takers because it is their privacy that is invaded, especially by personality tests that ask intrusive questions (London & Bray, 1980), and because of their lack of control over the use of the completed tests.

It is my contention that Autonomy is the most crucial principle with regard to the treatment of clients who are seen for clinical testing. Justice is an issue in ability and aptitude testing used to determine access to employment and educational opportunities insofar as such tests may discriminate or be used to discriminate against ethnic minorities. But with most test takers who are seen by psychotherapists and counselors, this is not the issue. Moreover treating these clients so as to protect and promote their autonomy will further all the other ethical principles as well. One way to do this will be described after a look at a definition of the term "test" and at some data regarding clinicians' degree of use of such instruments.

According to the *Standards for Educational & Psychological Tests* (APA, American Educational Research Association, & the National Council on Measurement in Education, 1974), a test is "any assessment device or aid that provides a systematic basis for making inferences about people" (p. 2). The 1985 edition of this booklet identifies three broad categories of test instruments: "constructed performance tasks, questionnaires, and to a lesser extent, structured behavior samples" (American Educational Research Association, APA, & the National Council on Measurement in Education, p. 4).

Tests are widely used by psychotherapists and counselors. According to a survey of 500 clinical psychologists, "Both objective and projective tests are used by clinical psychologists of all major therapeutic orientations with substantial percentages of clients" (Wade & Baker, 1977, p. 874). Only about 16.5% of the 236 respondents to the survey claimed that they did not use tests in either diagnosis or assessment of the nature and severity of the problems or as an aid in assignment to treatment. Vocational counselors rely heavily upon interest, ability, and personality tests in the counseling process, and marital counselors have a rich diversity of different tests to choose from for assessment and counseling purposes.

How can testing be conducted in such a way as to maximize the test taker's autonomy? The easy answer is to obtain the client's informed consent to take the tests. An elaboration of that procedure is contained in the preamble of Principle 8 of the American Psychological Association's "Ethical Principles" (APA, 1981a): "They [psychologists] respect the client's right to know the results, the interpretations made, and the bases for their conclusions and recommendations" (preamble). It is later noted that this right to know may be abrogated if "an explicit exception to this right has been agreed upon in advance" (Section a).

At least one psychotherapist has taken this principle to heart and has developed a system that fulfills both its letter and spirit. Following is a summary of the procedures developed by Ray Craddick (1975) who had taught personality assessment and carried on a private practice for most of the 20 years preceding his article.

Psychological Evaluation: Craddick's Approach

When the individual being seen personally by the professional is not the primary client, but rather someone to be evaluated, the primary obligation of the professional is to perform the evaluation competently and forward the results to the requesting person or agency. The obligation to the person being evaluated is secondary and is restricted to clarifying the nature and purpose of the evaluation, not necessarily to providing the results. Ray Craddick's much more open, coooperative approach is intended to make such evaluations, whether imposed on or solicited by the clients, a beneficial experience for them. It is not clear how realistic it is to utilize this approach in all cases, one problem being that it may require more time than the evaluator is able to negotiate to be reimbursed for. This could conflict with the Principle of Self-Interest, notably Justice to one's self; however, it is worthy of consideration as a model method to approximate and adopt to the extent possible.

Craddick (1975) points out that referred clients often come without "ever being told the reason for taking the tests or else being told something false" (p. 280). For example, a client may be told the tests are for purposes of job restructuring, when, in fact, the employer is thinking of firing the person. Another problem is that referrers may ask the therapist not to tell the client the results because they plan to interpret them to the client, as they see fit.

Craddick's procedures forestall any such deception or inadequate feedback. He asks the client to explain the reason for taking the tests and what he or she hopes to obtain from them. He then clears up any misunderstanding about the nature and purpose of the tests. As each test is introduced, Craddick explains what it attempts to assess, often going over various portions of the test beforehand in this clarification process.

At the end of projective tests Craddick asks the client to select a card or object that best represents himself or herself and other important people in his or her life, then a card or object that represents Craddick, and then one that represents both him and the client. If the client asks Craddick to do the same, he complies, and says why, even as he has asked the reasons for the client's selections.

At the end of testing, Craddick asks the client to leave a list of questions that he or she wishes to have answered. In return the client is informed of the questions asked by the referrer.

When they next meet, Craddick asks if there are any additional questions. He then reviews these and the previous questions, answering them as best he can in terms understandable to the client. He then reviews his answers to the questions posed by the referrer and may even dictate his report in the presence of the client. "Thus if there are any points of disagreement between us, these can be settled or not, as the case may be, and included in the report" (p. 281). A statement of this agreement, or lack thereof, is added to the report. Craddick has, on occasion, presented the test results simultaneously to the client and the referring person, for example, to the parent and the child who was tested, or the patient and the therapist who requested the testing. This, he claims, encourages trust between all parties because no secrets are being kept from the client.

Is this approach appropriate for "fragile" clients, such as those who are psychotic? Craddick claims it is. In support of that belief, he refers to a case reported by Jung, who found that giving the results of testing to a schizophrenic woman enabled her to clear her pathology and leave the hospital, never again to be institutionalized. In general, Craddick believes his approach is unworkable only for the severely mentally retarded who cannot comprehend the reason for being tested and that such persons should not be tested. Indeed, if such clients must be tested, their interests can only be protected by others, perhaps by proxy representation.

One of the notable advantages of Craddick's method is that it establishes a working relationship with referred clients that can be utilized on future occasions, should they arise.

AUTONOMY AND RESEARCH

Although it is the rare psychotherapist or counselor who actively engages in research, it is also the rare one who does not profit from the research that is conducted. Some initial confirmatory research is *de rigueur* before most therapists will consider adding a new technique to their repertoire. One of the hallmarks of being a professional is awareness of the important developments in one's field, many of which are products of, or have been screened by, research projects. Singer (1980) has claimed keeping abreast of recent developments in the research literature is "a central ethic of the profession" (p. 372).

Although a full ethical analysis of research bearing on the conduct of psychotherapy and counseling would be peripheral to the concerns of this volume, the salient feature of such an analysis is the central role of informed consent. And informed consent is, as has been noted, one of the major methods of promoting the principle of Autonomy. All the other principles are also involved, but as with testing, requiring informed consent of the potential participants implements them most directly.

The two most important sources for guidelines on the ethical conduct of psychological research are the regulations formulated in the 1986 *Federal Register* by the Department of Health and Human Services (DHHS) and *Ethical Principles in the Conduct of Research with Human Participants*, which was published by the APA in 1982.

The most important distinctions made by both publications are between those subjects of whom informed consent is normally to be required and those subjects who do not have to be informed of the research in which they are participants. Except in field research informed consent forms are typically used with all subjects and serve as a way of recruiting subjects as well as informing them of the project. However such forms are not mandatory: There are two classes of subjects who do not have to be informed of their participation—those who are at "minimal risk" and those whose naiveté is essential to the conduct of the research. Of the latter, persons who are deliberately deceived as to the nature of the research project in which they are taking part are of particular concern.

"Minimal Risk" Research

Subjects who are at "minimal risk" are distinguished from those who are "at risk" in both the DHHS regulations 1986 and the APA research publication (1982), as well as in APA's "Ethical Principles" (1981a). Following is the DHHS definition:

"Minimal risk" means that the risks of harm anticipated in the proposed research are not greater, considering probability and magnitude, than those ordinarily encountered in daily life or during the performance of routine physical or psychological examinations or tests. (Section 46.102.g)

"Minimal risk" research can be exempted from the review process required by DHHS for projects that it funds in whole or in part. This process determines if proper precautions have been used to protect human subjects from undue risk. Subjects "at risk" are normally expected to give their informed consent before participation in the project. A list of the components of informed consent agreements follows. It is based on the DHHS regulations and developed by the Committee for the Protection of Human Subjects of the University of Oregon (1982).

1. A statement that the study involves research, an explanation of the purposes of the research and the expected duration of the subject's participation, a description of the procedures to be followed, and identification of any experimental procedures

2. A description of any reasonably foreseeable risks or discomforts to the subject

3. A description of any benefits to the subject or to others that may reasonably be expected from the research

4. A disclosure of appropriate alternative procedures or courses of treatment, if any, that might be advantageous to the subject

5. A statement describing the extent, if any, to which confidentiality of records identifying the subject will be maintained

6. For research involving more than minimal risk, an explanation as to whether any compensation and any medical treatments are available if injury occurs and, if so, what they consist of, or where further information may be obtained

7. An explanation of whom to contact for answers to pertinent questions about the research and research subjects' rights, and whom to contact in the event of a research-related injury to the subject

8. A statement that participation is voluntary, refusal to participate will involve no penalty or loss of benefits to which the subject is otherwise entitled, and the subject may discontinue participation at any time without penalty or loss of benefits to which the subject is otherwise entitled

9. If physical injury is a likely risk the following statement or an acceptable paraphrase must be included:

Should you suffer physical injury as a direct result of participating in this project, you may file a claim against the State of _____. Questions regarding coverage and claims should be directed to _____.

With subjects unable to participate meaningfully or fully in the informed consent procedures by virtue of insufficient background or intellectual capacity to comprehend what is being asked of them, it is legally required to obtain consent from parties who can legitimately represent their best interests. Normally, children's "assent" is required as well as the "consent" of their representatives (Reese & Fremouw, 1984):

> The National Commission for the Protection of Human Subjects of Biomedical and Behavioral Research suggested, normatively, that although children cannot legally give *consent*, they can give *assent* [author's emphasis] and researchers should ask for the assent of children 7 years old or older. . . . However, this recommendation may be overridden under special circumstances, if the intervention is clearly in the children's best interest and is permitted by their parents or guardians. . . . For children younger than 7, obtaining their assent is not mandatory, but the children's objections and wishes should be respected if possible. . . . These principles are now federal policy. (p. 866)

Capacity to comprehend is a problem not only with mentally retarded individuals; as information becomes complex, many individuals may be unable to perceive the essential features of a research project as it applies to them. Indeed, perhaps because informed consent has become a legal and ethical requisite in so many projects, the forms developed to accomplish this have become too detailed to be understandable. In one study, which is a model for its incorporation of ethical concerns throughout its design and execution, the authors discovered that "in the end, the patients had to deal with consent forms comprising a total of approximately 2,000 words" (Imber et al., 1986, p. 144). Recognizing this potential problem, the researchers instructed the staff to interview all patients individually regarding their understanding of the program and to give them time to consider privately the written materials they received, including discussing them with family members and friends.

Coercion: Subtle and Otherwise

So far this chapter has touched on two of the three components of informed consent in research projects: transmission of essential information and capacity to comprehend. Now a few words on coercion as it might apply to participants in research in psychotherapy and counseling are appropriate.

One way of coercing clients into participation is permitting them to think or to suspect that if they don't participate they may not be accepted as clients, or, if accepted, that they may get reduced or less complete service than clients who do participate. To forestall such implications the informed consent form should state quite clearly that participation or nonparticipation has no bearing on eligibility for full, complete service. Also clients should be informed that they are free to ask the researchers questions at any time or to drop out of the research without penalty.

If, on the other hand, the research is of paramount importance, and service secondary, so that service will be reduced or not offered at all to nonparticipants, then that needs to be spelled out unequivocally. This may very well be the case in academic settings, such as clinics run by psychology departments whose primary mission is to train future therapists and researchers, and part of the training is in doing research or in participating in experimental treatment programs.

> In service contexts, in general, special care should be taken not to exercise subtle coercion upon clients by giving the impression that continued services are contingent upon research participation. The investigator must make explicit which services, if any, are by necessity contingent upon research participation, for example, if no treatment is possible other than the experimental one. (APA, 1982, p. 22)

Can Deception Be Justified?

Obviously the concern for the autonomy of research participants is overridden when they are deliberately deceived. As Sieber and Stanley (1988) put it in their insightful analysis of the various types of ethical issues involved in research, "*Informed consent* [authors' emphasis] or respectful communication between the scientist or purveyor of science and members of society are [*sic*] at issue at each stage of the research process"; whereas, "Deception at any stage of the research process is disrespectful" (p. 54). Diana Baumrind (1985) goes so far as to claim that intentional deception should be proscribed in research, based on rule-utilitarianism that takes into consideration the long-term and broad-range effects of any particular policy. These include the damage to the fiduciary relationship between researcher and subjects because subjects no longer trust researchers; the damage to the profession of the researchers because subjects, who become suspicious of what they are told, begin to play the roles they think the investigators want; and the harm done to society because undermining trust in scientists also undermines trust in authorities in general.

Certainly there is cognizance of this argument (cf. APA, 1982, p. 38), but it is definitely a minority view. The long-accepted, still-continuing, and projected future attitude of psychological researchers is that deception is essential to investigate many important areas of human functioning. Put in terms of ethical principles: Beneficence (toward humankind as a whole or large segments of society) is more important than Autonomy (of individual participants) as long as Nonmaleficence to the individual, the profession, and society seem to be insignificant factors.

Before deception is employed, it is essential to determine that no feasible, nondeceptive alternatives will accomplish much the same thing. If deception is employed, the APA's "Ethical Principles," (1981a) recommends that the deceived subjects should be informed about the deception and the reasons for it, and the researcher should attempt to ensure that there are no negative, enduring aftereffects of such deception. This debriefing should take place as soon as possible after the conclusion of the subject's participation, with the proviso that the subject not have the opportunity to undeceive other subjects who have not yet completed their part in the research.

> Methodological requirements of a study may make the use of concealment or deception necessary. Before conducting such a study, the investigator has a special responsibility to (i) determine whether the use of such techniques is justified by the study's prospective scientific, education, or applied value; (ii) determine whether alternative procedures are available that do not use concealment or deception; and (iii) ensure that the participants are provided with sufficient explanation as soon as possible. (APA, 1981a, Section 9e)

However, it is acknowledged in APA's special booklet for researchers that debriefing with regard to deception may not always be wise, and allowance is made for not doing so on occasions (APA, 1982, pp. 41–42).

Another feasible way of ameliorating the loss of autonomy in some research cases involving deception is to have the subjects designate relatives, friends, or anyone else they trust to act as their proxies in deciding if they should participate in a research project (Soble, 1978). This is not the same as having a legally appointed representative, because the subjects do the designating, and they themselves presumably would be capable of choosing whether to participate if they pleased. This could be referred to as "proxy autonomy"; whereas debriefing could be referred to as "post hoc autonomy."

Despite the official concern and the voluminous guidelines for conducting research involving deception, it is questionable whether, in fact, the guidelines are being followed. Adair, Dushenko, and Lindsay (1985) compared the methodological and ethical practices of empirical studies reported in the *Journal of Personality and Social Psychology* (*JPSP*) in 1979 to earlier surveys carried out in 1948, 1961, 1963, 1971, 1971–1974, and 1976–1978 (the first three surveys were of the *Journal of Abnormal and Social Psychology*, the predecessor of *JPSP*). They found an increase in studies involving deception, from 14.3% in 1948 to 58.5% in 1979. Only two thirds of the studies involving deception reported debriefing the subjects afterward, but Adair et al. point out that journal editors do not require such detail. What is astonishing is that, at least in the kinds of research reported in this journal, deception of subjects has become the norm rather than the exception! Moreover the authors point out that multiple deceptions, usually deceptions about both the purpose and the task, were employed in more than two thirds of the studies. Under these conditions the long-range, broad, negative effects of deceiving subjects seem indeed likely to be realized.

ISSUES

What major differences between group and individual clients bear upon autonomy?

How can group pressure be controlled?

Do groups composed wholly or in part of clients who also see the leader for individual treatment create any special problems?

How do psychodiagnostic testing and evaluation involve all the ethical principles of psychotherapy?

Why might Autonomy be considered to play the major role?

What elements of Ray Craddick's approach to evaluation make it a model for promoting the test taker's autonomy? Is it a feasible approach for all clients?

When is informed consent not necessary according to ethical and federal guidelines?

How is "minimal risk" research defined, and why is it mandatory to determine if the category applies?

How can the researcher "inform" participants who are incapable of full comprehension of the essential aspects of the research?

In what ways can the researcher protect participants against coercion?

When might deception in research be justified?

What hazards does overuse of deceptive research entail?

PART TWO

Fidelity

Intrinsic to the nature of any collaborative relationship is the mutual exchange of promises. Each party, implicitly or explicitly, promises to contribute certain functions or services toward the desired result of the relationship, and the total set of each person's promises structures that person's role in the relationship. According to the perspective of this book, keeping these promises is an ethical duty for all concerned parties, but because the subject matter primarily deals with the duties of the psychological care giver rather than the care receiver, I shall refer to the promises of the latter only insofar as it is necessary to clarify the duties of the former.

Part Two examines the major promises that counselors and psychotherapists make to their clients, explicitly or implicitly, promises which must be kept or risk the loss of the working relationship. Chapter Four will define the major premise of the relationship, namely that the therapist will help the client. Chapter Five is devoted to the promise of confidentiality.

CHAPTER 4

The Nature of the Relationship

THE BASIC PREMISE: IDENTIFICATION WITH THE CLIENT

The basic premise of the counseling or psychotherapeutic relationship is that the counselor or therapist is to help the client. But, as seen in Part One, this help should not threaten the client's autonomy, but rather promote it. To do so, the therapist must identify the changes sought by the client and establish goals with the client that the therapist is committed to helping the client reach. In other words the therapist *identifies* with selected interests of the client, so that it would be inaccurate to say either that the client's interest is subservient to the therapist's or that the therapist's interest is secondary to the client's. To maintain this balance, contrary and competing interests have to be reduced to a minimum.

But the therapist cannot focus on and identify with just any set of interests or just any aspect of interests. Internally directed interests are the special domain of psychological counselors. They help clients to cope with anxiety, depression, anger, and other emotions more rationally, to become more in control of expression of their emotions. For example, a client may come for help in getting employment. The counselor, to help him or her, qua psychological counselor, would have to translate that desire, with the client's agreement, into determining what part of the client's thinking, acting, and feeling is, or might be, interfering with the quest for employment. Is the client, perhaps, so obsessed with the importance of getting employment that he or she views every turndown as a major rejection and spends days recovering before being able to try again? Providing information about the external job market may also be very important, but counselors who do so step outside their role of psychological expert and take on the role of job market expert, that is, an expert on external, nonpsychological subjects.

To take another example, suppose a male client asks, as several have asked me over the years, to help him become a successful seducer of women. He is very frustrated with his inability to get women to go to bed with him and is jealous of all those "other guys" who seem to "score" at ease. This is not a proper interest for a therapist, qua therapist, to identify with, not only because it involves exploitation of women, which is reprehensible, but also because it involves a change in the external state of affairs, rather than in the internal, psychological functioning of the client. The client may indeed, at least for a while, be quite happy if he becomes a successful seducer without having to change himself in any way. But unless he is willing to change internally, psychologically, and to risk the hazards of that change (he may end up having to struggle with true two-way relationships), a therapist, qua therapist, cannot help him. The client may find out that women are not responsive to him because he is unresponsive, insensitive, or unaware of them and of what they want; and, in order to become sensitive to them he will have the difficult task of learning to relinquish his focus on his own desires and frustrations. Again teaching him how to dress, how to ask for dates, and so forth may be pertinent to his expressed goal, and even to any changed goals, but it involves a different sort of expertise and training, that is, a social skills training.

As well as being psychological experts, therapists can appropriately have several sets of expertises, such as in social skills training and/or job counseling. But, qua therapists or psychological counselors, their area of identification with their clients is the internal changes that are necessary for clients to achieve their desired goals of relief from psychological misery and augmented meaningfulness of their lives, happiness, and self-control. Insofar as a particular therapist agrees to help clients reach certain external goals by expanding their knowledge of the external world and their skills in dealing with it, these are separate promises that enter into the client–therapist relationship, requiring separate expertises from the therapist.

DUAL RELATIONSHIPS

The major threat to maintaining the therapist's focus on helping clients achieve their goals is the introduction of competing interests. Dual relationships introduce such other interests and thus threaten to interfere with, to dilute, or otherwise to diminish the purity of the concern that the therapist has for a client. Friendships, for example, are reciprocal, and thus would require the focus of the therapy to shift from one party to the other, from one set of interests to the other, and back again. Similarly with any other dual relationship: Romantic relationships bring in a whole host of distracting concerns; employer therapists are split between concern with job performance and client progress; teacher therapists may find it hard to separate their concerns with classroom performance from the therapy; and so forth.

Clients, in return, also will have divided attention in dual relationships; as friends or lovers they are obliged to consider the needs of their friend or lover, the therapist; as employees they must worry about their job performance; as students they are concerned about evaluation of their academic performance.

Duality of interests also is a fertile ground for exploitation and manipulation by therapists who hold dual power over their clients and by clients who can frustrate their therapists in dual ways. The ethical codes of the American Association for Counseling and Development and the American and the Canadian Psychological Associations recognize this fact by stating that dual relationships are to be avoided (CPA, 1986, Section III:23; APA, 1981a, Section 6:a; AACD 1988, B:13). The APA recently added the elaboration that barter of services is also to be avoided as a means of payment for psychological service because it puts the psychologist in the position of being the client's employer (Ethics Committee of the APA, 1986). Suppose, for example, that a client bartering yardwork for therapy does a tardy and incomplete job, what impact would that have on the therapy relationship? Barter of goods is also risky but is acceptable if the value of the goods is predetermined in some independent, fair manner.

An arguable contrasting point of view is that these theoretical claims are lacking empirical substantiation; that in actuality it is possible to hold dual relationships and still do a good job as a therapist. The greater investment may simply translate into more care and effort on the part of both parties. What data could contradict such contentions? Clinical experience, although not to be ignored, is rather untrustworthy because it is too often colored by the prejudices of the participants and commentators. Independent, empirical data are not available, however. To my knowledge there are no studies on the impact of friendship on therapy. Studies on sexual relationships between clients and therapists consist largely of accounts by clients who have complained in various ways, either to later therapists or to professional boards, or who responded to advertisements requesting information from persons who had experienced sexual intimacy with their therapists (Keith-Spiegel & Koocher, 1985). It seems likely that those clients who had no complaints, or who had positive things to report, would be less likely to be sampled by these methods.

Perhaps the largest, and in that sense, most representative study of the effects on clients relied on the results from a questionnaire sent to 4385 licensed psychologists in California (Bouhoutsos, Holroyd, Lerman, Forer, & Greenberg, 1983). Some 704 responded, of whom 318 had had clients who reported having sexual relations with former therapists. The sampled therapists were asked to evaluate the effects of the sexual relationships on their clients. The majority of the patients were assessed to have suffered harm of one type or another. Even so, some were assessed to have suffered no effects, and some were thought to have benefited. According to the clinicians, the patient's personality was adversely affected in 34% of the cases; the patient had negative feelings (29%); and/or the patient's sexual, marital, or other intimate relationships worsened (26%). However, in 9% of the patients there was thought to be no effect, and in 16% the patient was judged to have become healthier or to have improved emotionally and/or in sexual relationships.

Another larger, more recent study sampled the therapists' perspective and asked those who had had sexual contacts with one or more clients what they thought the effects were on their clients (Gartrell, Herman, Olarte, Feldstein, & Localio, 1986). A random sample of 5574 psychiatrists of the AMA resulted in 1423 returned, usable questionnaires. About 6% of these (84) admitted to such intimacies, which is almost the identical percentage found in most similar broad surveys of psychiatrists and psychologists. Of these individuals, 50 described the liaisons as caring, 29 as helpful, and 9 as therapeutic. Only 11 respondents thought they were exploitative, 8 harmful, and 5 inappropriate. It is important to note that most of these contacts occurred after formal termination of therapy (69%). Twenty-five percent of the therapists were pleased to have had the contact; 35% had mixed feelings; and 40% regretted it.

Regardless of the inconclusiveness of the evidence, the easily dominant opinion of professionals and laypeople alike is that such relationships clearly exploit clients. The codes of ethics of the professional organizations of both psychiatrists (American Psychiatric Association, 1986, Section 2:1) and psychologists (APA, 1981a, Section 6a), as well as those of social workers (NASW, 1984, Section 2:5) and counselors (AACD, 1988, Section B:14; National Board for Certified Counselors, 1987, Section a: 10), explicitly state that such relationships are unethical. This is true even if, as is frequently the case, the actual sexual contact occurs shortly after termination of therapy (Ethics Committee of the APA, 1986).

One reason for considering posttermination sexual contact unethical is that otherwise therapists might unilaterally and abruptly invoke termination when they decide to enter a sexual relationship with their clients because they know that doing so during the period of ongoing therapy would surely be highly unethical. But even with hurried termination, it is questionable whether clients are truly autonomous from their therapists' influence at any point in their subsequent existence, but especially shortly after termination when presumably the perception of therapist as wise and empathic is still salient. Sufficient time and events must pass in which clients find that they can truly function without their therapists' aid before a peer relationship can be realizable. Opportunities for clients to view their therapists as having "feet of clay" in other sorts of settings would abet this goal. Otherwise therapists threaten the client's ability to achieve autonomous functioning and violate the basic promise of the initial relationship: to help them achieve *their* goals.

Also the law has found such practices harmful in a number of well-publicized malpractice suits with the result that even the general public is now informed that this is considered an inappropriate extension of the therapeutic relationship. Moreover, insurance companies restrict or exclude coverage of such intimacies in their professional malpractice policies. If a counselor or therapist decided to practice otherwise and this became known, she or he would be unacceptable for membership in any professional organization or for state licensure, would receive no referrals from such professionals, and would be unlikely to attract a clientele.

The implicit promise of not expanding or not entering into other dual relationships, especially that of friendship, is not so well known or substantiated. Some codes specify that dual relationships other than sexual should be avoided but do not find them specifically unethical (NASW, 1984, Section II:4; AACD, 1988, Section B:11; APA, 1981a, Section 6a). Indeed, sexual intimacy with clients is about the only definitive, explicit unethical practice in most codes. Thus it is up to clinicians to inform their clients, as appropriate, of role limitations.

PREVIOUS RELATIONSHIPS WITH CLIENTS

When counselors are scarce and prospective clients do not have the means or time to travel far to see someone else, it may be necessary for counselors to accept clients whom they already know from another context, and who know them. To keep their respective roles straight, counselors need to sit down with such clients and reason out ways of minimizing the cross transference from one set of relationships to the other. Friendships can be put "on hold" by minimizing future contacts; less close relationships can be reduced to polite, routine transactions; other people can fill in to provide services where evaluation plays a role, such as doing the grading of a student's work for a teacher who is also that student's therapist. Sometimes, however, the only viable alternative is for the counselor not to accept the prospective client because of the high probability that one or the other of them will be hurt rather than helped by the additional relationship, that is, Nonmaleficence takes precedence over Beneficence in such situations. David Hargrove (1986) has written an especially sensitive treatment of this problem as it arises in rural mental health practice.

GIFTS FROM CLIENTS

The respective roles of the counselor and the client may also become unclear when counselors accept gifts from clients in addition to their regular recompense. The hazard is that the gift, either at the time of reception, or later, will acquire a significance that will alter the therapy itself. For example, it may signify to the client that the therapist now owes the client something special in the way of therapy. Other clients may feel they need to buy their therapist's devotion, that they are not worthy of it in their own stead. Still others may see this as an entry to establishing a social relationship with their therapists; in fact, gift giving and gift receiving are characteristic of such relationships. On the other hand, the routine refusal of all such offers of gifts would be inappropriate because it would also signify different things to different clients. In order to keep the roles clear as well as the promises that constitute these roles, therapists must determine, as best they can, both the client's current set of motives for any gift and how the client (and themselves) may be apt to perceive the gift in the future. Only then are they in a position to decide whether and how to receive or to reject the gift.

MULTICLIENTS

Sometimes a therapist's client is more than one person. This always occurs when treating families, couples, or miscellaneous others as a group, rather than individually. (This situation is not to be confused with the obligation to provide certain information about the client to third parties, which will be dealt with later.) The therapist's task in such instances is to identify with the common interest of all the individuals in the group, namely, to work together and in so doing to help themselves and each other, and in the case of families and couples, to improve their relationships with each other. This promise is usually quite explicit, and if all goes well, can be clearly maintained. The difficulty comes when one or more members of a group decide that they are no longer interested in the common goal of working together because it is interfering with their own individual goals of self-betterment or reduction of distress. This may even occur at the onset of counseling if one member of a family, for example, wants to leave the family and is there just to prove that working together won't work. Then the loyalty of the counselor risks division, for it is not necessarily the case that helping one individual in a group is going to benefit all the other members as well.

There are many ways to handle such situations clinically that would be infeasible to review here. From the viewpoints of Fidelity and Autonomy the important concern is that therapists make certain that the client understands what promises they consider primary and how they are going to proceed. Otherwise the clients have no clear concept of the goals they will be helped to achieve and may well misinterpret their therapists' subsequent actions and feel betrayed.

"INCIDENTAL" IMPLICIT PROMISES

A number of things are usually taken for granted in therapist–client relationships: punctuality for appointments, fair warning of anticipated absences, fair warning of any changes in scheduling or fees, and personal availability or prearranged coverage by others in cases of emergency. This does not mean that they are always observed, however. There may also be implicit promises to third parties such as to other therapists.

Fidelity to Other Therapists: How to Handle Clients Who Wish to Switch Therapists

Therapists obtain clients from other therapists and counselors through numerous different situations, each with its particular ethical concerns, as described in the following list:

1. *Therapist Actively Solicits Clients of Another Professional Counselor or Therapist.* This presents a host of ethical concerns including the possible damage to whatever benefit the clients were receiving from their current therapy, harm to the reputation of the current therapist, potential harm to oneself by inviting retaliation (all violation of Nonmaleficence), and the breaking of allegiance to one's colleagues (violation of Fidelity).

It might be justified if one were quite certain that the other therapist was harming clients through incompetence or other unethical practice. Even then, taking the client on oneself would smack of self-serving, and it would be better if referral were made to other qualified professionals.

2. *Therapist Obtains Clients by Referral.* This presents no ethical problem as long as the referral is appropriate and the client's autonomy has been preserved through awareness of the full range of possible alternative sources of treatment (Kelley & Alexander, 1985). Charging money for

referral is generally considered inappropriate, presumably because of its potential for abuse (Nonmaleficence to clients). The APA "Ethical Principles" (1981a, Section 6:d) and the code of the American Association for Marriage and Family Therapy (1982, Section I:3) specifically prohibit this practice, although the Federal Trade Commission recently found this practice to inhibit open competition for clients (Bales, 1988, March), the ethical basis for which finding is obscure to me.

3. *Prospective Clients Wish to Change from One Therapist to Another; Both Therapists Are Members of Same Mental Health Profession.* In this case because the client is not yet a client, the new therapist owes no allegiance to the client. However, if the other therapist is a colleague (a member of the same mental health profession), and especially if the colleague is a member of the same professional organization, there is a bond to be respected. Except perhaps in cases where the client's dissatisfaction arises from unethical behavior of the colleague, which will be discussed in Chapter 9, the ethical course of action would be to ensure that the colleague is aware of the situation.

This can be done in a number of ways. In some cases the client may have already told the therapist that he or she was discontinuing and why. In other cases the client can be prevailed upon to do so. In still other cases the client may not be willing to engage in such confrontation but is willing for the new therapist to convey the information. If none of these applies and there is no emergency, fidelity to one's colleagues would seem to require that the client be refused service.

4. *Same Situation Exists as in Situation 3, but New Therapist Is Not a Member of Same Profession.* In this case, unless there has been some sort of prior agreement, such as occurs when members of different professions work together in a variety of ways, there is no allegiance to be discharged to the former therapist. It would seem that the new therapist would be perfectly free to take on the dissatisfied client without further ado. However, a number of other ethical considerations must first be reviewed (see Situation 7).

5. *Client Belatedly Informs New Therapist of Abrupt, Unannounced Discontinuance of Therapy with Former Therapist, a Colleague.* In this case the therapist has already entered into a promissory relationship with the new client, and it would seem that this relationship should take precedence over any obligations to the client's former therapist. However, it could be argued that deception on the client's part, or, at the least, withholding of important information about the abrupt discontinuance of the former relationship releases the new therapist from observing such pref-

erence. There is no conflict, of course, if the client can be persuaded to return to the former therapist and explain the situation or gives permission to the new therapist to do so.

6. *Same Situation Exists as in Situation 5 Except That Former Therapist Is Not a Colleague.* This would be similar to Situation 4 in that there would be no formal obligation owed to members of other mental health professions except as a result of prior individual arrangements.

7. *Client Referrals May Involve Other Ethical Considerations.* Other reasons may exist for clearing transfers of clients from one professional to another. The following considerations deserve careful scrutiny:

A. Clients are likely to benefit from such openness of transfer in that they will learn that intimate relationships of any sort are usually best handled by above-board transactions. In fact, it may be deleterious to their future functioning to inadvertently learn otherwise. An open transfer is especially valuable to clients if they directly confront their former therapists and it is a successful experience. This assumes that, in such a situation, the former therapist does not act defensively and vindictively but uses the encounter as an occasion for mutual learning.

The confrontation may lead to a dissolution of the difficulties in their relationship, thus enabling the client to continue in the original therapy, and again both parties benefit from such continuance. This is especially true for clients who typically handle interpersonal conflicts and personal fears by running away. In such cases allowing the clients to do so does them no service.

B. Conversely if therapists take on clients who are running away from fears and conflicts aroused by current or recent therapy, without consulting with the former therapist to learn the details of the situation, they set themselves up for the same experience.

C. Not allowing other therapists to find out about the problems that led to their clients' abrupt discontinuance of therapy denies them feedback that may be of crucial value in improving their own service to future clients.

D. Unless such a feedback system prevails, likelihood is strong, especially in small marketplaces, that the unpleasant discovery of clients being "stolen" by another professional will strain relationships between mental health professionals. Strained relationships are likely to have deleterious effects on the entire delivery system for psychological counseling and therapy; whereas cooperative relationships are likely to benefit the consumer.

In conclusion, the preponderance of the ethical considerations falls on the side of providing feedback to other mental health professionals, whether colleagues or not, when clients wish to transfer from one therapist to another. However, in certain situations such feedback would still be con-traindicated: in particular, when there is reason to believe that the client would be subject to some sort of reprisal by the former therapist if such transfer were openly acknowledged; or if some sort of emergency situation were to exist requiring immediate acceptance of the client as a client, at least until such time as the emergency is taken care of. Alleged unethical behavior on the part of the former therapist might also obviate feedback, at least immediate feedback. Handling such complaints will receive special attention in Chapter 9.

What Do the Codes Say?

When clients of professional voluntarily seek out another therapist, different professions take somewhat different stances as to the "ethical" course of action. Three different perspectives follow.

The American Psychological Association's "Ethical Principles" (APA, 1981a) states:

> If a psychologist is contacted by a person who is already receiving similar services from another professional, the psychologist carefully considers that professional relationship and proceeds with caution and sensitivity to the therapeutic issues as well as the client's welfare. The psychologist discusses these issues with the client so as to minimize the risk of confusion and conflict. (Section 7b)

The *Code of Ethics* of the National Board for Certified Counselors (1987) includes this statement:

> If an individual is already in a counseling relationship with another profes-sional person, the certified counselor does not enter into a counseling re-lationship without first contacting and receiving the approval of that other professional. If the certified counselor discovers that the client is in another counseling relationship after the counseling relationship begins, the certified counselor must gain the consent of the other professional or terminate the relationship, unless the client elects to terminate the other relationship. (Section B3)

The National Association of Social Workers (1980) provides these guidelines:

1. The social worker should not solicit the clients of colleagues.
2. The social worker should not assume professional responsibility for the clients of another agency or a colleague without appropriate communication with that agency or colleague. (Section IIIK:1,2)

ISSUES

What essential promises define the therapist–client relationship?

In what ways can dual relationships violate the basic premise of the therapeutic relationship?

Are sexual relations between therapists and clients inevitably harmful and therefore unethical?

Why are such relations considered unethical even after termination of therapy?

When might it be better to allow dual relationships? How should they be handled?

What is ethically problematic about accepting gifts from clients?

How should a therapist ethically handle conflicting allegiances when seeing clients as a group (couple, family, therapy, or counseling group)?

What ethical concerns are aroused when a therapist:

1. Actively solicits clients from another professional?
2. Accepts referrals?
3. Accepts clients who wish to change therapists?
4. Allows clients to continue after discovering they have abruptly changed from another therapist?

CHAPTER 5

The Promise of Confidentiality

REASONS FOR CONFIDENTIALITY

In one-on-one, client–psychological counselor situations within the confines of a private office, the client generally assumes and the professional often explicitly states that whatever the client provides will be kept confidential, or even "strictly confidential." Exactly what this means may not be clear to the client, or even always to the professional, because there are so many possible exceptions. But the purpose of the promise is clear: It is to encourage the client to reveal openly and honestly anything relevant, no matter how private, to the professional. The assumption is that unless the client does this, the professional may not be in a position to help the client. Thus when counselors and therapists offer confidentiality, they expect their clients reciprocally to promise veracity, although this latter promise is implicit and may not be immediately realizable.

Interestingly, as the art of psychotherapy approaches science, we can expect that confidentiality will diminish in importance. Therapists will give clients the tools to diagnose and help themselves and will teach them how to use these tools; hence there will be no need to confide anything to another person except the general nature of their concerns. This is already done in psychoeducational classes in depression, controlled drinking, control of anger, handling of stress, and so forth. Even that limited disclosure will not be necessary if clients can make the desired changes by use of self-help programs that are fully presented in books, videos, or tapes. The increasing use of psychoeducational classes and the development of self-help programs attest to the vigor with which this approach is now being pursued. However, the traditional client–therapist mode of treatment seems far from fading away and, in fact, seems to be keeping pace with the new developments. So the issues of confidentiality should continue to be pertinent for some time to come.

DEFINING CONFIDENTIAL INFORMATION

There are a number of bits and types of information that could be covered under the umbrella of confidentiality. A partial list would include:

1. The status of the client—whether a former client or currently a client
2. The number of appointments, the starting date, and the intervals between subsequent appointments
3. The type of service—individual counseling, couple, family, group, or some combination of the foregoing
4. The reasons for the client seeking or receiving service and the client's diagnosis
5. The client's utterances during treatment in the therapy time and place; also the client's nonverbal behavior
6. The client's utterances and nonverbal behavior toward the therapist in other contexts
7. The verbal and nonverbal responses of the therapist, both within and without the treatment setting
8. The planned course of treatment and the actual course
9. The general opinions of the therapist about the course of treatment and about the results of treatment

Any or all of the above items may be requested by various parties, and release or nonrelease of them may make a difference to the client.

If clients were asked what they thought was being promised by "strict confidentiality," they would, no doubt provide a variety of answers. Almost all, however, might be expected to assume that whatever took place during the actual treatment sessions as well as whatever directly related to these sessions would be strictly between them and the therapist. Thus, even though clients might accidentally meet their therapists outside the office, as long as the topic of their conversation originated in the office sessions and their present conversation was private in that no one else was in hearing distance, such clients would probably assume that such conversations were also confidential.

In one sense, it does not matter whether all or only a minority of clients would make that assumption, as long as one might reasonably expect that some clients would so presume. Thus it is not necessary to conduct a large survey in order to determine what therapists and counselors should treat as confidential. If they are to "err," it should surely be on the side of secrecy in such matters.

There are also good reasons for keeping confidential such things as the status of clients and what is referred to as "appointment book information"—the number and timing of interviews. Unless there is a good reason to give this information to a third party, why disclose it? In some cases it may harm the client to reveal such information. For example, security-conscious governmental agencies look suspiciously upon applicants who have a record of counseling, believing it may indicate some more-than-usual mental problems that are still persisting, rather than a reasonable effort by a reasonable person to seek aid with certain problems. Private employers may well share the same prejudice according to Noll (1981):

> Acknowledging to present or potential employers and insurers that one is or has been a participant in psychotherapy may have fateful consequences for one's life opportunity.... The data obtained by Weinstock and Haft (1974) is of particular relevance. They found that regardless of type of position—executive, clerical, or maintenance—the hiring policies of those industries sampled would lead to rejection rates of up to 77% for applicants who were in psychotherapy. (p. 915)

Risking harm to clients in this way violates both the principle of Non-maleficence and that of Fidelity. The "Specialty Guidelines for the Delivery of Services by Clinical Psychologists" (APA 1981b, Sections 2.3.3.–2.3.5.) recognizes this by stipulating that such information is part of the confidential case record.

However, the law has typically separated appointment book information from client–therapist exchanges in cases of litigation and has made it more subject to disclosure. (Schwitzgebel & Schwitzgebel, 1980, p. 102)

Formal opinions about clients, such as contained in evaluative reports or diagnoses, usually have limited distribution—to other members of the treatment team, as in a psychiatric ward; to third parties who have referred the client for such evaluations; or to insurance companies, who generally require diagnosis and treatment plan. In many cases the client has already agreed to the release of such information, so the only promise is to limit the release to these authorized parties. In others it may be unclear whether the client has voluntarily and with comprehension agreed to such communication. Obviously, then, a collaborative relationship requires discussion with the client and clearly stated limits of confidentiality.

If the interaction between the counselor or therapist and the client consists only of evaluation for some third party, then the primary client is the third party and no promise of confidentiality can be made to the person evaluated other than to limit any release of information, from the evaluator's side at least, to the third party.

Many, perhaps most, such evaluations contain some degree of coercion of the persons being evaluated. They agree to such evaluations, for the most part, but only because the alternative is less palatable—increased jail time, loss of chance for a job, loss of chance for welfare benefits, and so forth. In such cases the evaluator is not functioning as a psychological care giver, but rather as the administrator of a "necessary evil."

If the evaluator makes any promise to the person being evaluated, it is to do a fair job, that is, to adhere to the Principle of Justice. The promise to the third party is to do a competent job, though not necessarily a thorough one because many times the funds and time allotted for the evaluation are severely restricted. Such evaluations presumably benefit society, at least in the case of governmental agencies; hence Beneficence is also a factor. They may or may not also benefit the ones being evaluated, but this is more likely to be true if Craddick's procedures are followed (see Chapter 3).

WHEN ARE INFORMAL OPINIONS APPROPRIATE?

Informal opinions are another matter altogether. Almost anyone who knows the client at all seems to feel entitled to the counselor's informal opinion on the client's progress. This is, of course, especially true of family or friends who may have informally referred the client for counseling. But unless it was stated otherwise at some point, this acquaintanceship and these referrals do not constitute what is referred to as "a need to know." The counselor's obligation is to the client and not to these others, no matter how well meaning nor how innocent their request may sound (or be). The problem with informal opinions is twofold: The therapist can never be sure how any given response will be interpreted or will be used by the inquiring party. Even a seemingly innocuous response such as, "She's doing fine," may be interpreted or passed on in some distorted fashion by the inquirer. Furthermore such a response may encourage requests for elaboration, for details.

However, not to respond at all or to respond with "I can't tell you without permission from the client" also risks a negative interpretation. So there seems to be a toss-up. But two "outs," preserve the primary duty in this situation, that of fidelity to the promise of confidentiality: One is to refer the person to the client for the answer, and the other is to discuss the issue with the client and ask the client how to handle such requests in the future.

Requests for informal opinions from a client's employer are a more serious matter. Employers seldom make such requests lightly and usually expect more than a simple, one-sentence generality in response. When anticipated, it is possible to head them off by making clear, in writing, that no information, however minimal, is available without the client's permission. If not anticipated, the principle is the same, but the skill required to reply with "No comment" is greater.

CATEGORIES OF DISCLOSURE

The various categories of people and agencies to whom disclosure is, at times appropriate, are as follows: Members of the treatment team, broadly defined; coclients, such as family members and group members; third parties, including referrers, insurers, courts, and, on occasions, clients themselves. The following sections examine the need to know of members of each category.

Disclosure to Treatment Team Members

A number of people may be privy to all or some items of information contained in the client–therapist relationship. Cotherapists who missed a session need to be brought up to date. Supervisors need full information in order to fulfill faithfully their obligations to train therapists and to enhance the clients' therapy, including protecting clients from therapist incompetence. Legally they are responsible for the trainees' treatment of clients, although trainees may also incur blame, especially if they hide vital information from their supervisors. Official treatment teams, as in many psychiatric care units, freely share information with each other in many ways, including periodic briefings and charts to which they have common access.

Others who are not normally "team members" may be brought in to provide a second opinion or some special expertise. These consultants may be internal or external to the agency or practice in which the treatment takes place. Often the need to know is restricted, consisting of only one aspect of the therapy, and the client's identity can be kept anonymous. However, the goal is to provide as much information as is necessary for the consultant to do a good job. For example, a psychiatrist who is asked to evaluate a client for the appropriateness of drug treatment may require information about the treatment to date as well as an interview with the client. Colleagues who are asked to judge the ethicality of some practice or to offer suggestions for breaking a client–therapist impasse will also sometimes need extensive information about the client. Consultants with more tangential expertises, such as lawyers or social welfare workers, will generally require more restricted, specific information.

Still another type of recruited team member could be a spouse, a parent, or a roommate who is asked, for example, to monitor the client's behavior for suicidal indications or to help the client make a behavioral change by not giving in to the client's pleas for money.

Because the constituents of the treatment team may not always be apparent to the client in any given situation, it is incumbent upon the therapist to point out each and every exception to "strict confidentiality" and get the client's permission to disclose what is necessary or advisable. Otherwise the promise of confidentiality will be violated. Many codes of professional psychological counselors and therapists recognize this duty (American Association for Marriage and Family Therapy, 1982, Section II:3; American Psychiatric Association, 1986, Section 4:2; APA, 1981a, Principle 5; Association for Specialists in Group Work, 1980, Section A-3 cited in Roberts, 1982; Canadian Psychological Association, 1986, Sections I:28–34; National Association of Social Workers, 1980, Section II:H).

The American Psychological Association addressed the issue more specifically when its Ethics Committee ruled that unless it is possible to keep clients' identity anonymous, they should be informed at the outset about any possible sharing of information with a supervisor or consultant and the nature of the information that may be shared ("Ethics Statement Issued," 1984).

Disclosure in Multiclient Situations: Couples, Families, and Groups

When the counselor engages in marital counseling, family therapy, or group therapy, then what is to be kept confidential from whom can become even more complex, especially if individual counseling is also involved.

With couples, for example, one counselor might see one spouse, a different counselor the other spouse, and still a third the two together. What should the counselors share with each other? In family therapy absent members may be talked about during a session. If they come to a later session, should they be told what was said? In groups, who guarantees that group members won't disclose to spouses and friends what other group members said and did in the group? What if the counselor sees some members individually, perhaps for emergency interviews in between group sessions, should that fact even be mentioned?

As one might guess, there is no single set of rules or procedures for handling any of these questions. With respect to couples being seen both individually and as a couple by the same therapist, some therapists ask their clients to sign waiver forms permitting them to use their "professional judgment'' about what to reveal when to other members of the family or to the other spouse when family members are seen separately, or when one or more is missing on any given occasion (Wendorf & Wendorf, 1985; Keith-Spiegel, 1986). My own preference is to promise confidentiality to each spouse but to point out the advantages of their sharing certain information with the other spouse if they are to develop an open, honest relationship. In my experience such information is inevitably voluntarily shared under these conditions.

When two or more therapists are involved in a family or marital situation, it is customary for each to get the client's permission to consult with the other therapist. The basic justification is that of Beneficence: counselors cannot do a good job, much less the best job possible, in helping their clients unless they have all relevant information at their disposal. These consultation waivers may also include a statement clarifying whether information disclosed by a client to one therapist can be disclosed to the client of another therapist, if desired. Such disclosure may well happen inadvertently when therapists consult with each other over members of the same family. In such cases permission to have professional discretion as to when to disclose information gained in this way might well be the most pragmatic solution.

Confidentiality within Groups

With groups the basic problem is that there is little or no leverage to ensure that members don't discuss group transactions outside of the group. The leaders can promise confidentiality, but they have no real control over the members in this respect. One can, of course, require members to sign a "contract" in which they promise not to break confidentiality, but implementing it is another matter. Such a contract has been copyrighted by R.K. Schwitzgebel and includes a provision for monetary reimbursement to "wronged" members. But the author admits that it may be legally toothless. Its primary value would seem to be that members would have in writing a clear statement of what is expected of them (Schwitzgebel & Schwitzgebel, 1980, Appendix M).

Pragmatically, studies have indicated that group members are typically not very worried about or very observant of "strict confidentiality." One survey of seven groups found that even when members were explicitly told that "anything said in the group was to remain in the group, 24 of the 57 members thought they could inform a friend and/or family member . . . 13 of these members actually told a friend what another group member said, and 12 told a family member" (Davis, 1982, p. 200). Slovenko (1977) conducted a number of interviews with group members and concluded that group members were far less concerned about confidentiality than their leaders.

This does not excuse group leaders, however, from at least clarifying the confidentiality issue at the outset of a group. In accordance with the following guidelines, the advantages and disadvantages of various limits of confidentiality can be frankly discussed and a consensus reached as to what limitations are realistic and desirable:

> Group leaders shall protect group members by defining clearly what confidentiality means, why it is important, and the difficulties involved in enforcement. (Association for Specialists in Group Work, 1981 *Guidelines for Group Leaders*: Section A-3, cited in Roberts, 1982)

> In a group counseling setting, the counselor must set a norm of confidentiality retarding all group participants' disclosures. (American Association for Counseling and Development, 1988, *Ethical Standards*: Section B-2)

Disclosure to Third Parties

Referral of clients does not, in and of itself, entitle the referrer to information about the client, even the knowledge of whether the client showed up. However, those agencies who pay for the client's treatment and evaluation normally require certain information before they will reimburse.

The information to be provided depends on the nature of the agency and the treatment. A private company, for example, may have an employee assistance program whereby the firm has a contract with a group of psychotherapists to provide employees with evaluation, short-term counseling and therapy, and referral as necessary. The identities of the employees may be kept confidential; the firm may require only statistical data such as number of employees serviced and the general types of service provided.

Another type of agency, such as a county's children's service division, may contract with selected private practitioners to provide specific programmatic treatment of sex offenders and may expect to be informed whether the referred offenders participated fully and with what degree of apparent success.

Regardless of the source, with a formal referral it is important to negotiate an agreement, put into writing exactly what information will be disclosed to whom, and get both the referrer and the client to sign. It might be wise to have this document cover the request for information "How is he doing?" opinions as well. As pointed out in Part One, Autonomy, if only evaluation is to be done, then the person being evaluated has the right to a full explanation of the nature of the evaluation, which stance is adopted by the APA (1981a):

> In the . . . utilization of assessment techniques, psychologists make every effort to promote the welfare and best interests of the client. . . . They respect the client's right to know the results, the interpretations made, and the bases for their conclusions and recommendations. (Section 8: Preamble)

If the referral is for treatment as well, or only for treatment, the contractual relationship for provision of information to the referrer—whether, for example, only a final report or also progress reports—needs to be clearly articulated to all parties, as is also succinctly stated in "Ethical Principles" (APA, 1981a):

> When a psychologist agrees to provide services to a client at the request of a third party, the psychologist assumes the responsibility of clarifying the nature of the relationship to all parties concerned. (Section 6b)

A third party may be entitled to information about clients even without having had a direct role in the referral of the client to the therapist. This is usually the case with carriers of the mental health insurance policies. Therapists should apprise clients exactly what information the insurers require in order to provide reimbursement. Some insurers promote such openness by requiring policyholders to sign the claim forms. This does not mean, however, that clients read the whole form or understand the routinely required diagnoses; hence it behooves the therapist to explain such terminology to the client in understandable terms. This would also be true of any further information that the insurer required to continue reimbursement. Sometimes it is possible to disclose less than what insurers request and still satisfy them. For instance, for purposes of quality control review, insurers may request all progress notes, but may accept a treatment summary instead.

Another issue is the disposition of information released to third parties. If the policy statements provided by the third parties do not make clear that the information goes to them only for specific, agreed-upon purposes, then, to protect the interests of the client (Nonmaleficence), such a statement should be in the release-of-information statement that all parties sign. If this is impossible, or there is evidence that these agreements are not adhered to by the third party, then, at the minimum, the potential client ought to be notified of the fact or not accepted at all under those conditions. Thus there are two sets of allegiances to consider in disclosure of information to third parties: those to the paying parties who may also have referred the clients, and those to the clients. Fidelity to the clients requires checking to see if they understand what information about them will be transmitted to the third party and truly agree to such transmittal, thus protecting their autonomy. Fidelity to the third party requires providing the information that is agreed upon. Fidelity to both requires the practitioner to do a competent job of both treatment/evaluation and transmission of information. The practitioner acts as the mediator in any differences between the clients and the third parties.

Release of Information to Parents or Guardians, Other Relatives, and Friends

Certain referrers may feel entitled to information about clients by virtue of their personal relationship with the clients. This is often the case with parents or spouses of clients, but sometimes also with other relatives and with friends. Those on whom the client is dependent, either financially or otherwise, are most apt to claim such privilege.

One all-too-common example is the situation created when parents call a college counseling center (or are referred to it by others in the administration of the college) because they are concerned about their children who are students at the college. Such parents often request that the counseling center contact their children and counsel them if they are not already doing so; if the students are clients, they want to know the nature and progress of the counseling. Does the counseling center owe the parents such information, especially if the parents are paying for their children's education? The legal answer to this question will be treated later in the chapter; at this point only the ethical issues are under consideration.

If the student is a client, then it is clear that the counselor owes allegiance to preserving the confidentiality of the relationship including, as was pointed out earlier, the fact of the relationship itself. Except in unusual circumstances, the counselor has a primary duty not to divulge information to anyone without first obtaining the express permission of their clients. The very fact that the parents find such calls necessary indicates that they have a less-than-open, less-than-satisfactory relationship with their offspring and thus are most apt to misuse whatever information they may obtain.

Should the parents provide what appears to be reliable information that potential suicide or homicide is imminent, then some disclosure may be made in the interest of preventing such action, but, normally, even in such circumstances the counselor would want to ascertain the validity of such information and try to do what is reasonable and agreeable to the client first. Paying for someone's education is not equivalent to paying for that person's therapy, nor do all parties, in such situations, sign contractual agreements that are to be honored. Certainly banks or other loan providers are not entitled to information about counseling. Tactful ways to handle parental inquiries include acknowledgment of the parents' concern and perhaps a promise to convey that concern if an appropriate opportunity presents itself, as well as a clear statement that the counselor–client relationship must be kept confidential to be effective.

Obviously if parents are not entitled to confidential information, neither are other relatives and friends. As pointed out earlier, the therapist can refer all such inquirers to the client for information about ongoing counseling or therapy.

Adolescent and Child Clients

What about clients who are teenagers or younger—are their parents entitled to information as to the nature and progress of counseling or therapy they receive? These clients cannot be presumed to be fully capable, or nearly so, of autonomous functioning; such clients may rely on their parents or guardians for more than just financial support. However, such reliance may be detrimental if the parents do not understand the child's needs or are incompetent to provide it. To a certain extent the counselor or therapist fills this role until such time that a transition can be made to others, perhaps to the parents or guardians. In this light it is arguable that the therapist must preserve and promote the client's autonomy *from* the parents until such time as this is no longer necessary. Also for the therapist to work with the child or adolescent, the client may need to be able to trust the therapist not to reveal information to the parents that may lead to negative repercussions on the client. Thus it would seem that the therapist must promise and maintain confidentiality for therapy to be of benefit. General information about the nature and likely duration of the treatment does not threaten the client's privacy and is reasonably required by any parent who has responsibility for the care of the child.

But, it can be asked, is it meaningful to young clients to promise confidentiality—can they understand what is offered? A recent review of the literature on confidentiality issues with minor clients (Gustafson & McNamara, 1987) has done what appears to be a thorough and accurate job in this area. The following comments are based mostly on this article and on similar articles already referred to in the discussion of Autonomy, most particularly those of Melton (1983) and Belter and Grisso (1984).

Gustafson and McNamara's (1987) thorough review of the literature in the area of competencies of minors is instructive; the studies discussed in this paragraph are all cited in this review. They point out that a number of studies have shown that minors aged 15 years or older are as competent to provide consent to counseling or therapy as adults. Below the age of 11 years, however, minors lack the necessary intellectual capabilities and have an undue deference to authority. One study with minors with learning and behavior problems found that they were capable of identifying relevant therapy risks and benefits (Kaser-Boyd, Adelman, & Taylor, 1985). Also two other studies indicate that adolescents respond more positively to treatment when involved in its planning and evaluation (Janzen & Love, 1977) and when they believe they have a choice about participation (Bastien & Adelman, 1984). It would seem appropriate, therefore, to extend confidentiality to minors, especially those aged 15 years or older. A task force of the American Psychiatric Association (1979) went even further, recommending that minors may give consent to release confidential information at the age of 12 years or older.

From this and other data Gustafson and McNamara recommend:

> To the extent that the adolescent is capable of understanding the importance and the limits of confidentiality and demonstrates an understanding that is equivalent to that of an adult, the clinician is justified in affording the minor the right to confidentiality in the therapeutic relationship. (p. 505)

They further suggest that those aged 14 to 15 years are generally as capable as adults. With preadolescent children:

> The therapist should consider the needs and desires of the child, the concerns of the parents, the particular presenting problem, and relevant state statutes in deciding what degree of confidentiality is appropriate. . . . [Also] the therapist should make an informal assessment of the minor's cognitive capacity. (p. 505)

Once therapists have decided the appropriate degree of confidentiality, they should arrange pretreatment family meetings where they explicate their decisions and the rationale therefor. Following that, whatever is agreed upon should be put into writing and signed by all parties. Parents should be encouraged to come in for future meetings any time that they develop concerns about the therapy.

What the parents will agree to and what the therapist thinks would be best for the minor client in terms of disclosure may not be reconcilable. Therapists have the right and the responsibility to refuse to provide treatment if they have good reason to believe that information provided to the parents or guardians is being used by them to the child's detriment; that is, Nonmaleficence is invoked. This, of course can occur sometime after therapy has begun, in which case it is up to the therapist to attempt to renegotiate the agreement.

Though not strictly relevant, it is instructive that the federal rules for conduct of research involving children recommend asking children aged 7 years and older for assent, albeit guardian or parental consent can override refusal if there is a determination that the research definitely benefits the child. Child "assent," however, is not to be confused with informed "consent," which is required from parents or guardians in any case (Department of Health and Human Services, 1983).

LEGAL CONSIDERATIONS

Laws in the United States generally recognize that it benefits society to protect the confidentiality of certain subject matter or transactions within certain relationships. According to Dekraai and Sales (1984) state laws protect confidentiality in a number of different ways. Some provide for confidentiality of certain subject matter, such as health-care information (Rhode Island) or medical and mental records (Virginia). Some protect certain classes of individuals such as the mentally retarded, the developmentally disabled, persons treated for alcoholism or drug abuse, persons institutionalized for mental illness, and sexual offenders. Some states protect the records of certain agencies, such as state-supported mental retardation programs or any facility treating the mentally ill.

Confidentiality for Minors

Laws have been established to protect the confidences of minors who come in for birth control and for drug counseling. Under normal conditions parents are not privy even to the fact that such counseling occurred. These laws are in a state of almost constant attack and revision so the exact status of the law may vary from legislative year to legislative year, as with any controversial area. Gustafson and McNamara's summary (1987) follows:

> Most jurisdictions allow minors to consent to treatment without parental knowledge in specific situations in which obtaining parental consent may jeopardize the likelihood that the minor will receive that treatment. . . . These specific situations include counseling or medical care for sexual abuse, substance abuse, pregnancy, sexually transmitted diseases, and contraception.
>
> In addition, the law has recognized four general exceptions to the requirement of parent consent for treatment of minors. . . . The first, the "mature

minor" pertains to minors with sufficient maturity to understand the nature and consequences of treatment. The second, "emancipated minor," refers to minors who are legally entitled to the rights and duties of adulthood for reasons that vary from state to state (e.g., a married minor). "Emergency treatment" is the third circumstance in which parental consent is not necessary. It is assumed that parental consent is implied because of the urgency of the situation. The final exception to obtaining parental consent is when treatment is court ordered.

Some states have gone further than this: Oregon, for example, allows minors, aged 14 years or over, "to obtain, without parental knowledge or consent, outpatient diagnosis or treatment of a *mental or emotional disorder* [italics added] or a chemical dependency . . ." by certain specified professionals (physicians, psychologists, registered nurse practitioners, and registered clinical social workers) or by approved community health programs (Oregon Revised Statutes 109.675).

What about counseling in schools: How protected are these sessions and the records thereof from scrutiny by parents? According to Schwitzgebel and Schwitzgebel (1980) "education records" that are "created or maintained by a physician, psychiatrist, psychologist, or other recognized professional or paraprofessional acting in his or her professional capacity, or assisting in that capacity" (pp. 211–212) are protected from direct scrutiny by both parents and the student clients, and are not to be disclosed to unauthorized third parties. The records will be disclosed to physicians or other appropriate treatment personnel chosen by the student to review them, upon request by the student. However, secondary and elementary school records for students under the age of 18 may be available to their parents.

Emergency situations, situations in which homicide or suicide seem probable, are treated somewhat differently (see Part Five, Nonmaleficence).

PRIVILEGE LAWS

"Privilege" statutes are a subarea of confidentiality laws. These state statutes protect the content of certain specified relationships from courtroom disclosure in the event of the client's involvement in some legal proceeding. Such information has typically already been protected from disclosure in other contexts but not in the courtroom, so a second type of law was created for this situation. Conversely, information that is protected from disclosure by privilege statutes is usually, but not always, also protected from disclosure outside the courtroom, even if no other confidentiality statute exists (DeKraai & Sales, 1984).

The laws vary extensively across states so it is not safe to say that any given relationship or any given subject matter is always fully protected or protected to the same extent in all jurisdictions (Wilson, 1984). Under common or case law—the law that has built up over the years through court cases—three relationships are privileged: attorney–client, husband–wife, and priest–penitent. Statutory law added the physician–patient relationship. Currently almost all states have a psychologist–client privilege, either separately or subsumed under some other relationship such as psychotherapist–client. As of about 1981, statutes in 17 states recognized the social worker–client relationship as privileged (DeKraai & Sales, 1982).

Because, as just noted, law can be created in a case-by-case fashion, mental health counselors and other psychological care givers not specifically covered under state statutes can, when called upon to testify, ask the court for privilege for their clients on the basis that their work is essentially the same as that of those professionals whose clients hold privilege. The criteria that justify the granting of a privilege are as follows:

> (1) The communications must originate in a confidence that they will not be disclosed; (2) this element of confidentiality must be essential to the full and satisfactory maintenance of the relation between the parties; (3) the relation must be one which in the opinion of the community must be sedulously fostered; and (4) the injury that would inure to the relation by disclosure of the communications must be greater than the benefit thereby gained for the correct disposal of the litigation. (Wigmore, 1940, p. 531, as cited in DeKraai & Sales, 1982)

Who Has the Privilege?

Although psychotherapists may claim privilege on behalf of their clients and should do so unless informed otherwise by their clients, it is the client who is the holder of the privilege. If the client wishes to release the information to the court, the therapist may try to persuade the client otherwise, if in the therapist's judgment such release would not be in the client's best interest, but the client has the final say. This is the case in most jurisdictions, but some states have modified this general rule, and arguments have been made to modify it even further. California and Missouri limit the client's ability to consent to disclosure by allowing discretion to the therapist in releasing the information (DeKraai & Sales, 1984). Everstine et al. (1980) and Slawson (1969, both cited in DeKraai & Sales, 1982) have argued for separate holding of privilege by the therapist on the grounds that therapists are in the best position to know what may be harmful to their clients. This latter position is an obvious example of Paternalism: Nonmaleficence and Beneficence over Autonomy.

Exceptions to Privilege

Exceptions to privilege are of three types (DeKraai & Sales, 1982):

1. *Judicial Discretion.* the law permits an exception whenever the judge rules that the interest of justice outweighs the interest of confidentiality. Some states grant judges this discretionary power.

2. *Limits According to the Nature of the Violation.* In some states privilege applies only to civil actions; other states extend privilege to both civil and criminal cases unless homicide is involved; still other states except cases involving child abuse or child victims of other crimes.

3. *Future Crime.* Exception has also been made, though not to psychologists, of information that shows intent to commit some future crime.

Waiver of Privilege

Clients automatically waive their privilege within the courtroom in some states in one or more of the following three situations specified in the Uniform Rules (federal) as cited in Cleary (1984, p. 245):

1. *Proceedings for Hospitalization.* There is no privilege ... if the psychotherapist in the course of diagnosis or treatment has determined that the patient is in need of hospitalization for mental illness.

2. *Examination by Order of the Court.* If the court orders an examination of the physical, mental, or emotional condition of the patient ... communications made in the course thereof are not privileged ... with respect to the particular purpose for which the examination is ordered unless the court orders otherwise.

3. *Condition and Element of Claim or Defense.* There is no privilege ... as to a communication relevant to an issue of the physical, mental, or emotional condition of the patient in any proceeding in which he relies upon the condition as an element of his claim or defense....

Marital and Family Counseling and Privileged Communication

According to Rule 504 of the proposed federal Rules of Evidence (cited in Knapp & VandeCreek, 1987):

(3) A communication is "confidential" if not intended to third persons other than those present to further the interest of the patient in the consultation, examination, or interview, or persons reasonably necessary for the transmission of the communications, or persons who are participating in the diagnosis and treatment under the direction of the psychotherapist, including members of the patient's family. (p. 170)

State statutes that follow this rule allow for privilege in marital or family therapy. "Most state statutes, however, do not provide the court with specific directions for communications in marital or family therapy" (Knapp & VandeCreek, 1987, p. 72). As a result these state courts must decide on common law grounds which communications are privileged, and case law is mixed in this respect. Distinctions have been drawn on the basis of whether the third parties who were present participated in the sessions, whether the communications were made to the therapist or from one client to another, whether both parties or only one party agreed to a waiver, and whether privilege statutes that cover marital and family counselors would also apply to other mental health professionals who saw couples and families.

Knapp and VandeCreek (1987) argue that privilege statutes should be extended to cover marital and family counseling in order to foster full participation of all relevant parties in joint sessions. Such participation may be limited if some members fear that what they communicate will later be used against them in court.

Group Psychotherapy and Privileged Communications

According to Slovenko (1977) communications made within group therapy have even less protection from disclosure in courtroom situations than those made in family therapy:

Thus, present-day privilege laws offer a modicum of assurance that communications in psychotherapy are shielded from disclosure in litigation of family matters, but they offer no assurance whatever in personal injury litigation where a group member makes his health a matter of issue. Likewise, should one group member assault another in the course of therapy, and suit ensue, the occurrence would not be shielded. (p. 415)

Since that writing, however, some progress has been made in this area. An amendment to a Colorado statute, for example, "prohibits the questioning of any persons who have participated in group therapy sessions 'concerning any knowledge gained during the course of such therapy without the consent of the persons or persons to whom the testimony sought relates' " (Schwitzgebel & Schwitzgebel, 1980, p. 209). Knapp and VandeCreek were able to find only one appellate court case on this issue, and it held that the communications within the group sessions would be privileged. They argue for such extension in all state statutes for similar reasons as for family and marital counseling—as a way of making group counseling maximally effective.

RESPONDING TO SUBPOENAS

One of the things that psychological counselors dread most is to receive a subpoena. Few feel competent to deal with today's legal system, and as a result the first impulse is to rush out and hire a lawyer. Although this is always a safe response, it may be unnecessary and expensive; there are steps that one can implement to reduce the role of an attorney or to resolve the matter without requiring consultation. Following are some step-by-step procedures that can serve as a general guide for responding to a subpoena. It is not a legal opinion appropriate to any and all particular situations (adapted from Schwitzgebel & Schwitzgebel, 1980, pp. 203–204, with review by Les Swanson, attorney, in a personal communication, January 21, 1983).

How to Respond When Served with a Subpoena

1. Determine the nature of the subpoena. Some governmental agencies or commissions may have subpoena power, others do not but use a subpoenalike form hoping to obtain information. If issued by a court and titled "Subpoena," it should be assumed valid and should not be ignored when properly delivered. Some subpoenas compel the production of records, others only require attendance. If the subpoena has the words *duces tecum* plainly on its face, it requires records and may or may not require attendance.

2. Whether the request is for records or for oral testimony, initially assert the privilege not to reveal any material pertaining to the client unless or until the client or the attorney of the client explicitly grants permission to do so, or the court orders you to do so. Failure to initially assert the privilege may result in legal action against you by the client. If the subpoena requires attendance at a legal proceeding, it is important to appear at the hearing in order to assert the privilege.

3. Alternatively, if an attorney was responsible for having the subpoena issued, the attorney can be contacted and informed of your intention to assert the privilege and may as a result, dismiss the subpoena.

4. If employed by an institution, notify the appropriate administrator. Do not destroy or tamper records to prevent disclosure. Tampering constitutes a misdemeanor or a felony.

5. Contact the client and/or the client's attorney. Explain the probable impact on the client of public exposure. If the impact might be detrimental, put this in writing and send a copy to the client's attorney and possibly to the client. If the client wants you to testify, request written authorization to release confidential information from the client, or the client's representative if the client is presumed incapable of making this judgment.

6. If the client does not give you written authorization or is not specific enough, or if the authorization is otherwise inadequate, two remaining options are:

A. Request a private conference with the appropriate judge. Seek clarification from the judge so that the information you provide will be limited to that essential to the court proceedings.

B. Provide only the information that the court requires you to produce. Subpoenaed records should be sealed and labeled "confidential" when submitted to the court, agency, or person that has subpoenaed the records.

Further advice is provided by "Specialty Guidelines for the Delivery of Services by Clinical Psychologists" (APA, 1981b) in cases where it seems unwise to release such information: "If directed by statute or regulations with the force of law or by court order, the psychologist may seek a resolution to the conflict that is both ethically and legally feasible and appropriate" (Section 2.3.5). Even if the client wants to provide the information, the psychologist has the responsibility "to discuss the implications of releasing psychological information and to assist the user in limiting disclosure only to information required by the present circumstance" (Section 2.3.5).

Is the Psychotherapist-Client Relationship a Fiduciary Relationship?

The professional psychological counselor–client relationship can be analyzed in terms of the promises, explicit and implicit, that characterize it. An interesting, though by no means decisive, commentary on this perspective could be provided by the judicial system. It has characterized certain duties and relationships as "fiduciary." "A fiduciary relationship exists when one party places trust and reliance in the other party who is obligated to act in the best interests of the party giving that trust" (DeKraai & Sales, 1984, p. 301). The physician–patient relationship has been so characterized by the law, and as Egar (1976, cited in DeKraai & Sales,

1984) argues, a stronger case could be made for the psychotherapist–client relationship because what is communicated is even more private in many instances. So far, however, there has been only one breach of fiduciary duty recognized as an appropriate action by a court.

ISSUES

What functions does providing confidentiality to clients serve? Are they necessary?

What reciprocal promises do clients implicitly make?

What types of information could conceivably be covered under the umbrella of confidential information?

Under what conditions, and from whom, might it be important to protect the various types from disclosure?

To whom is it proper to make disclosures, and how are they negotiated?

What are the respective rights of treatment team members, consultants, relatives, friends, referring agencies, and consultants to confidential information?

How are the rules of confidentiality/disclosure altered when more than one client is being treated simultaneously as in couple therapy, family therapy, and group therapy?

How is the ethical situation affected when there are multiple therapists—when different spouse or family members receive treatment from different therapists?

How does the client's being an adolescent or child affect the situation?

What does the research show about the capacity of minors to understand their rights in counseling?

What does the law say about confidentiality of health-care information and mentally disabled persons?

What laws cover protection of confidentiality for minors?

Do parents have the right to know about the counseling their children receive?

What do privilege laws protect from disclosure? When do they not apply? When are they usually waived?

How well does the law protect the confidentiality of multiclient (couples, families, and groups) counseling?

How should one respond to a subpoena to release information regarding a client?

Is the therapist–client relationship a fiduciary one?

PART THREE

Justice

Justice applies to all areas of endeavor where the concern is how humans treat each other. It is specifically relevant to counseling and therapy in the initial stage when determining whether a person is to receive services and whether they are to be comparable to services received by other individuals. It would also apply at any subsequent point in which a decision might be made to discriminate against or for particular clients. Justice becomes a legal issue if it involves clients' civil rights, sexual harassment, and other incidents of illegal discrimination.

CHAPTER 6

The Principle of Justice

DEFINING JUSTICE

Justice is the most elusive principle in terms of finding a single definition that satisfies all demands. Perhaps the most famous and the most succinct is Aristotle's: "Justice consists of treating equals equally, and unequals unequally but in proportion to their relevant differences" (Benn, 1967, p. 299). The problem with the definition is that the key terms—*equals, unequals,* and *relevant*—lack any content. One cannot determine equality or inequality without knowing what dimensions of comparison are relevant and how to measure differences on these dimensions. Once these determinations have been made, however, the definition becomes a useful guide.

Another way of looking at justice is as the fair distribution of benefits and burdens. This is called "distributive justice" (Beauchamp & Childress, 1983, p. 184). John Rawls (1971) argued that all *vital* economic goods and services ought to be distributed equally in a society unless it can be demonstrated that an unequal distribution would actually work to everyone's advantage. He also claimed that enlightened citizens (rational egoists) will recognize the value of this criterion for distribution, because otherwise they would become involved in destructive competition with each other.

To apply these guidelines to the provision of psychological counseling services and therapy in our society requires making two prior determinations: How vital and how scarce are the benefits of these services? If they are simply "frills" that result in a marginal and sometimes debatable improvement in the quality of life of the recipients, then there is no need to be concerned with their distribution. Likewise if these services are readily available to all who have use for them, then the distribution is not a problem. This chapter first considers the evidence for vitality, the importance of the benefits of psychotherapy and counseling in our society; then it looks at the evidence for scarcity and, if it exists, the reasons for it. Is it a matter of cost—that is, is it only scarce for those whose financial resources are quite restricted?

HOW VITAL IS PSYCHOLOGICAL COUNSELING
TO OUR SOCIETY?

There is no question that psychotherapy and counseling purport to treat problems that are endemic in our society. A partial list of them would include demoralization, depression, chronic anxiety, panic disorders, inability to concentrate, loss of self-direction, low self-esteem, compulsive behavior, obsessive rumination and worrying, delusional and hallucinatory thinking, marital and family discord, and effects of sexual abuse. However, there are reasons to question whether, in fact, the treatments work; if they don't work, they certainly can't be of "vital" importance.

The earlier discussion on diagnoses and autonomy (Chapter 1) noted Martin Gross's claim (1978) that many modern psychological "illnesses" have really been created by the practitioners who diagnose them; such illnesses often consist of transitory states, such as grief, that can be normal under certain conditions. The reason he can make this claim is the basically intangible quality of the complaints. Everybody, for example, is anxious at times—when is such anxiety a problem that must be dealt with rather than simply a tolerable discomfort and, indeed, one that may well diminish in intensity if viewed as temporary and to be expected? Similar questions can be asked about all of the other symptoms listed previously, even delusional thinking.

Another disturbing consideration is that there is actually no such thing as "psychotherapy" or "psychological counseling," or if there is, there is a *lot* of disagreement about what each refers to and how to distinguish between the two modes of treatment. There are several hundred schools of psychotherapy, each purporting to have "the best approach" to most of the common psychological disorders (Slovenko, 1981). Any of these schools of psychotherapy may be practiced by those who call themselves "counselors," which title is often simply a default appellation for persons not licensed to call themselves "psychotherapists." If people in the field really knew what they were doing in this broad treatment area, it seems likely that there would be greater unanimity of opinion as to which approach is best for what.

A third problem is that the evidence for the effectiveness of this collection of treatments referred to as "psychotherapy" is not very firm. Researchers have completed thousands of studies, but with few replications and with all calling for more research before reaching any definitive conclusions. The studies have generally been favorable, as substantiated by Smith and Glass in their mammoth meta-analysis of 520 studies selected for their apparent scientific rigor (1977).

However, because most clients invest considerable time, energy, and expectation in their treatment, one would anticipate that they would be likely to look for and report improvement in such intangible things as are measured by psychological tests and inventories. Their therapists' ratings would also be expected to show improvement for similar reasons. Additionally, one can presume that studies showing success in treatment are more apt to be submitted for publication, and as Mahoney (1977) has demonstrated, it is far more likely that such studies are published than are the exact same studies with negative results.

"Hard data," data based on tangible criteria, such as weight in pounds, number of alcoholic drinks consumed, and number of cigarettes smoked, indicate that modest progress is being made by various treatment programs in addictive behaviors, except perhaps in weight control. But the treatments that have been developed and show the most promise either use psychotherapy not at all or only as an ancillary (cf. Buie, 1987c, November).

Pursuing scientific proof of the value of psychotherapy may be a misguided and futile enterprise because the variables are so many, so complexly interwoven, and so transitory in effect that they will never allow definitive studies with regard to any of the more common, broadly defined, difficult, if not impossible to circumscribe, psychological concerns. This is the conclusion of at least one major writer in this field, who, as will be described in Chapter 8, has done some highly credible studies on the negative effects of encounter groups (Yalom, 1980):

> [One problem] plagues every psychotherapy outcome study. The more methods used to assess outcome, the less certain is the researcher of his results! How do researchers deal with this problem? One method is to increase reliability by asking fewer questions and to rely on a single source of data. Another . . . is to steer clear of "soft," or subjective, criteria and measure only objective criteria, such as amount of alcohol consumed, the number of times one spouse interrupts the other in some given period of time, the number of bites of food taken, galvanic skin response, or the size of penile tumescence while looking at slides of naked youths. But woe to the researcher who tries to measure the important factors, such as ability to love or care for another, zest in life, purposefulness, generosity, exuberance, autonomy, spontaneity, humor, courage, or engagement in life. Again and again one encounters a basic fact of life in psychotherapy research: the precision of the result is directly proportional to the triviality of the variables studies [sic]. A strange sort of science! (p. 24)

Because firm evidence of the efficacy of psychotherapy is lacking, it is necessary to turn to another, softer criterion—that of the status of psychotherapy in Western societies. It is clear, at least in the United

States and in most of Western Europe, that psychotherapy, most particularly psychoanalysis in Europe, is a recognized benefit. Psychiatry, clinical and counseling psychology, clinical social work, and other mental health counseling and therapy are well-entrenched professions in the United States; psychoanalysts, behavior therapists, and Rogerians, among others, are found in sizable numbers among the psychiatrists and psychologists in other Western countries. Also medical insurance policies frequently contain provisions for mental health benefits, and licensure of psychologists is well established in the United States and is making some headway in Europe. Clinical social workers, marriage and family counselors, and mental health counselors are also licensed or certified professions in a number of states and there are reasons to believe that this will spread extensively in the next few years.

There can be little doubt then that society has been generally persuaded that psychological counseling and psychotherapy are important benefits, and not just luxuries. Yet this is not a secure position; even as I write, there is a battle in the United States Congress over whether to delete mental health benefits from a proposed national "safety net" insurance system. Nevertheless, the professions that disperse such benefits are lobbying strenuously that such services are necessities, and they make similar arguments when they go to state and federal legislative bodies and ask for licensure or for parity as providers under laws regulating insurance companies. Accordingly, it would be inconsistent for such professions to take a different position when it comes to actually providing such services. From their perspective then, at least, these services are sufficiently basic that it is ethically important to determine a just way to distribute them.

DISTRIBUTING A SCARCE BENEFIT FAIRLY

Having put aside, if not laid to rest, the question of whether psychotherapy is a vital service, I now want to address the question of its scarcity, and the corresponding question of distribution. That psychotherapy and counseling are of limited availability in almost all sectors of the society is readily apparent: Public service agencies providing free, or relatively inexpensive, services typically have waiting lists that require them to limit the number of sessions clients can have. Also many clients simply do not receive treatment, either because they don't "qualify" for services for various reasons, or the agency has no group or individual treatment programs that will meet their needs, or their concern has to be handled in a timely fashion or not at all and they cannot be seen right away. Scarcity of services exists, at least for those who are not financially well off, as will be discussed later.

How then can a scarce benefit be distributed fairly? There are many ways of doing so, as outlined by Beauchamp and Childress (1983), whose suggestions I have generally adopted. One way is to give an equal amount to everyone, but this would not make sense with counseling or psychotherapy because the need for such services varies considerably from individual to individual and from time to time within the life of individuals. To provide one session per year per person, for example, would be unnecessary for many and too little for most of the others. Accumulating them over the years might be a better tactic, but to monitor such a system would create still other problems.

It seems more appropriate to provide according to need, if it is possible to determine a fair way of measuring "need." Currently, need is determined to be greatest in "crisis" situations, but this term is variably defined, depending on who makes the initial definition. Often clients simply declare themselves to be in crisis, and certain types of clients are more apt to make such a claim than others, the difference not always being in the direction of most need. At other times someone in contact with the client makes the determination, but that response may also be one of unjustified panic. By the time the professional, or in many cases, the paraprofessional, is involved, it is often easier to continue to deal with the client than to turn the client away because no real crisis (from the professional's viewpoint) is involved. Objective criteria are rarely available: Suicide attempts are usually discovered after the fact, and threats of suicide are also of variable definition ranging from vague allusions overheard and interpreted by third parties some time ago to explicit statements made by persons whose sincerity one would have no reason to doubt.

Diagnostic systems such as the *Diagnostic and Statistical Manual* of the American Psychiatric Association (DSM III-R, 1987) could provide another definition of need, but this first requires sufficient data gathering, often extending over several interviews, and administration of psychological inventories before diagnoses can be made with much assurance. Even then the more severe disorders, the chronic psychoses, are not usually very amenable to psychotherapy, so to provide such benefits here rather than at lesser need levels would be inefficient and inappropriate.

Other usable criteria are effort, achievement, and status—all of which are difficult to define in operational terms and therefore difficult to apply. However, some examples may clarify their possible use.

"The squeaky wheel gets the oil" describes a method of earning a service by effort, in this case by persistent supplication. People who make repeated requests for service over an extended period of time sometimes are able to bypass some of the barriers. Often this is done informally, but formal in-agency policies could be adopted such as, "If an applicant comes in three times, schedule the applicant."

Effort and achievement are combined when clients work their way up on a waiting list. The effort in this case is minimal: The client simply needs to come in the first time. The achievement is also minimal in that the client must only endure and be available when his or her turn comes up.

Still another criterion is status. Eligibility for services may be limited to achievers of a certain status, such as holding a job in a company that provides mental health services for employees. Various agencies and professionals can also simply confer status on someone, such as the status of being an ex-mental health patient of a state institution, which confers eligibility for state-provided aftercare services, or of having a drug abuse problem, which grants eligibility for state-provided drug treatment programs.

Perhaps the only sure way of earning access to mental health benefits is by having the money to pay for them, whatever they cost. Unfortunately, not everyone has equal opportunity or capacity to achieve this status, so it is problematic whether this is an appropriate criterion to use when attempting to dispense justice. In fact, overcoming many obstacles to become wealthy may demonstrate a mental toughness and health in the process that would belie such persons receiving treatment on the basis of need, if that were used as the basic criterion.

Rawls's (1971) proposal becomes relevant here. He claimed it is just to disperse benefits unequally if society as a whole benefits from such dispersal. Thus it could be argued that certain people perform such key functions in society that their mental well-being is more important to maintain than that of the average citizen. Such people normally also have sufficient financial recompense to afford such services, or they can receive such benefits through their employment, so it is seldom that this standard would have to be invoked in society as it now functions. Conversely, however, strict application of this standard would tend to shut out those who have not achieved the status of being "important to society."

None of the preceding criteria can be blithely disregarded, and, in fact, probably all of them have their place. Now it is necessary to consider how they apply to the increasingly dominant method for distributing the benefits of counseling and psychotherapy.

INSURANCE—BOON OR BANE?

On first appearance it would seem that provision of psychotherapy costs through reimbursement by insurance policies would be a purely positive contribution in that it would enable more people to have access to this somewhat scarce benefit. This would be true whether the payments were made through an ordinary medical insurance policy, a health maintenance organization (HMO), a preferred provider plan (PPO), an individual practice association (IPA), or some other yet-to-be-developed type of organization or policy. However, on closer inspection this development has opened up a can of worms of ethical concerns.

One problem that has already been mentioned is that insurance does not do away with the have/have not split. With the possible exception of some federal programs such as Medicaid, those who don't have jobs or don't have good, well-paying jobs, and are not dependents of individuals who do, are usually not covered under a health insurance policy at all, much less one that provides for psychotherapy. Ironically, this means those most able to pay don't need to, whereas those who can't pay are not eligible for insurance that would provide such services.

A confounding issue is whether or not psychotherapy is properly classified as a "medical treatment," which is the assumption made by including it under health care policies. If it is a medical treatment, then the providers ought to be medically trained, and the disorders should have a medical diagnosis. Prescriptions would seem to be in order and some sort of physical treatment might well be appropriate, such as drug therapy, lobotomy, or electroconvulsive therapy. But suppose this view is essentially wrong, that psychological disorders require an entirely different approach, one that must be done within a cooperative, rather than an authoritarian model, as was argued in Chapter 1, Promotion of Autonomy. Then the once dominant, and still all-too-typical, medical approach might well not benefit the "patients" at all and may actually make them worse. Danish and Symer (1981) argue in this vein in discussing the effects of assigning a medical diagnosis:

> One consequence of being labeled "mentally ill" is that . . . it may relieve the individual's family and support network of their responsibility. . . . If mental illness is labeled a *disease,* and not an interpersonal or competency deficiency, the causes are assumed to be biochemical or physiological. . . . Family and friends may feel they should not interfere in an area they know nothing about. . . . However, it is not just the loss of social support that adversely affects the patient. If individuals become convinced that they are

victims of mental illness, they may feel less able to master the problems themselves and therefore, less able to help themselves. (pp. 18–19)

The effect on the practitioner of utilizing medical model diagnoses also warrants scrutiny. In most cases to get reimbursed by third party insurance carriers, it is necessary to assign clients DSM III-R mental illness diagnoses that the carrier specifies as reimbursable. The therapist may not find such diagnoses useful except for this purpose and will be tempted, in any case, to "stretch" the symptomatology of clients to fit these reimbursable categories. For example, instead of saying the client is in need of marital counseling, a nonreimbursable category, the therapist selects the client's depressive symptoms and assigns the diagnosis of adjustment disorder with depressed mood. In terms of the principles, therapist Self-Interest takes precedence over Fidelity to the insurance carrier. To the degree that the diagnosis changes the client's self-concept or the concept of others regarding the client, or alters the treatment itself (such as in this example providing individual therapy instead of couple counseling), the diagnosis could adversely affect the client (violation of Nonmaleficence).

This and other problems were noted by the Oklahoma Psychological Association in 1981, leading to their proposal of a code of ethics for interacting with insurance reimbursers. The code prohibits a number of remunerative but unethical practices, including changing the diagnosis to fit the coverage, treating the client in a hospital rather than as an outpatient because the client's coverage only extends to inpatient treatment, and charging a higher than usual fee because it will be paid by the third party. This code was never adopted by the national organization; however, it was essentially reaffirmed in the 1988 report of the Ethics Committee of the American Psychological Association.

Another consequence of the huge role played by insurance payments in the field of psychological care is the fighting among professions over eligibility to be "providers" of such care and over the control of the referrals to the providers. But as this is primarily a matter of Justice with regard to the professional providers (Self-Justice), rather than of Justice to the clients, it will be discussed in the section Turf Battles between Professions, in Chapter 15.

The other ethical concern directly related to clients is the security of the information that is released to the insurers—in short, is confidentiality kept? Normally only date of service, type of service ("procedure"), and diagnosis are required, but if a quality control check is made, normally to detect fraud, then progress notes may be requested as well. The fear is that such information will be made privy to unqualified personnel who will misuse it in some way, or that it will be released to governmental agencies or employers without permission or knowledge of the client. Insurance companies pledge otherwise. CHAMPUS (Civilian Health and Medical Plan of the Uniformed Services), for example, promises to keep its psychiatric and psychological claims separate from other medical claims and not to release them to outside employers or to permit unlawful government access (Foltz, 1979). However, the suspicion remains. It is supported by sporadic disclosures of the illegal and questionable practices of the Central Intelligence Agency (CIA) and the Federal Bureau of Investigation (FBI), such as occurred in the once-famous case of Daniel Ellsberg, a vice presidential candidate who was replaced after the discovery that he had suffered from severe psychological problems over a period of time:

> The Daniel Ellsberg case should at least have taught us that if the government wants information on its citizens, it will stop at nothing to get it. This would be especially true if that information were resting innocently in the computers of its own agencies. (Roskam, 1979, p. 18)

This is primarily a matter of Fidelity, of keeping promises to clients and to therapists, but it is also a matter of Justice in that those who can afford to pay for their own psychological care don't run the same amount of risk of their confidences being betrayed because information about them, including the basic fact that they are or were clients, does not have to be released to any third party; thus the "burdens" of society are unfairly distributed (Herbert, 1979).

HOW TO HANDLE INDIGENT CLIENTS

Perhaps the most troubling problem for psychological care professions is what to do with those individuals who want psychotherapy and counseling but who can't pay the going rate for such services. In fact some of them can't, at least at the time and in the foreseeable future, pay anything at all. This situation provokes a naked confrontation between Self-Interest, on the part of the practitioner, and Justice, in terms of distributing benefits on the basis of need, to the potential clients. To a certain extent Self-Justice can be evoked by the professionals and by agencies that provide such services because a certain amount of income is necessary for them to survive economically. But beyond survival, what is a "fair" income to demand as a minimum? At what point does the attempt to administer justice to oneself unduly override doing justice to others? As of yet there are no generally acceptable guidelines for arriving at these figures. There are no widely endorsed and promoted formulas that specify "so many dollars [marks, francs, etc.] for so many years of education, training, and/or experience." What there is instead is the "going rate in the market place" or the "market value" of such services, which is often strongly influenced by what insurance will cover.

Lacking a simple, direct answer to the problem of poverty, the typical approach is to try to finesse the problem in a number of different ways. One way is to postpone payments until such time as clients can pay; another is to give reduced rates to those clients who can't afford the regular fee, the so-called "sliding scale" method; and still another is to refer impoverished applicants to special programs or agencies that receive public and/or charitable funding. One of the problems with this last solution is that it, in effect, "labels" these clients as somehow not being "worthy" of regular services, thus violating the principle of Nonmaleficence.

The most truly charitable approach is deliberately to accept some proportion of clients without charge, perhaps those who are most meritorious on other criteria such as effort or apparent need. Several codes recommend this altruistic approach including the codes of the Canadian Psychological Association (1986, Section IV:7) and the American Psychological Association (1981a). The APA's "Ethical Principles" states: "[Psychologists] contribute a portion of their services to work for which they receive little or no financial return" (Section 6d). The key word here is "contribute." Forced contributions, such as inevitably occur when clients default on payments, would not meet the spirit of this guideline.

The most comprehensive and elegant solution to all these problems would seem to be to provide nationally funded insurance for psychological care that would not be part of a "medical" health plan and that would be adequate to provide sufficient quality service for all who needed and could profit from it. Whether society could afford this is, of course, a real problem—although it could be argued that society can less afford the costs associated with the nonprovision of such services. Another major stumbling block, as previously noted, is how to select those who "need and can profit from" such services.

A step in this direction for the "chronically mentally ill" was taken at a recent convention of the American Orthopsychiatric Association. A paper coauthored by the retiring president John Talbott and Deputy Medical Director Steven Sharfstein proposed that the federal government develop a single administrative agency to coordinate all programs for this population. It would be initially financed by pooling all the monies that are now divided among a variety of federal programs (Bales, 1985).

JUSTICE TO ETHNIC MINORITIES

As the world population burgeons and international boundaries become increasingly permeable, it becomes harder and harder to maintain cultural distinctions. However, the twin barriers of poverty and language have not diminished, although constantly in flux, with the result that many immigrant groups, especially those who are refugees from persecution and poverty in other countries, arrive with very limited resources to integrate successfully in the "haven" countries. The United States hosts, albeit often unwillingly, refugee populations from Southeast Asia and Central America, among others, and Western Europe is hard pressed to take in refugees from Eastern Europe, Southeast Asia, and Africa.

Each country has, in addition, its own poorly assimilated cultural minorities. In the United States, blacks, Hispanics, and American Indians often have especially severe psychological and physical problems. Their needs are manifold: better housing, more employment opportunities, better health care, more education, and increased access to appropriate psychological care. Immigrant refugee groups have these problems and need language training as well.

To a certain extent the housing, educational, employment, and basic health care needs should receive priority attention, because psychological dysfunctioning is often directly traceable to such stressors. However, it can also be argued that supportive counseling and therapy may enable people to continue the struggle to obtain the other benefits, because passive resignation or acting-out behavior seldom accomplishes desired goals. Regardless, to serve Justice, it would seem that the need for psychological services should not be ignored.

The difficulty is that most therapists are ill equipped to deal with cultural minorities, especially individuals with language difficulties. A recent survey found:

> Only two of 105 APA-approved clinical psychology programs required a course on ethnic minority topics, [and] of 398 psychology departments responding to another survey, only 4.3% required courses or practica on assessment of ethnic minorities, and only 9.5% had electives in this area. (Suinn, 1987, p. 30)

The data appear to be similar with respect to counseling and school psychology and internship programs. Furthermore, only 5% of faculty and 11% of doctoral recipients came from minority groups. This is in contrast to the estimate that "soon, one of four Americans will be Amer-

ican Indian/Alaska Native, Asian/Pacific American, Black, or Hispanic''
(Suinn, 1987, p. 30)

Correspondingly, members of many minority cultures are ill acquainted
with the appropriate utilization of psychological counseling and therapy
because such resources were practically nonexistent in their native land
or in the environment in which they were raised.

With problems of this dimension it is obvious that national efforts must
be made to rectify the situation. Simply trying to accept more minority
candidates into graduate school programs is not enough. First there must
be a pool of candidates from which to draw. This will require offering
better economic, employment, and educational opportunities to all such
minority families and groups, starting at birth in many instances. Requiring
the introduction of courses and practicum in minority counseling and
psychotherapy is somewhat more feasible in the immediate future, although it too relies on having qualified instructors. This approach, plus
integration of multicultural concerns ''into all relevant aspects of the
curriculum'' has been strongly recommended by the American Psychological Association Training Committee at a recent APA conference on
graduate education in psychology (1987, p. 7). Private practitioners already in the field could be required to devote a certain amount of their
continuing education credits to cross-cultural training, once such training
is widely available, or such experiences could be doubly valued or otherwise encouraged.

In the meantime some innovative methods have been introduced to
breach the linguistic barrier. Acosta and Cristo (cited in Rogler, Malgady,
Costantino, & Blumenthal, 1987) treated Hispanic clients in a psychiatric
clinic with the aid of bilingual interpreters who were recruited from the
same neighborhoods as the clients and were trained in key concepts of
psychotherapy. Their efforts met with apparent success: The percentage
of Spanish-speaking clients doubled.

Even if the linguistic barrier is overcome, it may be that standard
psychotherapeutic approaches may be inappropriate for most minority
clients. How appropriate is it, for example, to do psychoanalysis with
someone whose life is in chaos because of environmental variables not
under their control? The same question might be asked of any insight-
oriented therapy. The answers are as yet lacking, and until what seems
to work best with whom becomes clearer, the best advice seems to be to
individualize the treatment process to the client, that is, to determine how
responsive each client seems to be to an approach before committing
oneself and the client to it. It may also be possible, assuming one knows
something about the cultural background of the client, to modify a treatment to the client's cultural values or beliefs. In one example reported

by Kreisman (Rogler, et al., 1987), the therapist working with two Mexican-American female schizophrenics who claimed to be bewitched concurred with them and invoked some folk remedies. This enabled the clients to accept and cooperate with the therapist in subsequent treatment.

There is much controversy over the effectiveness of psychotherapy for ethnic minority clients. But this debate must not obscure the basic ethical issue that such individuals should have access to therapy and to therapists of their choosing (Sue, 1988).

It is obvious that the application of the Principle of Justice is one of the more challenging for the psychological care professions and potentially one of the most personally rewarding.

ISSUES

Under what conditions is it relevant to require just distribution of benefits?

What is the nature and quality of the evidence that counseling/therapy are *vital* benefits in our society?

In what sense, to whom, are the benefits *scarce*?

What criteria can be applied to ensure fair distribution of the services of counseling and therapy?

What are the problems with applying each criterion?

What ethical problems are exacerbated when distribution of services is influenced by reimbursement from third parties, such as various medical insurance plans?

How can therapists ethically respond to the needs of persons who can't pay?

What must be done to provide ethnic minorities with appropriate, quality services?

What are some suggestions for handling such clients under current conditions?

What is the basic ethical issue for provision of services to ethnic minorities?

PART FOUR

Beneficence

The preceding principles, Autonomy, Fidelity, and Justice, although having relevance throughout the whole course of treatment, have an especial importance at the pretreatment and early-onset-of-treatment stages when prospective clients are informed what lies ahead, are explicitly or implicitly promised certain kinds of behavior on the part of their therapists, and are selected or not selected for treatment. Beneficence and the remaining principles of Nonmaleficence and Self-Interest are of roughly equal relevance throughout the course of treatment and posttreatment.

Beneficence is a "background" principle, the "bed" in which all the other principles lie. In theory it can be separated from Nonmaleficence, but in practice the two inevitably intertwine, so much of the material in Part Four could as well be in the section on Nonmaleficence, and, indeed, some cross-referencing will occur. However, a valid difference in emphasis does exist in many areas and separation of the two principles is thus of pragmatic value.

CHAPTER 7

The Principle of Beneficence

ASPECTS OF BENEFICENCE

If any principle is the core duty of a help-providing profession, it is the duty of beneficence. Indeed, some ethical codes have an explicit statement to that effect, such as this one from that of the American Association for Counseling and Development (1988):

> The member's *primary* (italics added) obligation is to respect the integrity and promote the welfare of the client(s), whether the client(s) is (are) assisted individually or in a group relationship. (Section B.1)

Yet, parceling out the various aspects of the roles of the helpers according to other principles leaves very little to assign primarily to Beneficence—it is almost as if it were a disappearing phenomenon. Beauchamp and Childress (1983) avoided that problem by assigning active removal and prevention of harm to Beneficence and left only passive avoidance of doing harm to Nonmaleficence, which division is certainly permissible, but admittedly arbitrary. Ross's (1930) formulation of Nonmaleficence did not separate out the various ways of ensuring that one did not do harm, but I find it more in keeping with his formulation to put all harm-oriented reduction under Nonmaleficence: removal of present harm, prevention of future harm, and the passive avoidance of harm. This leaves only the doing of good to Beneficence.

Thus what remains is sort of a figure–ground relationship where the apparent importance and clarity of Beneficence shifts from figure to background when the other principles are considered, with one exception: altruism, or self-sacrifice on behalf of others. Altruism is properly judged from an external viewpoint because the persons who are "sacrificing" may feel they are doing so for selfish reasons; that is, they are personally gratified when they help others. However, daily altruistic behavior hardly seems like a reasonable duty to ask of those who have elected to pursue help-providing professions, and, indeed, no ethical code demands it.

Some self-sacrifice of a particular kind is expected of psychological care givers, however. They, like their counterparts in physical care giving, the physicians, are expected to be available for emergencies, either personally or through prearranged backup services of comparable quality. They acknowledge this duty in a number of ways, such as providing their personal phone number to clients who appear suicidal and recommending crisis hotlines to others in less serious straits if they are apt to need frequent reassurance and reality checks. Strictly speaking, such measures are taken more in the interest of Nonmaleficence, or prevention of harm to clients, than of Beneficence. Therapists may also take them to reduce the possibility of a malpractice suit on the basis of negligence, in which case Self-Protection is being served.

A purer example of altruism concerns indigent clients, those who can't pay for psychotherapy. "Ethical Principles" (APA, 1981a) clearly states that some provision should be made for such clients: "Psychologists . . . contribute a portion of their services to work for which they receive little or no financial reward" (Section 6e). The new code of the Canadian Psychological Association has a similar guideline (1986, Section IV:7).

Free or for-cost lectures, workshops, and other presentations are ways of manifesting altruism. They may also, in some cases, be a way of advertising the professional's or the agency's services. When the initial presentation is free, but subsequent ones, described in glowing terms, are costly, it is likely that altruism is not involved at all.

Most other aspects of Beneficence have or will be mentioned in connection with the other duties. Thus, a primary way to promote the welfare of others is to promote their functioning as autonomous individuals. Similarly, under the rubric of Fidelity, clients benefit when their therapists or counselors identify with their concerns and help them achieve their goals of self-improvement and relief from misery. The promise of confidentiality and its implications, such as claiming privilege on behalf of the client when asked to divulge confidences in the courtroom, is based on the premise that keeping such promises will act to the benefit of the client. Therapists who act justly to clients and avoid doing injury to them also do so to their benefit.

Some categories of activities, however, that clearly fall under Beneficence and its almost inevitable companion, Nonmaleficence, have received or will receive inadequate attention in the other sections of the book. This short list begins with Paternalism.

PATERNALISM

Paternalism is usually defined as an imposition on client autonomy—that is, the professional decides what is best for the clients, rather than letting clients decide that for themselves. This is done both for reasons of enhancing the benefits that clients will receive and to avoid harm that may occur if they decide "wrongly," as defined by the professional; thus both Beneficence and Nonmaleficence are involved and seen as superseding Autonomy.

Paternalism is clearly invoked when the client–therapist relationship encourages dependency on the therapist's judgment. Therapists routinely usurp the choice of technique, the choice of focus, and the determination of when the client is ready to make certain decisions. Indeed, these can be seen to be the responsibility of the therapist.

Clients with particularly diminished capacity for self-direction are frequently put into institutions, often without their agreement, by establishing that they constitute a danger to themselves, because they are suicidal or are unable to care for themselves, or that they constitute a danger to others. Institutions make many choices for their inmates. They impose getting-up times, mealtimes, type and frequency of various group and individual activities; they give or revoke canteen privileges, trial visits to the community, work release passes; and they decide when to terminate treatment. As a result some inmates become "institutionalized"; that is, their capacity to make autonomous decisions is so eroded that they are unable to function outside an environment that makes such decisions for them. This is not the intent of the institutionalization, which normally is to protect the clients until such time as they are able to return to autonomous functioning, or, at least, improved functioning, but it is almost an inevitable consequence of prolonged or repeated institutionalizations. To prevent this type of dependency, modern psychiatry, psychology, and social work promote short-term community-based treatment programs. Also, outpatient care is generally preferable to inpatient care, if feasible; albeit, at times there is risk of overriding this approach when the client's insurance will cover inpatient care, but not outpatient.

Paternalism exists in many other situations as well, some of which are described in the following sections.

RECORD KEEPING

One area in which Beneficence plays an obvious role is in the keeping of client records. Counselors probably originally kept notes on interviews and other interactions with their clients simply because they learned that, unless they did so, they were apt to forget important details of these transactions. The awkward or embarrassing result was that sometimes they either had to ask the client for aid in remembering what had happened or they had to pretend they remembered when they didn't. They also weren't as competent as they might otherwise have been; therefore, both Self-Interest and Beneficence were not being well served. Test results and other data were also put in such files. Thus if clients came back, it was possible to avoid some historical rehashing and perhaps to avoid retaking some psychological tests. Also, a record of current or past counseling was handy if the client called in for emergency counseling and her or his counselor wasn't available. In any instance, records facilitated transition to other counselors. As society became more complicated, clients sometimes needed to verify that they had received treatment, or they wanted specified information from their files sent to some third party, such as to another counselor whom they were seeing. Thus it became important to keep files for extended periods of time. Finally, extensive notes are necessary if one hopes to learn from one's attempts at helping the client. Freud used to document the dreams of his clients carefully, for example, and used his notes for constructing a theory of how to interpret such dreams. This theory then became useful to him and others in treating additional clients. For these and perhaps still other reasons, keeping such treatment records has become a routine part of most psychotherapy and counseling.

Being that such records contain sensitive information, it is imperative to establish policies and methods of retention and of transmission that protect the confidentiality of the information therein and best promote the welfare of the clients. The "Specialty Guidelines" (APA, 1981b, Section 2.3.5) developed by the American Psychological Association for service providers recommends that psychological service units develop a written record retention policy. What should or should not be in the records, how long they should be maintained, how they should be secured, and other concerns come to the fore.

Recommendations for Record Keeping

These concerns are addressed in the following recommendations (adapted from Thompson, 1983, pp. 104–106).

1. *Keep Only Essential Records.* With the advent of computerized data banks, it has become apparent that the more information there is on file the more administrative and research questions can theoretically be answered. Therefore the types of information preserved by agencies, especially those devoted to research, in anticipation that they will sometime prove useful, threatens to expand geometrically. In our homes this preservationistic attitude has led to overflowing closets, garages, attics, and even to rental of additional storage units. In the office it leads to additional

computer and paper files with additional filing cabinets and greater computer memory. As a result the chances of misplacing something dramatically increase, and misplaced data is not secure data. Periodic reviews of files with consequent systematic purging and shredding need to be established.

Some facts are best left out of records altogether, unless they are of clear clinical importance. These include descriptions of sexual practices and illegal behavior, which, if brought to light, would tend to embarrass or harm the client.

2. *Write Behavior Descriptions, Not Speculations in Your Case Notes.* It is just as simple and more useful in the long run to write down the basic facts of client-provided information than to write down the derivative speculations. For example, instead of writing, "Client appears to have paranoid delusions," write, "Client reports frequent suspicions of being followed by strangers and of being talked about behind his back." The behavior description will probably evoke the speculative diagnoses at any given future date, whereas the reverse is not apt to be true—the particulars are likely to fade in memory and suffer distortion.

Also behavior descriptions may be understood more readily and correctly by any other party who has legitimate access to the file. Even colleagues may have theoretical orientations that differ enough to cause inaccurate transmission of diagnostic speculations.

The focus in record keeping should always be on facts:

> The developing right of clients to gain access to their records, and the widespread release of records to third-party payers and others emphasize that records should focus on facts and not hunches or value judgments. (Cohen, 1979, cited in Soisson, VandeCreek, & Knapp, 1987, p. 500)

3. *Document the Important Decisions.* There are certain decisions, such as whether to inform the authorities of a client's suicidal or homicidal tendencies, that should be justified at the time they are made in order to ensure that this material will be maximally accurate and available in the event of some future request for such justification. This documentation would consist of the description of the behavior and the basis for the interpretation, including a report of any consultation the therapist received. It is appropriate here to record any speculative interpretation because it constitutes a primary part of the basis for the decision. But most important are the facts used in arriving at the interpretations and conclusions, including the presence or absence of environmental controls. For example, if the client lives with others who can readily observe the client's behavior and intervene in any crisis situation, there would be less

need to worry about suicide than if the client lived alone. Knapp (1980) states:

> Careful documentation of the treatment and the treatment plan reduces the likelihood of a successful malpractice suit. Complete records can aid the psychologist in court. Records should include detailed notes of symptomatology, a diagnosis, treatment, all aspects of consent, relevant consultations and their outcomes, and descriptions of significant sessions.
>
> Psychologists should seek professional consultation with difficult or life-threatening clients. (p. 611)

Cohen (1979, cited in Soisson et al., 1987, p. 500), also with a view of protection against malpractice suits, recommends that client files should contain:

> At the minimum, a descriptive summary of all contacts, regular summaries of progress, available psychological tests, notations of informed consent to all aspects of treatment, notes concerning phone contacts and conversations with significant others in the client's life, and copies of all correspondence with the client. (p. 500)

Obviously, the primary concern here is Self-Protection for the clinician rather than promotion of Beneficence to the client, except insofar as seeking consultation may be helpful. Gutheil and Appelbaum (1982, cited in Soisson et al., 1987) also recommend keeping such detailed records with certain clients as a protection against malpractice suits.

4. *Follow the Official Policy on Record Retention That Applies to Your Situation.* If you work in a governmental agency, whether local, state, or federal, the policy for record retention is probably already fixed by the relevant governmental authority. If you are in private practice or work for an independent private agency, the APA "Specialty Guidelines" (1981b) recommend:

> a. That the full record be retained intact for 3 years after the completion of planned services or after the date of last contact with the user, whichever is later; (b) that a full record or summary of the record be maintained for an additional 12 years; and (c) that the record may be disposed of no sooner than 15 years after the completion of planned services or after the date of last contact, whichever is later. These temporal guides are consistent with procedures currently in use by federal record centers. (Section 2.3.5)

Why should practitioners follow such institutional policies and governmental regulations and laws? Two principles are primarily involved:

Beneficence in that clients may profit from recourse to such records at a later date, and Self-Protection in that should the records be subpoenaed for some reason, *not* to have followed official regulations leaves the practitioner and/or agency in a difficult-to-defend position.

Shadow Records

Many therapists keep shadow records containing personal speculations about their clients. Some clinicians find them useful in formulating their thoughts and planning future strategies for their clients. Obviously such records must also either be kept secured or be coded to prevent identification of the clients. The legal status of such records is largely undetermined. According to Soisson et al. (1987), in Illinois such notes are protected by statute and are immune from subpoena (Mental and Developmental Disabilities Confidentiality Act, 1979). They were unaware of any court test of dual records in states without explicit protection. However, subpoenas can specify release of *all records* on specified clients, and judges may consider such records as potentially germane to the case, especially if the records on file are sparse.

Client Access to Records

It is strange to think that confidentiality, or the keeping of secrets, has come so far that it extends to the exclusion of clients themselves, the original providers of the secret material and the supposed beneficiaries of the protection from disclosure. Yet it is exactly this argument of Beneficence over Autonomy, that is, Paternalism, that is used to keep clients from accessing their own files and other records about themselves.

At first blush this does not seem to make sense, but even in the priest–parishioner confessional model the priest would, if asked, have basis for refusing the request of a parishioner who wanted to know the priest's unvoiced reactions and private thoughts about the confession. It is these aspects of the client's records plus information the therapist may have received in confidence about the client and information that is not readily interpretable to laypersons—diagnoses, theoretical speculations, and test results—that are kept from direct client access.

It is feared that some clients might not be able to understand and would distort the portions of their records generated by others if they had direct access to them. An alternative, which may or may not be satisfactory to some clients, is to provide an interpreted version of the records to the clients, one that edits out the allegedly harmful portions. As seen in Part One, promotion of client autonomy would seem to require at least this much. Indeed this stance has received some recognition in the law. According to Schwitzgebel and Schwitzgebel (1980):

> Several states give statutory permission to . . . mental patients to examine and copy . . . their medical records. Most states with access statutes explicitly prohibit disclosure of records of patients in mental hospitals . . . except . . . upon request of the patient's attorney. Access may be further limited to a professional intermediary, such as an independent psychiatrist or psychologist retained by the patient to examine the record and report relevant conclusion.

> In states without statutes granting mental patients access to their medical records, a review of the record by the patient is likely to be difficult unless the institution or practitioner voluntarily agrees. . . .

> Finally, some distinction may be made between records such as transcripts or test protocols, in which the patient has a proprietary interest, and the more informal professional products such as technical notes, comments, or uninterpreted data, which are meaningful only to the practitioner. Those informal products are usually in the sole possession of the practitioner or assistants and are not accessible to or transmitted to other persons. (pp. 212–213)

A similar distinction is made with respect to educational records. The revised Family Education Rights and Privacy Act of 1974 gives students aged 18 years or older or those attending a postsecondary educational institution the right to inspect some educational records, but not records of treatment "created or maintained by a physician, psychiatrist, psychologist, or other recognized professional or paraprofessional acting in his or her professional capacity" (Schwitzgebel & Schwitzgebel, 1980, pp. 211–212). Upon request of the student, however, such records are to be disclosed to an appropriate treatment professional chosen by the student.

Although some practitioners write their notes in such a way as to make them quite understandable to their clients and freely provide such records to the clients, this is the exception rather than the rule. Most are reluctant to reveal directly what is in the records. This protective stance is supported by the APA "Specialty Guidelines" (1981b):

> Users have the right to obtain information from their psychological records. However, the records are the property of the psychologist or the facility in which the psychologist works and are, therefore, the responsibility of the psychologist and subject to his or her control. (Section 2.3.5)

Ironically, protecting clients from misinterpreting their files also may prevent them from discovering errors in these records which could adversely affect them. So the argument of Nonmaleficence can be made both for and against direct access. Direct release of files may also be contrary to the Self-Interest of the practitioner or the agency, at least in the short run, because they may contain information that would embarrass the practitioner or agency or even serve as a basis for a malpractice suit. The only investigation of which I am aware in this area comes down on the side of client access:

> After conducting extensive inquiries and holding hearings on the issue [the commission] reported that "not one witness was able to identify an instance where access to [one's own] records had an untoward effect on a patient's condition. . . . In fact, several officials . . . believed that clients' potential access to the files actually improved the quality of the notes, because their personnel were striving to enhance accuracy and exclude irrelevances. (Report by the federally appointed Privacy Protection Study Commission, cited in Plotkin, 1978, p. 10)

WAYS OF ENHANCING COMPETENCY

A certain minimum level of competency is expected of any practitioner for without it there is danger not only of failure to help clients but also of actually harming them. In fact, it is doubtful that counseling or psychotherapy can be "neutral" experiences though measuring the complex of possible impacts on the recipients is difficult. If clients are not helped, they are probably harmed, if only in that they have wasted some time and money in the effort. Also the constantly changing societal context of counseling and therapy inevitaby impinges on the success or failure of any given treatment approach. For example, to establish rapport with and communicate clearly with teenage clients, it is necessary to keep abreast of the nomenclature in their peer group. Therefore to ensure competency, clinicians must continually "enhance" their skills and knowledge: They cannot rely solely on what worked in the past.

Beneficence (and Nonmaleficence) thus requires a commitment to continuing education—workshops, reading, lectures, and coursework. Ethical guidelines for counselors and psychotherapists routinely recognize this fact, as exemplified by the following excerpt (American Psychiatric Association, 1986):

> A physician shall continue to study, apply, and advance scientific knowledge, make relevant information available to patients, colleagues, and the public, obtain consultation, and use the talents of other health professionals when indicated. (Preamble to Section 5)

As suggested by these guidelines, seeking consultation and referral are two other ways to benefit and protect clients. Such actions are appropriate any time that the practitioner fears being incompetent in assessing or treating any particular client, or simply believes that he or she could do a better job by gaining additional knowledge from consultation, or judges that the client would be better off if seen by another available professional. Sometimes referral can be made for a particular part of the client's concerns, such as assessment for brain damage or for physical disease, or a referral can be for a limited amount of time, such as for general counseling or psychotherapy before attempting vocational counseling.

Carrying this policy to the extreme, however, threatens the livelihood of the practitioner. This is especially true for those therapists who are just starting out in practice and are unsure of their skills. Thus Self-Beneficence would require retaining some clients even though they might get more experienced help elsewhere.

The same can be said with regard to having practitioners-in-training see clients. It is Self-Interest, more precisely Self-Beneficence for the profession, as well as Beneficence for future clients, that justifies provision of what can be assumed to be less-than-optimal service to the clients. Supervision of such trainees is the "guarantee" for the client that the service will be beneficial, as much as this can be guaranteed in any case, and not harmful.

Proper Working Conditions

The psychological and physical environment in which services are rendered can have a profound impact on the quality of the services. For example, if an agency requires that therapists see a certain number of clients in a week, or even a certain number consecutively in any given day, it may well be that those clients who are seen at the end of the shift will receive less focused attention than those seen earlier. If clients are seen in noisy conditions, or in inadequately ventilated, or in obviously restricted spaces, this may also impact adversely on both the therapist and the clients. Thus Beneficence and Nonmaleficence require attention to such variables. This is recognized in APA's "Specialty Guidelines" (1981b):

> **4.1** Providers of clinical psychological services promote the development in the service setting of a physical, organizational, and social environment that facilitates optimal human functioning. (Section 4.1)

Beneficence and "Team Members": The Use of Family, Roommates, Peer Supervisors, and Others as Consultants

The discussion on confidentiality (Chapter 5) pointed out that the concept of the treatment team is an expandable one and can include in various ways and to varying degrees consultants, both colleagues and those of other professions, family and friends of the client who are asked to monitor or encourage certain behavior, as well as co-workers and cotherapists—in short, anyone who contributes some significant portion of the treatment program of the client. Because this was in the context of protection of confidentiality, the emphasis was on sharing information about the client, as necessary, to implement the treatment, but with the client's knowledge and consent.

What was not emphasized, but is obvious, is that these team members were used with the intention of benefiting the client; hence, Beneficence is the controlling principle. In some instances a variety of individuals may be called in to protect the client from harm, such as when a roommate, spouse, or parent is instructed what to do if the client appears irrational. Then Nonmaleficence would be the primary motive.

Using colleagues as peer supervisors serves the duties of both Beneficence and Nonmaleficence. All too often once therapists graduate from internships the only additional training and supervision received is in continuing education workshops, if that. Such "supervision" is a sporadic and inadequate means of monitoring daily practices. Yet nobody is without blind spots or insensitivities and anyone may do a less than competent job and perhaps even an injurious one with certain clients, especially if the therapist is having personal problems at the time.

To protect clients from these human frailties, it seems reasonable, if not obligatory, that counselors and therapists seek out a group of colleagues whose judgment they trust and regularly present difficult cases to them and vice versa. Such a practice could go a long way toward maintaining sensitivity to individual proclivities that subtract from work with clients.

Not every horse can be led to the water, however, and those who are there may not drink. So for those therapists who give indications of unethical or incompetent behavior but are not willing to discuss it or apparently do anything about it, stronger measures have to be taken. These will be discussed in Chapter 9.

BENEFICENCE IN GROUP COUNSELING

How does one ensure that a group experience will be beneficial to the participant? As with individual counseling there are no absolute answers to this question, but certain procedures promote this result. Selection of the applicants via a screening interview is one of these procedures. It has already been discussed under Autonomy (Chapter 3) because such interviews also serve the purpose of providing information regarding the group objectives and means of reaching them. Only those applicants who appear able to focus on the concerns of others, as well as their own, would be apt to profit from and contribute to a group experience. Other criteria include the ability to use criticism constructively, to control the tendency to interpret neutral comments negatively, and to withstand group pressure.

It may be possible to offer applicants who "fail" these criteria pregroup individual counseling or training to help them develop decision-making skills and independence of judgment, as recommended by Zimpfer (1971).

Even the most thorough screening, however, will not completely take care of the problem of differential readiness for a particular group experience.

> Group members do not start ... from the same "starting line" and run breast to breast only in passing.... Some members at any given point in the group process are apt to "be out of it," and not getting any benefit from the group experience. (Thompson, 1983, p. 209)

It is not always possible for the leaders to be aware of this, and even if they are, it may not be appropriate to disrupt the group process which is benefiting the other group members in order to try to bring in the retarded ones.

One way of handling this problem, particularly if it is a persistent one with certain group members, is to provide special in-between sessions for them. Those members who didn't "finish" at the same time as the other group members may need posttermination individual sessions or referral to another group in order to consolidate their gains. This is the policy recommended by the Association for Specialists in Group Work (Roberts, 1982):

> Group leaders shall provide between-session consultation to group members and follow-up after termination of the group as needed or requested. (Section B-10)

There are many other group counseling concerns, such as the effects of ostracism on group members, the risks of experimental group treatments, and the negative fallout from too much group- or leader-induced pressure. These will be taken up in Chapter 8 because the emphasis is on finding procedures to prevent harm, rather than simply on promoting benefits.

ISSUES

Why might Beneficence be considered the core or primary duty of psychotherapists and counselors?

In what ways are therapists expected to be altruistic?

What is paternalism and how is it reflected in psychotherapy?

How is record keeping a natural response to Beneficence?

Explain the reasons for keeping certain kinds of information. Why should the therapist avoid speculative comments? When should they be part of the record? What decisions should be documented, and how?

What are the official guidelines for record retention, and why should they be followed?

What is the value of "shadow records?" What is their legal status?

Should clients have access to their files, and do clients have the legal right to view them?

Why might continuing education be considered an ethical obligation and not just a "plus"?

How can giving clients to practitioners-in-training be justified?

What is the relevance of working conditions of the therapist to the welfare of the client?

How does Beneficence require that the concept of the "treatment team" be expandable?

What essential role do "peer supervisors" play in such a team?

What special procedures ought to be followed and what criteria must be met to ensure the beneficial treatment of group clients?

PART FIVE

Nonmaleficence

In a sense all ethical principles can be reduced to two—Beneficence and Nonmaleficence. We either help our fellow humans or we harm them, and we behave ethically when we act in ways that are apt to help and not to harm. Promoting autonomy, keeping promises, and acting justly are usually helpful. Promoting dependency, breaking promises, and acting unjustly usually cause harm. Likewise, competence is apt to help, and incompetence is apt to harm. Protecting against incompetence and unwarranted risks then are the major foci of this part of the book. As will soon be evident, more attention has been given to the prevention, diminution, and removal of harm than to any other aspect of ethical practice or counseling and psychotherapy.

There are seven chapters in this section, five of which have strong legal components; two—Chapters 11 and 12—are initially framed by the legal issues.

Chapter 8 introduces the case for developing means of protecting individual and group clients from the hazards of thoughtless, overenthusiastic, and incompetent practitioners. Various types of potential harms will be identified.

The next three chapters describe the major ways of regulating mental health professions to prevent, ameliorate, and compensate for harm. Chapter 9 reviews the attempts of professional associations to regulate their members. Chapter 10 details the pros and cons of licensure as a means of protecting the public from unethical and incompetent practitioners. Chapter 11 reviews the role of malpractice suits, their components, and their potential effects on practitioners.

The last three chapters in Part Five depict the particular issues raised by physical and perhaps psychological violence. The *Tarasoff* case and its consequences form the focus of Chapter 12. Chapter 13 reviews the laws on reporting child abuse and their possible conflicts with ethical practice. Chapter 14 analyzes the moral and legal aspects of suicide.

Potential Harmful Effects of Psychotherapy on Individual and Group Clients

HARM-PRODUCING ASPECTS OF PSYCHOTHERAPY

The injunction not to do harm has been associated with the helping profession since the early history of medicine. The Hippocratic Oath: "I will use treatment to help the sick according to my ability and judgment, but I will never use it to injure or wrong them" is sometimes confused with an admonition of unknown origin: "Above all, or first, do no harm" (*primum non nocere*) (Beauchamp & Childress, 1983, p. 106). Ross (1930) concurred with *primum non nocere:* He asserted, other things being equal, that Nonmaleficence should take precedence over the other duties.

At first it was thought that psychotherapy had no harm-producing aspect, that it was purely a beneficial treatment, or rather a beneficial array of treatments. However, it is now generally admitted that some clients actually are worse off following psychotherapy than they were beforehand. Bergin (1971) estimated that the mean rate of deterioration was 10% compared to 5% of controls in individual therapy samples studied, and the Stanford study of encounter groups (Lieberman, Yalom, & Miles, 1973) revealed a similar negative fallout rate. Licensure of psychotherapists and counselors is a tacit admission that society needs to be protected from incompetent and unethical practice of psychotherapy. The ever-burgeoning number of successful malpractice suits against psychotherapists also attests to this conclusion. The next sections briefly sketch some ways in which psychotherapy may cause harm.

PSYCHOLOGICAL ABUSE OF CLIENTS: INDIVIDUAL THERAPY

People generally think of psychological abuse in connection with parental treatment of children or institutional treatment of relatively defenseless inmates, such as may occur in private boarding schools, orphanages, or institutions for the mentally defective. But as pointed out earlier, the very nature of the client–therapist relationship puts the client in a vulnerable position. The therapist, as the expert on psychological disorders, determines the presence or absence of a disorder, defines its nature and severity, and both recommends and controls the remedy or treatment. In that process clients' concepts of reality, of self, and of their relationships to others may be questioned and altered according to the therapist's views, and, indeed, must be so altered in order to bring about what the therapist would consider sufficient positive change. Thus, for example, clients who come in because of emotional distress may be told that their problems can only be successfully treated by 6 months to 2 years of intensive therapy, whereas a single interview may suffice. Without opposing opinions from other experts, or without a strong sense of self and some prior experience in psychotherapy, such clients are at the mercy of the therapist's judgment.

Sometimes clients have already committed themselves to extensive exploration before their therapists inform them that they "need" treatment of a certain duration and type, perhaps both long and expensive. At such a point it is apt to be even more difficult to reject the therapist's opinion, because, as discussed in Chapter 2, the one-sided disclosure of intimate revelations has placed the client in a dependent, trusting position. Yet without such revelation, psychotherapy cannot proceed.

Ethically sensitive therapists everywhere are well aware of the dangers of psychotherapy, as is revealed by a survey of Swiss psychotherapists (Thompson, 1987). Their list of the possible results of unethical practices included disintegration of the personality structure of the client, loss of client autonomy, loss of self-esteem and confidence due to sarcastic or demeaning remarks by the therapist, enrichment of the therapist at the client's expense, and imposition of sexual relationships on clients.

Other negative effects of psychotherapy include damage to the client's relations to others, such as spouses, which may occur as an unintended side effect of therapy-induced changes in the client (Hare-Mustin et al., 1979); loss of previously sustaining religious faith, again as an unintended side effect of most therapists' secular orientation and most clients' religious orientation (Bergin, 1980; Jensen & Bergin, 1988); negative self-labeling or labeling by others as a result of misunderstood diagnoses (Danish & Symer, 1981); and failure to reintegrate fully after exposure to a high-powered, ill-advised, and incompetently applied therapy procedure (e.g., Kitchener, 1984; Reilley, Dupree, Rodolfe, & Kraft, 1987).

Giving advice in a noncontrolled context, such as occurs in talk shows or other media presentations, may also be ill-conceived and misapplied

(APA, 1981a, Section 4k). This cautionary note brings to mind the many "how to cope" pop psychology books on the market, the effects of which have not been researched.

Of all the areas of potential negative impact by therapists, by far the largest amount of attention has been given to sexual relations between clients and therapists. Other types of dual relationships with the danger of exploitation by the therapist of the client, such as soliciting free investment advice from clients who are financial advisors or who are successful in their investments, are less involved and pose less danger to the client. As stated in Chapter 4 evidence of actual harm in such relations is spotty. However, the potential for harm is clearly there in view of the intensity of the involvement that may result. Such a relationship threatens to subordinate any therapeutic concerns, as therapists may become more interested in satisfying their sexual desires than in considering their clients' welfare. Certainly the initial attraction is unlikely to be based on therapeutic grounds. Clients, on their part, may seek such relationships as a way of equalizing the power differential in their interactions with their therapists, which in turn may perpetuate inappropriate ways of handling such discomfort.

Three other areas of special concern are homicide, child abuse, and suicide. Because psychotherapy is utilized as a mode of treatment for participants in these destructive acts, it is important to examine its role. Homicide will be covered in Chapter 12 on *Tarasoff*, child abuse in Chapter 13, and suicide in Chapter 14.

PSYCHOLOGICAL ABUSE: GROUP THERAPY

Groups differ from individual therapy in many dimensions, but perhaps the most important one in terms of potential for harm is the amount of social pressure they can place upon the individual to conform to a group norm. Groups can both support individuality or undermine it, depending on how the group is conducted, but when the leader and all other members cohere and attempt to force their will upon a solitary member, it takes an unusual individual to withstand that coercive pressure. The norm may be to disclose some intimacy or some shameful event; or it may be simply to display a certain level of emotionality; or it may be to confess to harboring some anger or resentment to some other member; or it may be to "abandon" oneself, to act uninhibitedly in some group exercise; or it could be any of a myriad of other demands that the group has decided signify "progress."

When pressure for emotional expressiveness or disclosure is extreme, it is hard to know whether it is really authentic. A natural consequence is the elicitation of superficial and nonauthentic support. A more dangerous result is that of disabling depression or anxiety in the premature discloser. (Lakin, 1986, p. 458).

Unfortunately, both compliance or noncompliance can precipitate a psychotic reaction or other serious disturbance in the one singled out for such focused treatment. Such a reaction may occur and/or become obvious and full-blown only after the group meeting, and subsequent intervention may be too late to be effective.

Another danger is that instead of helping individuals to change and engage in less negative self-labeling, groups may actually do the opposite. Group members may be summarily characterized on the basis of their interactions with other group members at an early point in the group's functioning and be forever after referred to in those terms, regardless of changes in their behavior.

A distinct advantage of group treatment is the potentiality for flexibility in roles taken by a participant. . . . However, participants gravitate naturally even to socially disparaged roles, such as the "blocker," the "group clown," or the "group foul-up." Moreover, role interchange is not easily achieved, because a group tends to persevere in perceiving a given individual in a given role because it has predictable social characteristics. (Lakin, 1986, pp. 457–458)

With groups whose members may meet socially outside the official meetings, there is a danger that some members who are attracted to each other will form cliques which, in effect, ostracize other members. To the degree that approval from group members has become important to any member's self-perspective, this will impact negatively on the left-out member. This would be especially true if members of the "in group" allude to their joint out-of-group activities or are allowed to function as "teams" within the group meetings, paying attention to and showing approval of only each other's contributions.

With institutional groups who not only meet together for counseling or therapy but plan and execute other activities together, ostracism can be particularly potent, as is demonstrated by a report about one member of a "resocialization ward" who was punished by his ward group for not attempting a behavior they prescribed. He was not allowed to participate in a long-anticipated trip to town and subsequently suffered a marked regression in his behavior (Galinsky & Schopler, 1977, p. 92).

There are no easy solutions to such problems. For example, getting groups to promise not to socialize outside of group sessions, or only to socialize if all members are invited, is one thing, but to monitor and enforce it is another, with perhaps undesirable side effects. Like complete confidentiality, this would be an unrealistic standard for most groups. With some groups it may make sense actually to encourage socializing between members. Research is largely lacking in this area and would be apt to be inconclusive in any case given the complexities involved. Freedman (1976) reports one survey of group members of an outpatient community health center indicating that the functioning of members of groups where socializing was discouraged was superior to that of those where socializing was encouraged.

Not only individual members of groups, but groups as a whole may risk psychological and physical harm under certain conditions. The most dramatic example of recent years is the group suicide that was carried out in the Guyanese jungle by a religious cult under the leadership of Reverend Jim Jones ("Mistrial in Peoples Temple Case," 1981). Closer to home are the cults for psychotherapists that the Temerlins (1982) studied and which were reviewed in Chapter 2. Here the cults as a whole cultivated a paranoid way of thinking with regard to outsiders and within each cult developed a highly dependent, in some cases even a self-abasing, attitude toward the leader. Members, therapists in their own rights, acted as household servants for their leaders and relinquished to them such decisions as whom to marry and whether to seek a divorce.

Less dramatic but more common is the tendency for groups to form in accordance with the latest psychological fad. With today's accelerated rate such a phenomenon may boom and bust within a few years or may survive a decade or more by migrating with its leaders to those parts of the United States or other countries that have not yet been exposed to the new phenomena.

Experimentation has its place, but only under carefully controlled conditions when any real risks are involved. Not all clients, for example, are appropriate for group therapy marathons, for nude encounters, or perhaps even for "acting out their aggressions" by hitting other members with pillows in a group setting. Experimenting with mind-altering drugs as a group experiment is obviously risky in more ways than just a psychological sense; yet not so many years ago all these behaviors, plus many others, were the "in" thing to do. At that time it was also argued that a "hands off" policy was appropriate for the profession to follow regarding the encouragement or the discouragement of such experimentation.

The law sets limits on the behavior that one individual may show towards another, and these limits will surely apply within a group if its members call for aid. If they do not seek the protection of the law, then can we, as psychologists, set limits when the individual does not? Can we deny to any psychologist—or to anyone else—the right to lead a group based on his own responsibility, any group whatsoever, with whatever goals? Can we set *ethical* limits on whether a trainer should be able to choose to assault a group member, or to strip her, if in the situation, he thinks it appropriate, and she elected to accept it. . . .

I think we cannot interfere, *provided*—and here we do encounter a principle that cannot and must not be violated—the individual in the group has freely chosen to join it, and to accept its styles. (Verplanck, cited in Patterson, 1972, p. 93)

Corsini takes a similar position:

I think that the best thing right now is *hands off.* It is probably best not to try any policing. We just don't know enough. . . . We are in a period of uncontrolled growth, development and experimentation, and I think this is good. (cited in Patterson, 1972, p. 93)

A more cautionary attitude emerged following the publication of the Stanford study of 210 students who enrolled in an encounter group course (Lieberman et al., 1973). The students were divided into 17 different groups using 10 different approaches including a National Training Laboratory model, Gestalt therapy, and "Esalen Eclectic" (Esalen being the mecca of such groups at the time). Using a number of different instruments the researchers attempted to determine both the differences in group processes and the result for the individual members. They discovered that, overall, the "casualty" rate was nearly 10% for those students who completed 50% or more of the group meetings. A casualty was defined as:

An individual who, as a direct result of his experience in the encounter group, became more psychologically distressed/or employed more maladaptive mechanisms of defense. Furthermore, to be so defined this negative change must not be transient, but enduring, as judged eight months after the group experience. (p. 171)

In addition one student committed suicide. He was not technically a "casualty" because he was also receiving therapy from two sources and was a member of another encounter group, so no direct connection could be made to the encounter group in the study.

The casualty rate was not evenly distributed across the 17 groups; rather those groups with a leader "whose style is characterized by high aggressive stimulation, high charisma, high individual focus, high support, and high confrontation" were most apt to have casualties in their groups

(p. 174). Furthermore the group leaders were, by and large, much less sensitive to the negative impact of the group experience on individuals than were fellow group members. Leaders identified only 2 of 16 casualties, whereas group members picked out 12 of them in response to the question, "Who was hurt by the group?"

Further studies and further documentations followed (e.g., Croghan, 1974; Duncan, 1976; Gaza, Duncan, & Sisson, 1971; Patterson, 1972; Peters, 1973; and Zimpfer, 1971). The American Psychological Association adopted special guidelines for growth groups (APA, 1973) and the American Association for Counseling and Development adopted protective procedures in its 1981 code (Sections B8, B13). More extensive guidelines were adopted by the Association for Specialists in Group Work (ASGW) in 1980 (cited in Roberts, 1982). The following injunctions perhaps contain the essence of these guidelines as they pertain to prevention of harm:

1. Screen all prospective group members and select only those "whose well-being will not be jeopardized by the group experience." (Section A-2)
2. "Protect member rights against physical threats, intimidation, coercion, and undue peer pressure insofar as is reasonably possible." (Section B-1)

An example of how this can be done is reported in the Stanford study (Lieberman et al., 1973):

One Type B leader who led a low-risk group, very explicitly asked each member repeatedly to make the choice of what he wanted to work on and how far he wished to proceed in a particular meeting. This is in marked contrast to Type A leaders who made that choice for their members and developed a hot-seat, no-escape-hatch format. (p. 26)

The Type B leader operated in the fashion recommended in Chapter 3 for implementing informed consent in ongoing group situations. This can be supplemented by encouraging group members to express reservations about group process and by modeling how to express negative reactions to group members in behavior-focused ways, rather than by characterization of the person.

It is also essential to establish the right of members to withdraw temporarily or to leave altogether. The potentially negative impact on the other members of unexpected and/or unwanted departure of group members may be attentuated by asking, but not demanding, that they present their reasons for leaving, thus giving the group a chance to negotiate a continuance. Different writers take different stances on this point: Corey and Corey (1987), for example, emphasize keeping the group intact, whereas Lakin (1986) favors supporting individual choice, as do the ASGW guidelines (Roberts, 1982).

Many group disruptions are not predictable, even to the most experienced leader. There are various ways of handling such unexpected events. One is to present them to the group as a common problem requiring solution; another is to consult individually with the disruptive member(s); and still another is to ignore the matter judiciously and let it take its course. The one unethical approach would be for the leaders to "stick their heads in the sand," hoping for things to clear up by themselves, thereby foregoing a reasoned decision based on full awareness of the facts (Thompson, 1983).

ISSUES

Is there evidence that individual and group psychotherapy can cause harm?

In what way does the therapist's role as psychological expert give rise to danger of harm to clients?

What types of harm can be inflicted?

Why are therapist–client sexual relationships potentially more harmful than other dual relationships?

What hazards to group clients arise out of peer pressure?

Does out-of-group socializing create special hazards for members?

What are some modern instances in which physical and psychological harm resulted from closely knit groups?

Are groups composed of psychotherapists immune from harmful functioning?

Under what conditions is experimentation within groups safe? Unsafe?

What types of encounter group leaders are most apt to produce high "casualty" rates? What types produce low casualty rates?

What guidelines have been proposed for conducting safe groups?

CHAPTER 9

Regulation by Professional Associations

ETHICAL CODES OF PROFESSIONAL ASSOCIATIONS

Professional associations are formed when individuals with similar training, skills, and interests band together. By a sort of "lifting oneself by one's bootstrap" phenomenon they first establish and then continually refine their professional identity, both by the actions they take as an association and by their increasingly stringent membership requirements. They thus separate and raise themselves ever more from the public mainstream and from other similar professional groups. At the same time they continually strive to add to their membership in order to increase their political clout.

This desire for power and identity may or may not be accompanied by a strong desire to serve the public and to do so in more effective ways, even though the profession espouses such goals. The immediate, often tangible, benefits of protecting and enhancing one's prestige and one's political and economic status may often be more powerful incentives than those of good service to the public. Should the two conflict, or appear to conflict, the latter is apt to give way.

Increased public awareness may have caused this pattern to change somewhat in recent years. It has become a matter of Self-Interest for professional organizations of psychotherapists and counselors to actively promote ethical regulation of their membership. A primary vehicle for doing so is the adoption of ethical codes to guide and govern the behavior of the members. The American Psychological Association has adopted four types of codes: one for all members ("Ethical Principles of Psychologists," 1981a); two for practitioners, a general code (*General Guidelines for Providers of Psychological Services,* 1987b) and codes that elaborate on these standards for the specific disciplines of clinical, counseling, industrial-organizational, and school psychology ("Specialty Guidelines for Delivery of Services by Clinical Psychologists," 1981b); and one for researchers (*Ethical Principles in the Conduct of Research with Human Participants,* 1982). The APA bylaws list the sanctions that can be applied in the case of errant, harmful behavior.

Corresponding codes for other organizations with some members who practice psychotherapy and counseling are the *Standards for the Practice of Clinical Social Work* of the National Association of Social Workers (1984), *Ethical Standards* of the American Association for Counseling and Development (1982), *The Principles of Medical Ethics with Annotations Especially Applicable to Psychiatry* of the American Psychiatric Association (1986), and the *Code of Ethical Principles for Family Therapists* of the American Association for Marriage and Family Therapy (1982).

The effectiveness of these codes depends on four main factors: (1) the benefit that members perceive in retaining their membership; (2) the effectiveness of the association in communicating the code and a sense of its importance to its members; (3) the willingness of members to monitor the behavior of fellow members and to apply the sanctions when appropriate; and (4) the efforts by the profession to educate the public as to what constitutes competent and ethical behavior by its members and to support any legitimate complaints about such behavior by members. In recent years it has also been recognized that the helping professions, especially medicine and psychology, would do well to identify and assist those practitioners who are impaired in their own functioning because of physical and psychological problems.

INCENTIVES OF MEMBERSHIP IN PROFESSIONAL ASSOCIATIONS

The benefit of membership is the fulcrum factor in a voluntary organization. Unless members perceive loss of membership as being significant, they will treat any application or threatened application of a sanction for unethical behavior as a reason for resigning rather than as a reason for complying.

Advantages of membership in most voluntary organizations are often more intangible or potential than concrete and immediately operative. Potential benefits arise mostly from the expanded contacts members may enjoy with others in their profession. Such contacts could prove important in the search for and procurement of new employment, in increased referrals of clients, in intellectual enrichment, and in new or enhanced social relationships. In addition, the organization's publications provide a means of keeping apprised of recent developments in the field. All these are "iffy" benefits that apply to lesser or greater degree to different members.

More concrete benefits include access to lower cost group insurance policies such as malpractice liability insurance, reduced rates on organizational journals and other publications, and access to and reduced rates on various professional training experiences.

Should these or other considerations constitute sufficient incentive, then members will be inclined to accept and abide by sanctions that might be levied against them for violation of the organization's ethical code(s). These sanctions might include all or some of the following (cf. Hall & Hare-Mustin, 1983, p. 1505):

Education of members who commit unintentional violations

Reprimand or censure

Order to cease and desist

Supervision, rehabilitation, training, or psychotherapy from designated programs or individuals

Placement on probation with referral to state or local organization for monitoring

Suspension for stipulated period of time or until certain tasks have been accomplished (such as completion of a drug rehabilitation program)

The ultimate sanction, expulsion from membership, is invoked only in severe cases where it is believed that none of the lesser sanctions will work or that they are inadequate in light of the nature of the offense (Hare-Mustin & Hall, 1981). The effect of expulsion may be minimal in itself, but it is enhanced by the simple act of publication. Lists of expelled members including stipulation of the grounds for their expulsion can be distributed to all other members of the organization or even released to the public media. Also, when legal violations are involved, the appropriate legal authorities, such as state licensing boards, can be apprised of the violation (Hare-Mustin & Hall, 1981).

It is also possible for members, acting on their own, to impact on other colleagues. If the offending member is a fellow employee in an organization, the supervisor or administrative head could be approached. Therapeutic supervisors should be informed in any case because it jeopardizes their own license and professional standing if they do not intervene when a supervisee acts in an incompetent or unethical manner. It may or may not be appropriate to inform other management personnel and employers, depending on their commitment and sensitivity to ethical principles.

If the colleague is exclusively in private practice, the most vulnerable point may be the sources of his or her referrals. How far to pursue informing such sources, or which to inform, is a very ticklish matter, both ethically and legally, and depends on many factors such as the degree of certainty that an offense was committed and the nature of the offense. At the least, however, colleagues who directly know of the offense can choose not to refer future clients to the errant colleague until such time as the situation has changed.

One problem with supporting a client's apparently legitimate complaint against a colleague is that it places the current therapist in the dual role of being the client's advocate and the therapist. An ingenious solution to that problem has been described by Alan Stone (1983). He proposes that therapists who are convinced that their clients have been victimized suggest to the clients that they both consult a third party, an "administrator." If the client agrees and the consultation takes place, from that point on the consultant takes on the responsibility of working with the client to further any legitimate complaint, including obtaining any necessary waivers of confidentiality. This may be somewhat less threatening than immediately referring clients to professional organizations or licensing boards.

PROMOTION OF THE CODE

Simple adoption of a code does not, in and of itself, ensure that the members will thoroughly familiarize themselves with it and its applications. It is necessary to promote and publicize the code by referring to it frequently in articles and at workshops on ethical issues, and by establishing *ad hoc* and standing committees to examine its relevance to current practice with a view to its extension and revision as necessary. Perhaps the most effective promotion, however, occurs when, as a by-product of its publicized application to various members, an association lists expelled members along with the reasons for expulsion. This is currently done in both the American Psychological Association and the American Psychiatric Association.

National organizations with clout can also indirectly promote attention to ethical issues by demanding that educational and training programs must provide a firm grounding in practitioner ethics in order to receive the endorsement of the organization. Even in the American Psychological Association, which does indeed carry and use such clout in promoting attention to ethical concerns, recent reports indicate that a sizable portion of members and of psychologists in training are ill informed regarding a number of ethical violations. The chair of the APA's ethics committee asserted that "A substantial minority of psychologists judged as guilty of violating the Ethical Standards of Psychologists appear to have done so without intent or awareness" (Keith-Spiegel, 1977). Also a survey of 294 randomly selected members of Division 29, Psychotherapy, of the APA showed considerable discrepancy as to whether certain practices were unethical and how serious a concern they represented (Haas, Malouf, & Mayerson, 1986).

This ignorance of what constitutes an ethical violation does not necessarily reflect an unawareness of the codes themselves; it could result from lack of clarity within the profession as to what is ethical and what is unethical and/or how to interpret the codes. In fact, one study (Tymchuk et al., 1982) found that 99% of the clinical psychologists who responded indicated familiarity with the profession's ethical code, but 58% did not consider themselves well enough informed about ethical issues in psychology. This was perhaps the reason there was considerable variation in their responses to some of the hypothetical clinical situations presented to them. A major impetus for this book is to provide a system of principles better suited for analysis of ethically novel and complex situations than the ones offered by present ethical codes.

WILLINGNESS OF MEMBERS TO POLICE THEIR COLLEAGUES

The willingness to monitor and correct unethical and incompetent behavior by colleagues is difficult to instill or to encourage. Yet without such willingness the entire structure collapses. Many, if not most of the ethical violations by professionals come to the attention of fellow professionals when clients seek them out, sometimes to remedy the wrong that was committed, but more often because their original problem was not satisfactorily resolved. The clients may not even be aware that they were mistreated because they lack the requisite knowledge of professional standards. Their current therapists can choose to ignore the matter, actively try to persuade clients that no real wrong or harm was done, pursue the matter themselves (normally with the client's permission), or support their clients' efforts to do so. Which course of action is chosen is crucial, in the aggregate, in determining the effectiveness of the profession's self-policing.

One way in which to gauge the willingness to implement the ethical code is by determining how many complaints are received and how they are treated. Statistics on such data are difficult to obtain, but some have been publicized and these indicate a substantial increase both in complaints and in severity of action in recent years. For example, the Ethics Committee of the American Psychological Association (1986) reported that the cases brought before it increased from 68 in 1984 to 93 in 1985. Also, according to the published summaries sent to each member, the number of members expelled from the association for ethical violations went from 3 in 1983 to 13 in 1987.

The American Psychiatric Association reported 82 charges, 12 convictions, and 6 members expelled from the time span of 1950 to 1973. From 1972 to 1983 the corresponding numbers were 382 charges, 86 convictions, and 27 expulsions. Even after correcting for the substantially greater number of members in the latter period (more than double), it is clear that corrective actions have been geometrically rising. Nevertheless they are still minuscule: "Even if the number [of serious misconduct cases] is underreported by 10 times, only 1% of our membership would have their ethical conduct questioned in a year" (Moore, 1985, p. 1046).

Another way to determine the willingness to report fellow professionals is to describe various hypothetical situations involving ethical violations and ask selected respondents first what they "should" do and then what they think they actually "would" do. Bernard and Jara (1986) did just that with 170 graduate students from 25 APA-approved clinical training programs. Approximately half the students admitted that they would do less than they thought they should. A replicate of this study sampling clinical psychologists obtained similar results (Bernard, Murphy, & Little, 1987): 63% to 74% thought they would do what they should do, depending on the situation.

According to another recent survey of psychologists and psychotherapists, a substantial number of them (14%) found it unethical, except, perhaps in rare circumstances, to file an ethics complaint against a colleague (Pope, Tabachnick, & Keith-Spiegel, 1987). Unfortunately it is not clear why they held this opinion.

EFFORTS TO EDUCATE THE PUBLIC

The final method by which an association can promote adherence to its ethical standards is by informing the public of these standards, encouraging the public to complain if the standards are not met in contacts with members of the profession, and providing easily used, efficient, and effective complaint procedures. Ralph Nader's organization, Public Citizen, has deemed it necessary to establish a model consumer–therapist contract that specifies client rights (Adams & Orgel, 1975). This would indicate that the various professions practicing psychotherapy have not done a good job in this respect. Even the increased number of complaints that the APA and the American Psychiatric Association have received in recent years, for example, is not a lot considering their thousands of practitioner members and their millions of clients. It seems unlikely that their practice is so free from ethical error. Of course, some clients may have chosen to complain instead through state or district organizations, state licensing boards, or the courts. If the following study is any indication, however, it is not likely that these recourses are utilized to any great extent either, or that those who attempt to utilize them are satisfied with the response.

A Study of Clients Who Were Sexually Involved with Their Therapists

In a recent study Vinson (1987) investigated the complaint procedure apparatus in California for clients who were sexually involved with their psychotherapists during the course of treatment. Such relations are perhaps the most widely publicized area of ethical violation in psychotherapy as well as being one of the few violations that are clearly specified as such in most ethical codes for psychotherapists. If these offenses do not find redress, one would seriously wonder which would.

There were two parts to the study. In the first part Vinson interviewed 30 board members and staff concerned with handling complaints regarding psychotherapists in California, including 12 representatives of the three state boards who license psychotherapists (medical, psychological, and social workers/marriage and child counselors) and 16 representatives of the corresponding professional associations. According to the three state licensing boards a total of 12 therapists were disciplined for sexual involvement with patients in 1982: They included 3 psychiatrists, 3 psychologists, 4 marriage and family counselors, and 2 psychotherapists who were jointly licensed as psychologists and as marriage and family counselors.

In the same year the state professional associations disciplined 4 members for such offenses, some of whom may have also been among those disciplined by the state licensing boards. This figure of 12 to 16 members is hypothesized by Vinson to represent only 0.5% of the 2200 therapists whom one would estimate on the basis of previous surveys as being sexually active with their clients and only 0.2% of the potential complainants. However, she seems to have assumed in making these calculations that all the therapists who did have sexual relations with their clients at some time during their professional careers did so in 1982, rather than at other times. Perhaps 20 times 0.5% or 10% would be a more accurate figure; in any case, far fewer were disciplined than could be expected to warrant such discipline.

Both members of the licensing boards and representatives of the professional organizations admitted that lack of money prevented them from actively pursuing many of the complaints that came to their attention, much less to ascertain if there were other, unreported complaints.

Another factor that discouraged investigation of complaints, especially by professional associations, was the potential impact of countersuits by members under investigation or who had already been disciplined. In fact, experience with and fear of such suits in the future caused the disbandment of the ethics committee of the California Psychological Association in 1986. Professional organizations in other states have also either disbanded or curtailed the functioning of their ethics committees because of the excessive cost of getting adequate liability insurance for members and for the organization in the event of such suits (Menustik, 1986).

The second part of the study consisted of interviews with clients who had been sexually involved with their therapists. Twenty-eight such clients responded to ads placed in 11 of San Francisco's newspapers and news-letters, including 21 women who had had male therapists, 5 men who had had female therapists, and 2 clients, 1 man and 1 woman, who had been sexually involved with same-sex therapists. The study concentrated on the 21 women, 20 of whom claimed that the sexual relationship seriously disrupted their lives.

Three facets of the clients' experiences are of special interest: the degree of awareness of the clients that their therapists had committed an ethical and possibly also a legal violation; where such complaints, if any, were initiated; and the clients' satisfaction with the complaint procedures.

Only five of the 21 women were aware at the time of their involvement with their therapists that such involvement constituted an ethical viola-tion. All five of these women were employed in health or mental health fields. None of these five chose to pursue a complaint procedure.

Ten of the other 16 women became aware afterward, 2 by virtue of hearing about malpractice suits based on similar grounds. These 2, plus 1 other, contacted attorneys. How the others gained awareness was not specified in the article, but the fact that they did so might attest to the increased awareness overall in our society that such relationships are taboo (cf. Pope, Tabachnick, & Keith-Spiegel, 1987). Five turned to li-censing boards to register complaints, and 2 to professional organizations. Thus all 10 decided to pursue a course of action.

The three who went to attorneys met with varying response: One at-torney initiated a malpractice suit, but the other two women were informed that it was too late for civil action and were not apprised of any alternative complaint procedures.

Four of the five who turned to state licensing boards were satisfied with the response of the boards. The two who registered complaints with a state professional organization were disappointed: One was told nothing could be done; and the other was referred to another association, the one her therapist belonged to, but the case was still unresolved as of April 1986.

Obviously this sample is too small to make any generalizations as to where to initiate complaint procedures. The type of violation would also have to be taken into account because not all ethical violations clearly involve legal aspects. However, it is interesting to note that those women who registered complaints with the licensing boards were the most sat-isfied with the response.

TREATMENT OF IMPAIRED THERAPISTS

So far the emphasis has been on what can be done to educate and discipline the therapist and to protect the client through information and support during the complaint process. Another way of approaching this complex problem of how best to regulate a profession is to recognize that incompetent and unethical behavior by professionals in any field is often a function of the professional's own psychological dysfunctioning. Such dysfunctioning is not often remedied through either educative or disciplinary actions but may succumb to psychotherapy and other rehabilitative efforts. In recent years this fact has received increased attention and a number of programs have been set up to accommodate the need (Beck, 1983; Kilburg, Nathan, & Thoreson, 1986; Stadler, Willing, Eberhage, & Ward, 1988). Generally such programs are staffed by professional colleagues who volunteer to work for little or no fee on a limited basis. Use is also made of appropriate rehabilitation programs, such as alcohol or drug abuse programs.

ISSUES

Do "helping professions" necessarily have the best interests of the public at heart?

What role do professional ethical codes play in promoting ethical regulation of members?

What major factors determine whether such regulation is effective?

Why might it be important, ethically, to maintain strong incentives for membership in professional organizations?

What corrective sanctions can professional organizations apply?

How can practitioners as individuals diminish the impact of their colleagues' unethical behavior?

How can therapists who wish to help their clients make legitimate complaints avoid being both client advocate and therapist?

How can/do professional organizations promote their ethical codes?

How informed are therapists regarding their profession's ethical codes?

Is being informed equivalent to knowing how to apply the code?

How willing are clinicians to police their colleagues?

Have professional psychotherapists and the public they serve shown increased awareness of ethical practice in recent years?

Does it seem likely most offenses are being reported?

What obligation do professional organizations have to educate the public regarding their ethical standards?

Which clients decide to complain about sexual involvement with their therapists, and what happens to their complaints?

Why have the ethics committees of some state organizations largely curtailed their complaint-processing activities?

Why is the physical and psychological well-being of practitioners an ethical issue? What is being done about it?

CHAPTER 10

Licensure and Protection of the Public

THE PURPOSE OF LICENSURE

The primary purpose of licensing laws has been to protect the public health, morals, safety, and general welfare. . . . Licensing attempts to accomplish this by eliminating quacks, charlatans, incompetents, and unethical practitioners from the field, which is done through strict entrance requirements, enforcing discipline, and preventing unlicensed practice. (Hogan, 1979, p. 237)

Whether licensing laws for psychotherapists accomplish this purpose is highly debatable. However, it is clear that what they do seems quite related to their purpose. This includes setting educational and training standards, establishing minimum standards for specific and general knowledge as measured by written and oral tests, adopting professional codes of ethics, setting up systems for receiving and investigating complaints, and developing procedures for educating and disciplining errant practitioners. In addition licensed practitioners have to earn set amounts of continuing education credits on an annual basis or risk losing their licenses.

The exact nature of the education and training standards will vary from profession to profession, and from state to state within professions. The professions that have licensing laws that include the practice of psychotherapy include medicine, psychology, social work, marital and family counseling, pastoral counseling (New Hampshire), social psychotherapy (Texas), and recreational therapy (Utah). Virginia has a law that includes professional counselors, certified alcoholism counselors, and certified drug counselors. Mental health technicians, and other mental health counselors of various kinds who hold master's or bachelor's degrees are also licensed to practice psychotherapy in several states, but often only under the supervision of other licensed health-care professionals. The variety and type of licensing is a constantly changing phenomenon; thus information in this section may soon be, if it is not already, outdated.

The activity of psychotherapy is often only implied as being among the activities covered under the licensure laws in many professions, such as medicine and social work, or it may constitute only a small portion of the explicitly defined scope of practice. Psychology licensing laws, although also broad in scope, are more specifically tailored to include the practice of psychotherapy, so the clearest picture of how this practice is regulated to protect the public will emerge from study of its laws. Also the laws are more apt to be quite similar from state to state because the national organization—the American Psychological Association (APA)—provides a model law that the various state chapters strive to get enacted by their state legislatures, given the legal context provided by the other laws of the state (APA, 1987c).

Perhaps the first point to clarify is exactly what is licensed and how that is accomplished so as to protect the public. Unlicensed individuals are prohibited either from performing certain activities altogether, or from performing them under certain conditions. These activities are described in the "scope of practice" statement that is essential to each licensure law. The scope of practice statement proposed in the model act reads as follows:

> 3. *Practice of psychology* is defined as the observation, description, evaluation, interpretation, and modification of human behavior by the application of psychological principles, methods, and procedures, for the purpose of preventing or eliminating symptomatic, maladaptive, or undesired behavior and of enhancing interpersonal relationships, work and life adjustment, personal effectiveness, behavioral health, and mental health. The practice of psychology includes, but is not limited to ... psychological testing and the evaluation or assessment of personal characteristics, such as intelligence, personality, abilities, interests, aptitudes, and neuropsychological functioning; counseling, psychoanalysis, psychotherapy, hypnosis, biofeedback, and behavior analysis and therapy; diagnosis and treatment of mental and emotional disorder or disability, alcoholism and substance abuse, disorders of habit or conduct, as well as of the psychological aspects of physical illness, accident, injury, or disability; and psychoeducational evaluation, therapy, remediation, and consultation. Psychological services may be rendered to individuals, families, groups, and the public. The practice of psychology shall be construed within the meaning of this definition without regard to whether payment is received for services rendered. (See Section J for exemptions.)

> 4. *Psychologist:* A person represents himself or herself to be a psychologist if that person uses any title or description of services incorporating the words *psychology, psychological,* or *psychologist,* or if he or she possesses expert qualification in any area of psychology, or if that person offers to

the public or renders to individuals or to groups of individuals services defined as the practice of psychology in this Act. (p. 2)

It is clear from this scope of practice statement that there is very little that *is not* included; in fact, the scope is so broad that it includes many of the daily activities of parents with their children, or salespersons with their customers. Who, in fact, doesn't observe, describe, evaluate, interpret, and attempt to modify other people's behavior for the purposes of preventing or eliminating undesired behavior and of enhancing personal relationships? This being the case, Section 4 becomes of primary importance in making this proposed definition an enactable one. It suggests how to identify the *unlawful* practice of psychology, namely by prohibiting people from referring to themselves as psychologists or otherwise using the prefix "psycho" to describe their activities. State legislatures have made this connection explicit: For example, Oregon's licensing statute reads:

"Practice of psychology" means the rendering or offering to render to individuals, groups, organizations or the public any psychological service *while representing oneself to be a psychologist* [italics added]. . . . (Oregon Revised Statutes, 1985, 675.010, Section (4))

Another important modification is the reference to exemptions from the model act (APA, 1987c). These include:

Persons engaged solely in teaching, research, or provision of psychological services to organizations, . . . members of other established professions, such as physicians, attorneys, and clergy, . . . school psychologists who are certified by the state education agency. (p. 5)

It also exempts "graduate students, interns, postdoctoral trainees, and applicants for licensure" (p. 5) who function under the supervision of a licensed psychologist and may therefore use such titles as psychological intern, and psychological trainee.

Laws that are devised to make clear that the improper use of the title is prohibited, not the activities themselves, are referred to as "title protection acts." There are some activities, such as psychological testing and evaluation, which seem specific enough to be limited to a certain profession, but many such tests are customarily administered by non-PhD personnel and even interpreted by such personnel because, as a matter of fact, they do not require extensive psychological knowledge or training to give or to interpret. Some tests are even self-administered and self-interpreted with the aid of written instructions. Computer programs for interpretation of certain standard personality inventories, such as the Minnesota Multiphasic Inventory, abound, and it is not at all clear at this point how much expertise is needed to select and use various programs, how much expertise is needed to know when such "canned" interpretations should be modified, or how many supposedly qualified users actually are in a position to make these choices or interpretations. Hence if test interpretation is to be limited to psychologists, it will be necessary to specify *which* tests are involved and *what* kind of training is necessary to qualify the psychologists to use them.

Several ways have been discovered that protect the practice of certain activities and not just the titles associated with them. One such approach is illustrated in the language of a bill that passed the Oregon Legislative Assembly (1987) but was vetoed by the governor (Senate Bill 266, 1987):

> As used in paragraph (b) of subsection (1) of this section, "practice clinical or counseling psychology" means the use, for money or other consideration, of psychological principles for the purpose of assessment, diagnosis and testing for and the prevention, treatment and amelioration of mental or emotional distress or disorders and behavioral disorders of individuals and includes the psychological evaluation and psychological treatment of neuropsychological and psychophysiological disorders. (Section 2 (2))

The crucial words here are "for the purpose of . . . prevention, treatment, and amelioration of. . . ." It can be argued that such specification of purpose allows others to employ psychological principles for other purposes germane to their concerns. Thus parents can employ psychological principles to raise their children, employers to motivate their employees, and so forth, without being accused of usurping the province of the practice of psychology.

Another approach is illustrated in another bill that the Oregon Legislative Assembly (1987) passed and the governor vetoed whose purpose was to establish licensure for "professional counselors" (Senate Bill 260). The relevant language is as follows:

> "Professional counseling" means providing counseling services to individuals, couples, families, children, groups, organizations or the general public through the therapeutic relationship, . . . "Professional counseling" includes, but is not limited to, the following:
>
> (a) Application of counseling theories and techniques designed to assist clients with current or potential problems and to facilitate change in thinking, feeling and behaving. . . . (Section 1 (4))

"Clients" and, perhaps, "the therapeutic relationship" are the crucial words here. This again does not foolishly try to prohibit ordinary citizens who also have varying degrees of acquaintanceship with various counseling theories and techniques from employing such theories and techniques in their relations with their friends, relatives and employees or other "nonclient" relationships. Lawyers and others who have clients would not normally characterize their relationships with their clients as being essentially "therapeutic" but as businesslike and helpful in other specific ways.

Such legislation or, at this point, attempts at legislation, also protect certain titles, such as "psychologist" and "professional counselor," even as the titles of other professions, such as "medical doctor," are protected. How does such title protection protect the public? The answer is, in part, that by restricting the use of certain titles to people with prescribed qualifications, the public can be reasonably sure that users of these titles are competent practitioners and not quacks or well-meaning bunglers.

Secondarily, and of increasing importance, only such titled persons are apt to be eligible for providing services that are covered under the consumer's insurance policy. Thus the two matters of licensure and insurance coverage are again interwoven. Finally, certain agency positions or other jobs may be open only to licensed practitioners. Many agencies hire nonlicensed individuals to function as psychotherapists but become eligible for third-party reimbursements by placing licensed individuals in supervisory positions.

Licensure laws may also license individuals to practice at several levels, with full licensure being reserved for those who have graduated with doctoral degrees from board-approved educational and training programs and have passed the requisite written and oral exams. Those with lower level licensure typically may only practice under supervision and/or have their practice limited to certain specialties.

In order to administer the application process, to give the oral examinations, to collect the licensure and exam fees, and to establish procedures for these activities, states typically establish state licensing boards. State governors normally appoint members to such boards from recommendations made by the relevant professional organizations in their states. One or more public members may also be appointed. These boards have the additional responsibilities of setting up procedures for processing complaints, either of licensed members about unlicensed practitioners engaging in unlawful practice, such as claiming to offer "psychotherapy," or of unethical or incompetent practice of licensed professionals. The boards are also authorized to administer certain sanctions designed to correct or to eliminate the faulty behavior.

THE INJUSTICE OF ARTIFICIALLY HIGH
STANDARDS FOR LICENSURE

Because licensing of professions has the effect (and the intention) of limiting the profession's practice to certain qualified members, it is a matter of justice whether the licensing requirements are artificially high. Such standards may exclude those who don't meet them even though such persons may be equally competent to practice the proscribed activity. Is it really necessary, for example, to have a PhD or an MD with a boarded specialty in psychiatry in order to practice psychotherapy competently? Is it necessary to have passed certain exams that require extensive and perhaps arcane knowledge with highly problematic relationships to performance competency?

This question is also a matter of justice with regard to the consumer (see Chapter 6). The higher the level of standards to be met, the fewer persons meeting them, and the more they can arguably charge as their "just due" for their services; thus the higher the price is apt to be to the consumer and the fewer will be the consumers that can afford the services. In other words, licensure threatens to increase the problems of fairly distributing the benefits of psychotherapy by making such services scarce and expensive.

Even though licensure, especially of the title protection type, does not prohibit consumers from going to persons who use nonprohibited titles such as "counselor" (without further specification such as "mental health counselor" or "professional counselor"), it does effectively exclude such counselors from being eligible recipients of third-party reimbursement. This in turn reduces the chances that consumers who can afford to pay for professional counseling, that is, those with jobs with good group insurance benefit packages and those who can afford such individual policies, will seek out such generic counselors. As a result many perhaps perfectly competent counselors and therapists may not even seek to practice or, if they do so, will not be able to sustain a livelihood.

HOGAN'S ALTERNATIVE TO LICENSURE

Hogan (1979) argues that present-day licensing does, indeed, create injustice by creating irrelevant, artificial barriers to the practice of psychotherapy. He would do away with licensure of psychotherapists of all kinds and replace it with a registration system regulated by the evaluations of consumers. He contends that at this stage of our knowledge licensure is inappropriate and has proven to be an inadequate means of regulating psychotherapy. He points out:

> Psychotherapy is a complex, highly amorphous, somewhat artistic, and not well-understood activity. . . . Although its history is long, no such thing yet exists as "current psychotherapeutic theory." Rather, a wide variety of theories vie for acceptance, and a seemingly endless succession of techniques and methodologies comes and goes. . . . [Furthermore] empirical evidence indicates that those in the helping professions bring about similar results no matter what techniques are used, no matter what the purpose of their methods is, and irrespective of type of academic training. (pp. 343–344)

He holds little hope for change in the near future as a result of research.

> The disagreement among psychotherapists about basic outcome criteria, the difficulty of operationally defining these criteria, the problem of finding an adequate test methodology, and the difficulty of conducting research to adequately examine whatever methodology is chosen, ensure that no consensus is likely to develop in the near future. This fact has significant implications for all regulatory proposals. It means that attempts at licensing or other restrictive regulations, no matter what method of selection chosen will be based on a process that has little reliability or validity and about which no consensus exists as to its value. It means that if traditional academic and experience requirements are relied upon, the public is likely to be receiving very little protection for its money. (p. 346)

Hogan further sets the stage for his proposal by arguing that not only does licensing fail to protect the public because the selection criteria for licensure have no bearing on actual performance and because a "woefully inadequate" (p. 348) disciplinary system more often takes action to protect the good name of the profession than to protect the public, but licensing also has a number of negative side effects, such as "exacerbating shortages in the supply of personnel" (p. 348) and aggravating problems in the geographical distribution of practitioner.

What then can be done? Hogan proposes "licensing through registration":

> Any person desiring to practice as a psychotherapist should be required to register with the state. The registration fee should be nominal, and practitioners should not have to meet any educational, experiential, or other prerequisites before being granted the right to practice. They would, however, have to provide the state with their name, address, and other information related to their intended field of practice, such as relevant experience

and academic training, the methods they intend to use, the goals of treatment, their fees, and a statement of their ethical beliefs. The registration laws would be administered by a board of registration that would also be responsible for disciplinary enforcement. (p. 361)

In order to effectively monitor the actual practice of psychotherapy, further laws would have to be passed, including laws requiring the practitioners to distribute evaluation forms to clients regarding the services they received. These forms would then be submitted to the regulatory board. A sufficient number of negative comments or ratings would bring about a disciplinary inquiry or hearing. The boards themselves would be adequately funded and would not depend on registration fees for their operation. They would not be dominated by practitioners or their representatives, but would be balanced by inclusion of members of the public, clients, and government officers.

Special laws could be passed for specific concerns—for example, a law could be enacted making sexual intercourse between psychotherapists and their clients a criminal offense. Finally, research should be conducted to evaluate these, or any other, methods of regulation.

This proposal at this point in time is more envisionary than realistic. The professions seem committed to traditional licensure as a way of gaining status and claiming competency, an approach that Hogan regards as a return to a guild society. Nevertheless what is possible tomorrow may be different than what is possible today, and in any case, some aspects of his proposal could be included as modifications in current licensing regulation, such as the mandatory distribution of client evaluation forms and the more balanced representation in regulatory boards of all kinds.

THE VALIDITY OF KNOWLEDGE-BASED EXAMS IN MEASURING COMPETENCY

Another criticism of licensing laws on which other writers have focused, and which would be bypassed by a simple registration system, is the relevancy of taking and passing exams that test the applicant's familiarity with certain subject matter. The Examination for Professional Practice in Psychology (EPPP) has especially come under attack. The nature of the test itself, the relevance of the various topics that are covered, and the overall scoring system have been questioned. First of all the test is admittedly a test of knowledge and not a measure of performance. As Flexner (1910) observed:

There is only one sort of licensing test that is significant, viz., a test that ascertains the practical ability of the student confronting a concrete case to collect all relevant data and to suggest the positive procedure applicable to the conditions disclosed. A written examination may have some incidental value; it does not touch the heart of the matter. (p. 169)

Two arguments can be brought to bear in response to this attack. The first is that there are no comprehensive, cost-effective tests of "practical ability." Cost-effectiveness is, however, a relative matter. In view of the costs associated with trying to pass the current exams, especially the EPPP, as is detailed later in this section, it might actually be cheaper to develop and use performance-based exams. Ann Howard (1983) has sketched such exams and notes that licensing procedures can incorporate work samples and simulations even now.

The second argument is that performance ability must have some grounding in knowledge, albeit precisely which concepts and facts are most relevant may not be known. Wiens and Menne (1981) argue this position with respect to the EPPP:

We believe that passing this exam is a necessary but certainly not a sufficient condition for licensing. . . . The examination is only a check to see that the candidate has some knowledge of that basic corpus of knowledge which is the science of psychology. A passing grade on the exam does not necessarily tell us how much someone knows, but failure indicates that something is wrong, either with the candidate or with the institution from which the candidate graduated. (p. 394)

The EPPP is not a static test; its items change from testing to testing; also the number of items that come from various subareas of psychology may change. Some of these subareas seem remote from the planned practices of many of the applicants, and it is with great reluctance that they review and update themselves, just for the purpose of passing the exam, on topics that they had last briefly studied in freshmen survey courses. Psychology of learning, of perception, and statistics, for example, may be seen as relevant only to those planning to do research of particular kinds. Their importance to practitioners is an issue that is not readily resolved.

Also because the exam changes from one semiannual testing to another, most states use a floating cutoff score rather than a fixed number of items or a fixed percentage of items that must be passed. Either the mean score of all the applicants taking the test at that testing, one standard deviation less than the mean, or some proportion of one standard deviation less than the mean is set as the passing score, depending on the state (Reaves, 1982). If the mean score is used, approximately one half of all the applicants will fail the test, regardless of how well they have done in terms of number of items that they have answered correctly.

To make it possible for more first-time applicants to pass the exam, some states have established separate norms for them, such as comparing them only to each other, or reducing the passing score for these applicants.

The net effect of using a floating cutoff score is to raise the level of knowledge and test sophistication required to pass the test. In view of the allegation years ago that the level was artificially high, when taking the preparation workshops was not necessary, how much more likely is it now that current cutoff scores have no relationship to what is necessary to be a competent practitioner?

One of the side effects of using a floating point criterion has been to make the test, and preparation for it extremely competitive. This has engendered a test preparation industry. Four-to-five-day workshops covering the major subareas in the exam are offered at key cities in the United States by large organizations that have sprung up simply to provide this "licensure exam review" service. For those who can't afford the time or money to attend, "independent study programs" are also for sale and can be ordered by mail.

As of this writing, the fee for the full on-site workshop offered by one of these organizations was $795 and the home study materials cost $395. When the costs of travel to one of the national test sites and lodging there are included, it becomes problematic how accessible the licensing system is for applicants who are relatively impoverished, especially because each state also adds on its own licensing fees for exams and processing.

Related to this issue is the question whether the EPPP discriminates unfairly against minority applicants and older applicants. State employment officials in California, one of the states that uses the mean as the cutoff score, conducted a study of the results of the April 1980 administration of the EPPP in San Francisco (Foltz, 1981). They discovered that over half of the white applicants passed, compared to one fourth of the blacks, and only one sixth of other minorities. This is a serious matter, if true, in view of the data presented in Chapter 6 on justice and cultural minorities, where it was shown how woefully inadequate are the instructional and delivery systems for minority clients. Also those applicants in their 20s did the best, with performance uniformly declining in succeeding decades. Examination of the test itself revealed that only 6% of the items concerned treatment planning, intervention, implementation, and evaluation. It could be argued that pursuing Nonmaleficence (protection of clients from incompetent practitioners) and Self-Interest (on the part of the already licensed practitioners and the test preparation industry) may have resulted in lack of Justice, both to would-be therapists and to their consumers.

In recognition of these criticisms the American Association of State Psychology Boards has devoted a major part of its resources to research on the validity of the EPPP (Wand & Weaver, 1983).

REGULATORY BOARDS—DO THEY WORK?

One of the issues that Hogan raised was the tendency of guild organizations to be more concerned about their public image than the public's welfare. Therefore he argued that the regulatory boards, whether for licensure or for registration, be comprised of a *minority* of representatives of the profession to be regulated rather than a majority. This rather radical proposal has not, to my knowledge, been adopted as yet with regard to regulation of psychotherapy, but increasing numbers of public members have been placed on such boards. Such members have even served to chair the boards, as is true of the current Oregon Board of Psychologist Examiners.

Another issue Hogan raised is whether such boards need to be funded from state revenues or solely from licensure fees paid by licensed professionals and applicants. To date, the latter source of funds seems woefully inadequate to do the breadth or depth of investigation of complaints that is necessary in our increasingly litigious society. A single contested application of a sanction brought against a professional after thorough investigation of the charges and due process for both sides can exceed a licensing board's budget for several years. Hogan recognized this fact also in the following statements:

> *Licensing Fees.* If the state believes that licensing is important to protect the public, then it should be willing to underwrite the costs of that protection. For this reason and because high licensing fees operate in discriminatory fashion, licensing fees should be minimal. Funding for the administration of the licensing process should be derived from general state funds. . . . (p. 376)

> *Adequate Funding.* A major reason why disciplinary boards have not been effective is lack of funds. Without reasonable financial resources it is impossible to hire investigative officers, train staff, or prosecute important cases. Even the matter of record-keeping is seriously hampered. (p. 377)

Having sufficient funds to investigate and prosecute is not enough to ensure truly effective boards. Both the practitioners in the field and the public must have ready access to the board with their complaints about unethical and incompetent practice and must be adequately educated to know both what constitutes a proper complaint and how to register one. This sort of educative function requires funding also. Regulation may also be strengthened by legislation that would make certain acts, such as sexual intercourse between therapists or counselors and clients, illegal, as is the case in Minnesota (Bouhoutsos, 1985), and laws that would require practitioners to make available to their clients evaluation forms that contain information of where to send them, as Hogan suggested.

Finally, the boards themselves and the professionals they represent need to have the "will" to effectively monitor, educate, and sanction. As Wiens and Menne state with respect to the role of the boards (1981):

> The competency assurance that licensing boards can provide consumers of psychological services is directly proportional to the vigor and dispatch with which a licensing board remediates, disciplines, or removes the license of an incompetent, unethical, negligent, dishonest, or unprofessional practitioner. (p. 391)

As indicated earlier, the sanctions available to licensing boards are not limited only to "punishment," nor should they be. The fuller the range the more flexible and appropriate the response can be. In some cases all that may be necessary to correct the behavior, assuming investigation has shown the complaint to be justified, is to educate the practitioner by a warning or reprimand and to monitor subsequent behavior. Other options could include conditional probation, such as requiring the practitioner to submit to care, counseling, or treatment by a board-designated professional, suspension of the license for a specified period of time, requirement of restitution to the wronged party, and ultimately, revocation of licensure (APA, 1987c).

CURRENT DEVELOPMENTS

Another way in which to gain competitive standing in the marketplace of those offering psychotherapy and psychological counseling is that of certification by national organizations. A case in point is that of the National Board of Certified Counselors (NBCC). The NBCC was established by the American Association for Counseling and Development in 1982 as a result of its "professional concerns and efforts in the area of credentialing" (National Board of Certified Counselors, 1988). As of May 1987 it had certified approximately 17,000 counselors, who are bound by the

NBCC Code of Ethics and can claim exclusive rights to the title, "National Certified Counselor" or "National Certified Career Counselor." Practitioners who use such title without NBCC authorization "may be denied the right to future certification or may be subject to legal action" (p. 1). Presumably the latter would only apply in states whose laws protect such titles.

As might be guessed, the NBCC actively promotes efforts to obtain licensure for its members in all the states in which it is active. It can be expected that more and more such certifying bodies will arise and petition state legislatures for title protection. To the degree to which they are successful, especially if this also enables them to become eligible for third-party reimbursement for their services, the more choices consumers will have. Also the more attractive and sensible Hogan's registration system appears.

ISSUES

What is the primary purpose of licensing laws?

How might the purposes of professional groups seeking licensure differ from the primary purpose?

What aspects of and activities associated with licensure are most germane to protection of the public?

Is it possible to license the activity of psychotherapy or psychological counseling as one might license the practice of surgery?

What is a "scope of practice" statement, and what function does it serve in licensing laws?

What is the function of "title protection" legislation?

What are some ways scope of practice statements can be written to clarify who can do what to whom under what conditions?

How are licensure and third-party reimbursement intertwined?

Are there dangers that licensure unjustly promotes the status and financial security of some practitioners or professions over other equally competent and ethical practitioners and unjustly restricts the distribution of the benefits of psychotherapy and psychological counseling?

Why might Dan Hogan's registration system be more equitable to all concerned?

How does his proposed system protect the public?

Can parts of his system be transposed to present licensing regulatory systems?

Why are knowledge-based exams, such as the EPPP, of dubious validity in assessing practitioner competency and ethics?

Does using a floating mean as the passing score pose special ethical problems?

Is there evidence that the EPPP discriminates unfairly? Against whom, what groups of applicants?

Are EPPP test preparation workshops a way of ensuring competency or do they work instead to exclude financially disadvantaged applicants?

Why not develop competency-based exams?

Do licensing boards effectively regulate licensed practitioners? If not, why not, and what can be done about it?

Why is it important for such boards to have a broad array of sanctions at their disposal?

What current developments threaten to alter the current licensing system by bypassing or expanding it?

CHAPTER 11

Malpractice

THE THREAT OF MALPRACTICE

At times it seems as if a panic mentality has set in among psychotherapists in private practice with regard to the threat of being sued for malpractice. In response to the high degree of concern that is evident, and feeding into it, is a spate of books, articles, and workshops on the subject. Few are reassuring; almost all provide good information but promote panic by emphasizing the geometrical increase in malpractice suits against psychotherapists and sometimes by promoting overkill precautionary responses. It is my hope to approach this serious matter in a more reasoned way, but more important from the standpoint of this book, in a way that acknowledges the potentially valuable aspect of malpractice suits in promoting the principles of Nonmaleficence.

Probably the primary purpose of malpractice suits is to ameliorate and redress the harm suffered by injured clients. A secondary purpose is to prevent such harm from befalling future clients. This purpose is served only when the public and the professions are educated by reviewing malpractice suits for what is legally considered harmful, and when the threat of such suits discourages clinicians from practicing in ways that may prove harmful to their clients or to other parts of the public.

A logical starting point for such education is a brief, analytical review of the incidence of malpractice suits that pertain to professional psychotherapists, the types of suits, and the possible reasons for the recent rise in such suits. Following this review is an examination of the legal and the financial contexts for bringing malpractice suits, their legal components, and some moderate recommendations for avoiding such suits.

INCIDENCE OF MALPRACTICE SUITS

Hogan (1979) could only find 300 psychotherapeutic malpractice suits from 1850 to 1977 that had reached the appellate court level. His review of these cases led him to despair over the efficacy of such suits to impact on basic psychotherapy, which involves only talking:

> Unfortunately, it is still the case that virtually no reported decisions exist in which a psychotherapist has been successfully sued for negligence in what was said to a client during the therapeutic process. As long as therapists restrict their practice to talk, interpretations, and advice, they will remain nearly immune from suit, no matter how poor their advice, how damaging their comments, or how incorrect their comments, or how incorrect their interpretations. (Volume 3, p. 27)

Since that time there is evidence that the incidence of malpractice suits against psychotherapists has grown considerably and that psychotherapists cannot deal with certain types of clients, notably those who pose danger to themselves or to others, simply with "talking therapy" and expect to escape malpractice suits. They are expected, in some of these cases, to breach confidentiality, if necessary, in order to protect the client or the public.

The best data on incidence come from the statistics kept by the APA Insurance trust, which covers cases brought against members of the American Psychological Association, most of whom, it can be assumed, have liability coverage through the trust. A number of articles have reported this data and analyzed it in different ways.

From 1955 to 1965 there were no claims, and there were less than 3000 participants (policyholders). From 1975 to 1980 there were 122 claims with an average claim value of $3,571, and the number of participants had risen to 16,000 in 1980 (Wright, 1981a). From 1976 to 1981 there were 266 claims, and the claims increased from 1982 to 1984 to an average of 153 claims per year; also there were 26,000 participants in 1984 (Fisher, 1985). The most recent data show that from 1975 to 1985 there were 998 suits against psychologists (Pope, 1987; Turkington, 1986), 850 of which resulted in some expenditures.

During this time the number of clients has also increased geometrically. In 1955 only 233,000 persons were reported as being treated in psychiatric outpatient clinics. That number has now swelled to about 4 million seen in such clinics and in community mental health centers (Cohen, 1979). Cohen also estimates that approximately 7 million persons in the private sector obtain psychotherapy-related services from mental health professionals and nonprofessionals. This latter figure can be compared to another estimate that in 1979, 2 million people were in psychotherapy annually (Deardorff, Cross, & Hupprich, 1984).

Data from the trust also show that 71% of those who are awarded more than $1 million in damages suffered significant physical injuries such as paralysis, permanent brain damage, wrongful death, amputations, or burns.

Furthermore half of the initial jury awards decreased after trial. Finally it is estimated that the chance of any given psychologist being sued is less than one half of one percent (Turkington, 1986, November).

Data regarding other mental health professions are less helpful insofar as what is available is not specific to the practice of psychotherapy. Psychiatry, for example, typically involves one or more physical treatment components, such as drug therapy, electroconvulsive therapy (ECT), and physical therapy, and it also involves suits for wrongful commitment or release. Social workers in private practice also are not necessarily involved solely or mostly in doing psychotherapy. What is known is that relative to other medical specialties psychiatrists are least apt to be sued. Cohen (1979) reports that "the average American psychiatrist is sued once for every 50 to 100 years of practice, whereas the average neurosurgeon can expect to be sued once for every two years of practice" (p. 8). Klein and Glover (1983) reporting perhaps more recent data state: "Only about 1.5 claims are filed per 100 psychiatrists, annually, as opposed to about 25 claims per 100 physicians annually for other practitioners" (p. 132). Furthermore they claim there were no reported cases for negligent psychotherapy. The number of psychiatrists has also increased dramatically over the past 40 years, going from less than 5,000 in 1948 to over 34,000 in 1988, with an increase of over 10,000 in just the past 10 years (data provided by Robert McDevitt, Chair, American Psychiatric Association Ethics Committee, 1988).

According to Besharov and Besharov (1987) social work liability is a relatively new thing. Up to about 15 years ago there were almost no lawsuits, but in the short span of 1982 to 1985 they went from fewer than 1000 malpractice suits to more than 2000. Nevertheless they can still get malpractice insurance for from $46 to $138 (Frey, 1988), whereas psychologists now pay about $450 per annum (Buie, 1987, December).

Thus it seems safe to conclude that although the incidence of malpractice suits against professional psychotherapists has increased manifold in recent years, at least part of that can be attributed to sizable increases in the numbers of clients and the number of practitioners during the same span of time. Also, relative to malpractice suits against some other professionals, particularly physicians, the danger of such suits is relatively small. Nevertheless, this phenomenon is a remarkable one and deserves some attempt at explanation.

Most Frequent Grounds for Action

Although one cannot strictly break down all suits into mutually exclusive categories, it is instructive to note the results of the attempts to do so because it will indicate the areas of practice most prone to legal and perhaps also ethical violations. Again the study of the suits filed against participants in the APA Insurance Trust from 1975 to 1985 provides the most definitive data in this arena (Pope, 1987).

The 10 most expensive-to-litigate types of cases, listed in order of expense, are as follows:

1. *Sexual Improprieties.* This represented 18.5% of the total cases but 44.8% of the total paid out for all claims. It is clear that modern courts have no sympathy for the argument that sex between clients and therapists is a matter of "consenting adults." Of all the sexual malpractice suits that have been filed in this sample, in only one was the therapist exonerated (Cummings & Sobel, 1985). Perhaps for this reason APA's contracted insurer has limited its total liability in such cases to $25,000. This coverage includes former as well as current clients, attempts at erotic sexual contact and proposal as well as actual contact, and relatives and members of the same household as the client. Back in 1985 the malpractice insurance available through the American Psychiatric Organization discontinued providing any coverage for sexual misconduct ("Insurance No Longer Covers," 1985).

2. *Incorrect Treatment.* Inappropriate interventions accounted for about 15% of all cases.

3. *Death of Patient or Others.* This category is primarily the result of incorrect assessment and follow-through with regard to potential suicide and accounted for about 9% of the cases.

4. *Diagnosis.* Inadequate or incorrect diagnosis was the primary factor in about 6% of all cases. It is not necessary to make a formal diagnosis, but there must be evidence of some sort of clear conceptualization of the client's difficulties.

5. *Loss from Evaluation.* Clients who lose the opportunity for certain jobs or positions because of unfavorable psychological evaluations may sue, and will win, if there is sufficient evidence that the evaluation was inadequate or otherwise incorrect. Only 3.2% of all cases were of this nature, but they accounted for 9.6% of the expenditures.

6. *Breach of Confidentiality/Privacy.* This category accounted for about 7% of the cases.

7. *Failure to Warn.* Despite all the publicity over the *Tarasoff* rulings, there were only four successful malpractice suits in this category.

8. *Bodily Injury.* There were 21 cases in which client collected for bodily injury (2.5%).

9. *Countersuit for Fee Collection.* This used to be the most common type of case (Cummings & Sobel, 1985). Now it accounts for only 5.9% of the cases. Apparently psychologists have become more sophisticated in this area.

10. *Assault and Battery.* There were nine (1.1%) such suits.

If the view of malpractice is expanded to include "mental health practitioners in all settings," Slimak and Berkowitz (1983, p. 291) claim that the six most prominent types of malpractice suits were: faulty diagnosis, improper certification in a commitment proceeding, failure to exercise adequate precautions for a suicidal patient, breach of confidentiality, faulty applications of therapy, and promise of a cure. The latter may form the basis for a breach of contract suit as well.

Psychiatrists have been found liable for damages that resulted from electroconvulsive therapy, drug therapy, physical therapy, sexual therapy and sexual contact with patients, patient suicide, and acts of patients who harm others (Klein & Glover, 1983).

Common lawsuits against social workers are treatment without consent (i.e., clients claim they were somehow coerced into or poorly informed about treatment they received), inappropriate treatment, failure to consult with or refer to a specialist, failure to prevent a patient's suicide, causing a client's suicide, failure to protect third parties, inappropriate release of a client, false imprisonment, failure to provide adequate care for clients in residential settings, assault and battery, sexual involvements with clients, breach of confidentiality, defamation, violation of client's civil rights, failure to be available when needed, abrupt or inappropriately timed termination of treatment, and inappropriate bill collection methods (Besharov & Besharov, 1987).

It is evident that Hogan's observation that psychotherapists who restricted themselves to talking therapy were virtually secure from malpractice suits does not apply today. Incorrect treatment, suicide, faulty diagnosis, and failure to protect the public from client actions are among other actions or inactions that can serve as grounds of action that might even apply to "pure" psychotherapy.

Reasons for Increase in Malpractice Suits

There are a multitude of different reasons, speculative and otherwise, for the exponential increase in malpractice suits in recent decades. The following are not necessarily listed in order of their importance:

1. *Self-Regulation Has Been Inadequate.* Perhaps the basic reason is that it has become increasingly apparent that the professions have not

done a good job of regulating themselves. This is claimed both by Hogan, as already seen, and by Robert Plotkin, legal consultant for the APA who states (1979):

> But as pyschology continues to exert greater influence on special social institutions and on wider issues of public policy, it too may feel the public's clamor for increased regulation and accountability.
>
> If so, the reason is likely to be in large part because psychology, like the medical profession, lacks a truly effective system of accountability for licensed practitioners. Present regulation is oriented to controlling the formal structure by which licenses are granted: the accreditation of educational programs and the setting of minimal licensure standards. This system presumes that, once licensed, a psychologist becomes the immutable equivalent of an honest and ethical practitioner. (p. 10)

2. *The Base Rate of Malpractice Suits Has Been Low.* In such a circumstance it is easy to double or triple the amount during any given 10-year period. Much of the increase can be accounted for by the tremendous growth of practitioners and clients during the same time periods.

3. *"Talking Therapy" Is Giving Way to More Prescriptive Therapies.* The nature of psychotherapeutic interventions, especially for psychologists and other nonmedical therapists may be changing from that of doing mostly or exclusively talking therapy to that of more active prescriptive therapies. Tyron (1976) warned that behaviorally oriented clinicians needed to be especially cautious or they might experience an increase in malpractice suits "because, among other reasons, of the specificity of behavior modification therapies ..." (p. 468) Also the populations such therapists work with have expanded from persons with strictly psychological problems to a mixture of psychological and physical problems, thus increasing the likelihood of a claim for physical damage, which is easier to demonstrate and prove to the satisfaction of a jury or a judge than emotional damage.

Knapp and Vandecreek (1981, p. 679) claim that the new breed of "health psychologists" who work in conjunction with the medical profession, often in medical settings, are particularly vulnerable to malpractice suits. They list a number of reasons in addition to the possibility of physical harm, which include the lack of a close emotional bond between therapist and patient, the decreased social stigma for such patients if they testify in courts, and the decreased likelihood of emotional blocks, such as dependency and low self-esteem, which otherwise might mitigate against initiating or following through with a malpractice suit.

4. *Acceptance and Legal Recognition of "Emotional Distress" as Grounds for Malpractice Have Increased.* As will be noted later, the supreme courts of Hawaii and California abolished the traditional requirement that there can be no recovery for the negligent infliction of emotional disturbance alone (Thompson, 1983). The California Supreme Court stated: "The jurors are best situated to determine whether and to what extent the defendant's conduct caused emotional distress" (*Molien v. Kaiser Foundation Hospitals,* 1980).

5. *There Has Been a Change in Case Law Affecting the Statute of Limitations.* "There used to be a 3-year statute of limitations on all malpractice cases. However courts have now consistently ruled that the statute of limitations starts when the emotionally disturbed patient begins to realize his or her rights" (Cummings & Sobel, 1985, p. 186).

6. *Distrust of Authority in General Has Grown in Our Society.* It has been precipitated in part by Watergate, Irangate, disclosures of illegal insider trading in stock market, scandals in labor unions, business, and so forth (cf. Cohen, 1979).

7. *Lawyers Are Abundant.* Although "ambulance chaser" lawyers may be scarce in any arena, and more so in that of possible psychological trauma, it certainly is easier these days to locate an attorney who has the time and the skills to find a basis for action.

8. *Litigation Is in Vogue.* It is safe to say that one of the first thoughts that cross people's minds who feel that they have been wronged by a professional is whether they can or should sue the professional. There are almost daily headlines of multimillion-dollar suits of all kinds in our newspapers, many of which are malpractice suits. As a result the public has become very sensitized to this option.

LEGAL CONTEXT: MALPRACTICE AND TORT LAW

According to Cohen (1979) there are three kinds of law: constitutional (federal and state), statutory (enacted by federal and state legislatures and by federal and state administrative agencies), and common law, otherwise referred to as "case law" or "judge-made law." This last kind of law consists of decisions in areas not specifically covered by other kinds of laws. When a higher court has already made such a decision, it establishes a precedent that has the effect of law.

Another way in which to categorize law is to divide it into criminal law and civil law. Criminal law defines acts that are offensive to society in general. Civil law is concerned with acts offensive to specific individuals under certain conditions. Because the sanctions for criminal acts may be severe, establishing that such an act was indeed committed by a certain party or parties requires proof "beyond a reasonable doubt"; whereas civil offenses require only "a preponderance of evidence."

Malpractice suits fall under common law and are concerned with civil offenses of the tort type. A tort (Latin *tort(um)* = "wrong" or "injustice") is variously defined. Cohen (1979) cites Krauskopf and Krauskopf's definition: A tort is "a harm done to an individual in such a way and of such a type that the law will order the person who did the harm to pay damages to the injured party" (p. 314). The body of law that has been built up over the centuries through the common law process is referred to as "tort law."

It is perhaps easier and clearer for now to think of torts as harms or offenses to individuals which, if proven to have occurred by application of the standard of "the preponderance of evidence,"will result in the awarding of monetary compensation to the injured party.

Historically it was important to determine if the tort was an "intentional" one or an "unintentional" one, and malpractice suits originally comprised only unintentional torts. Assault, battery, and defamation are intentional torts, and negligence is unintentional. However, Cohen claims this distinction has not been holding up.

FINANCIAL CONTEXT: COSTS OF BRINGING
SUIT AND DAMAGES AWARDED

Because a tort is not under criminal law, the government does not initiate the prosecution; it is up to the party who feels wronged to do so. This can be prohibitively expensive, and many parties who would have a good chance of recovering damages would not be able to pursue this course of action except that many lawyers agree to take on such cases for a percentage, usually one third, of any awarded damages. The lawyer, in effect, bears the brunt of the cost of the legal proceedings in the calculated risk that the suit will be successful. This is known as a "contingency fee" arrangement.

An important factor in deciding whether to file such a suit, besides the estimated chance of winning it, is the amount of money that might be awarded. This in turn is partially a function of the ability of the parties being sued to pay out large amounts. Therefore it is customary to name an extensive array of defendants, especially those with "deep pockets"— that is, with a large financial reserve, such as persons who have large liability insurance policies and institutions. Ironically, defendants who are so incautious as not to carry liability insurance are less apt to be sued, unless they were under the umbrella of some institution when they allegedly committed the tort or unless they are independently wealthy. On the other hand, any suit is more apt to financially impoverish noncovered defendants.

Another factor that enters in is the likelihood of being awarded punitive damages in addition to the customary damages awarded in successful suits. Punitive damages, also referred to as "exemplary damages," are awarded when more than simple negligence is found, such as when assault or some other intentional tort is proven. The purposes of punitive damages are to punish the perpetuator effectively so that she or he will never again be tempted to repeat the act and also to set an example for other would-be perpetuators. Such damages can be in the millions of dollars.

Other damages that may be awarded are specific, general, and attorney fees. The specific damages are documentable actual costs that the plaintiff suffered as a result of maltreatment or insufficient care. Receipts for prescribed drugs or payments to other therapists for remedial treatments are examples of such costs that might apply in professional psychotherapy malpractice suits. General damages are estimates of future costs that can reasonably be expected to result from the maltreatment. They are more difficult to determine because there is no precise way to measure many such costs, such as continued pain and suffering, except as they might manifest themselves in tangible ways, such as loss of future earnings. Finally, there are attorney fees, but these are usually awarded only if punitive damages are also assessed (Cohen, 1979).

LEGAL CRITERIA FOR PROVING MALPRACTICE

Proving malpractice is no easy matter, especially in the practice of psychotherapy, as will be soon evident. In brief there are four legal criteria (Thompson, 1983, p. 155). They are:

1. The defendant owed a legal duty to the plaintiff.
2. The defendant's conduct violated that duty by failing to conform to a legal standard established to prevent unreasonable risk or harm.
3. There is a sufficient causal connection between the conduct of the defendant and the harm suffered by the plaintiff.
4. The harm to the plaintiff is an actual personal injury that can be measured in economic terms.

Establishment of Duty

Establishment of a duty occurs when the therapist has agreed to accept someone as a client. This would only be an issue if it is not clear that such an agreement was made.

Standard of Care

Establishment of violation of duty is more complex. In the case of professional malpractice the legal standard of care is higher than that required of the nonexpert or the ordinary citizen. For a nonprofessional, the giving of advice or any other activity that might fall under the rubric of "psychotherapy" would be measured against the standard of what a "reasonable" person would do in the circumstances that obtained at the time. For the professional the standard of care is that of "good professional practice" or "customary and usual practice." For the professional-in-training the standard would presumably fall somewhere in between.

Professional standards of care may vary according to the geographical area. Thus in remote rural areas where practitioners may have to stretch the limits of their expertise or else refuse to serve many members of the local population, who would have nowhere else to turn, the standard may be lower than in a metropolitan area where referral to specialists is readily feasible.

Professional standards will also vary according to the level of expertise one could reasonably expect from a practitioner with similar qualifications: Thus professionals who have special certificates, such as psychologists who have diplomas in the specialty areas of clinical and counseling psychology from the American Board of Professional Psychology, or psychotherapists who give workshops to other professional psychotherapists in practitioner ethics might be held to a higher standard (Woody, 1983).

As a practical matter, it is very difficult to determine exactly what the professional standard of care is because the field of psychotherapy is so ill-defined and so multifaceted. The usual procedure is to call on experts to render judgments as to whether the standard has been met in any given malpractice suit. But the more esoteric the type of therapy that was administered, the more difficult it is to find professional therapists who know enough about the treatment to be able to say whether it was conducted appropriately. Even as one needs fellow heart transplant surgeons to testify if a transplant operation was botched, so one would need fellow primal scream therapists to determine if one of their colleagues malpracticed, insofar as the issue is how well or expertly he or she followed prescribed procedures. This would not be true, however, in blatant violations of general rules of psychotherapy, such as the therapist's gossiping about a client in a public forum or consistently showing up for therapy in an intoxicated condition.

Another problem that arises with utilization of expert witnesses is that the usual screening procedures employed by lawyers on both sides will frequently result in contradictory testimony. The lawyer for the defense, for example, is likely to sound out several psychotherapeutic experts until one or more are found who generally support the defense's position. The lawyer for the plaintiff will do the same to gather support for the plaintiff's position, with the result that it appears that each side has "hired" its own experts (and, indeed, the experts are paid by each side respectively) and that there is no truly expert opinion. This problem is, of course, not reserved for malpractice suits but is a consequence of our adversarial legal system.

Alternatives to Using Expert Witnesses to Determine Standard of Care

This type of situation has led a legal expert, Professor William Prosser (1971, p. 164), to support the proposal of several medical and bar associations that the medical profession establish panels of qualified and disinterested experts who could be available to testify in court. Their fees would come out of some general fund. This proposal could be adopted by any profession that is frequently called on to provide expert testimony in legal proceedings. On the other hand it can be argued that the adversarial system does not create differences in expert opinion, it merely discovers and emphasizes them; whereas any other system would tend to mask or plaster over such differences.

The ethical codes of the various professions that practice psychotherapy make another approach available to the courts. When the defendant's conduct clearly violates some provision of such a code, then the need for expert testimony is negligible. Of course this depends on the comprehensiveness and the specificity of the codes. Adding to most of the professional codes the explicit provision that sexual relations between therapists and their clients is unethical may well have increased the chances of finding malpractice if such a relationship existed. Certainly the insurance companies have decided as much by writing in specific exemptions from coverage in such instances.

Legal Causal Connection

Even blatantly unethical acts do not, in themselves, guarantee that the third or fourth criterion will be met. The third, legal causation, requires that whatever damage is claimed to have occurred must be a result of the unethical or incompetent acts of the therapist and not the result of other factors not under the therapist's control. Simple establishment of a sexual relationship, for example, does not necessarily result in damage to the client. In fact, as seen in Chapter 4, even the studies that have reported that clients are typically harmed by such relationships have also disclosed that a subset of clients appear not to have been harmed, and perhaps were even helped, by the sexual relationship with their therapists (e.g., Bouhoutsos et al., 1983). Again, in order to establish whether harm has come to the particular client at issue, recourse is usually made to expert witnesses.

Economically Measurable Harm

Finally, tort law requires that a plaintiff's injury be real and measurable in monetary terms. Fright, shock, emotional distress, and disturbance that do not lead to actual physical injury are hard to determine in such terms, and the claim to suffering from them is often greeted with skepticism. Even physical symptoms that are frequently allied with psychological stress such as dizziness, headaches, rashes, and nausea are, at the worst, easily faked and, at the best, variably incapacitating.

Sometimes tangible damages can be claimed, such as loss of salary, payment of child care expenses, physicians' charges for investigating a possible physical base for symptoms, physical treatment of symptoms, and medication, but in the final analysis the jury needs to be convinced by the weight of the testimony that the mental suffering is real and not faked or substantially exaggerated, and that it results predominately from the therapist's failure to conform to the appropriate standard of care. When the California Supreme Court abolished the traditional legal requirement of proving physical consequences for emotional injury before recovery is possible, it stated: "The jurors are best situated to determine whether and to what extent the defendant's conduct caused emotional distress" (*Molien v. Kaiser Foundation Hospitals,* 1980).

RECOMMENDATIONS

These are the facts, as best as I can ascertain them. The task now is to interpret them and translate them into recommendations for prudent, ethical practice. Therapists must take care to ensure that ethical duties toward clients are not overshadowed or usurped by self-protective actions that are designed, often mistakenly, to protect themselves from malpractice suits, for surely neither the law nor ethical theory would wish to promote such an eventuality.

In one set of circumstances Nonmaleficence to oneself, that is, Self-Protection, appropriately comes to the fore, and that is when the client is clearly contemplating or has already taken steps to initiate legal action against the practitioner. A separate set of recommendations at the end of the chapter deals with this situation.

The following recommendations are gleaned from the many different sets of recommendations that I have reviewed in arriving at a comprehensive, yet reasonably succinct set that conforms to the criteria of ethical practice. Annotated in brackets are the ethical principles, besides Self-Protection, most germane to the recommendation.

1. Be clear and aboveboard with clients about all aspects of their treatment. As Plotkin (1978) says, "All professionals must be trained to treat clients like the consumers they are and to strive for positive, open relationships that will foster trust." (p. 10). This includes being able to provide your rationale for their treatment to clients or to anyone else whenever requested (Woody, 1983). This in turn includes the way you conceptualize their problems in theoretical terms (i.e., your diagnosis) and its relationship to their treatment. [Autonomy]

When clients are seen essentially for evaluation, and not for counseling or therapy, it is important to share with them the results of that evaluation and your recommendations. Such sharing will prevent the repercussions that come about when the impact of the results unpleasantly surprises the client, and it provides an opportunity to resolve differences and misunderstandings (Wright, 1981b). Craddick's model (1975), as presented in Chapter 3, is relevant here. [Autonomy]

Communications with others, of whatever nature, should also be reviewed and shared with clients. In fact, clients can take the responsibility in most instances of forwarding such communications, such as mailing in the relevant insurance forms (Woody, 1983). [Autonomy]

2. Keep abreast of your profession, especially the arena within which you practice. This includes keeping abreast of legal developments that may impact on your practice, ethical codes, and agency and institutional policies (Besharov & Besharov, 1987; Slimak & Berkowitz, 1983). [Beneficence, Nonmaleficence]

3. Maintain a consulting, supervisory relationship with someone or some group—a "place" where you can bring your difficult cases and where you can get feedback that you respect (Woody, 1983). This could be a group of colleagues who mutually serve this function for each other as described in Chapter 9. [Beneficence, Nonmaleficence]

4. When you have an especially difficult case, especially one that involves danger to the client or to others, consult one or more respected

colleagues (Deardorff et al., 1984; Knapp, 1980; Slimak & Berkowitz, 1983; Wright, 1981b). [Beneficence, Nonmaleficence]

5. Document this consultation and all other pertinent data regarding such cases, including the rationale for whatever decisions you made and actions you or the client took (Besharov & Besharov, 1987; Deardorff et al., 1984; Knapp, 1980; Slimak & Berkowitz, 1983).

6. If unsure of the legal aspects of such cases, seek legal counsel.

7. Be clear about all aspects of fees with clients, preferably providing them with a written statement of your policy. Do not let unpaid bills build up unless you are willing to write them off. Otherwise the formation of an additional relationship—creditor–debtor—will threaten to negatively impact the primary therapist–client relationship. On the other hand, do not abandon any clients still in definite need of therapy. They are your responsibility, both legally and ethically, until such time as the completion of therapy or suitable referral elsewhere. [Autonomy, Fidelity, Justice]

8. Do not, under any circumstances, make sexual advances or proposals to or enter into sexual relationships with clients or former clients who can be presumed to be still under your influence. [Autonomy, Fidelity]

Suppose, in spite of all precautions, a client threatens suit. What should/shouldn't you do? Following is an edited list of recommendations from those proposed by Roger Wright, an early member of the American Psychological Association's Insurance Trust (1981b):

1. Do not express your dismay to the client or the client's attorney or attempt to resolve the issue by any sort of direct communication. It is probably too late then, and what you say may be used against you (Woody, 1983).

2. Don't discuss the case or consult with colleagues, much less confess to them your fears of having botched it up in some way. They may provide moral support at the time, but later they may be subpoenaed and required to disclose what you said.

3. If in a personal crisis, seek out professional help from a respected colleague.

4. If you must consult with someone and do not want professional personal counseling, consult with a colleague who is in no way connected to the present situation.

5. Notify your malpractice insurance carrier promptly and then be patient. The wheels of justice often grind slowly.

6. Once you know what the defense strategy is, get a second opinion from an attorney with expertise in professional malpractice suits.

7. Assemble all documents in a logical fashion and don't expose them to anyone but your legal advocate.

8. Review scientific and professional literature relevant to this particular issue and type of case.

ISSUES

What ethical purpose is furthered by malpractice suits?

How can practitioners further such purpose?

How great is the rise in incidence of malpractice suits in recent years? What is the best way to interpret this phenomenal increase?

What are the most frequent causes of action in malpractice suits against psychotherapists?

Why is restricting practice to "talking therapy" no longer a secure protection against such suits?

Where does professional malpractice fit in the legal system?

Financial considerations play what role in bringing such suits?

What is the purpose of punitive damages?

How is the standard of care determined for any given professional? Why do some professionals have higher or lower standards of care?

Why are expert witnesses so intrinsic to the determination of culpability?

What alternatives are proposed or exist already to supplement and reduce the need for expert witnesses?

Do blatantly unethical acts necessarily secure the plaintiff's case? If not, why not?

How can psychic harm be measured in economic terms?

Based on a thorough understanding of malpractice actions, what preventive measures are recommended, and what ethical principles are most intimately associated with these measures?

Should a suit be threatened or enjoined, what steps can maximize Self-Protection?

CHAPTER 12

The Tarasoff *Case*

ATTITUDES TOWARD *TARASOFF*

If a single name strikes fear in the hearts of practicing psychotherapists, it is the name "Tarasoff." More anguish has been felt and more words have been written about the *Tarasoff* case than probably any other case in the annals of psychological and psychiatric history. Yet, as might be expected, that which frightens close up can be fascinating from a more distant perspective. The purpose of this chapter is to enable practitioners to gain cognitive distance from this legal phenomenon so that they will not act hysterically, that is, distort their practices unnecessarily and nontherapeutically in response to the fear that they, too, will be found wanting in the courts of law because one of their clients seriously harmed or killed someone else.

From an ethical perspective *Tarasoff* pits the duty of Nonmaleficence to third parties versus that of Autonomy for the client. Insofar as following legally questionable procedures may result in a malpractice suit against the psychotherapist or counselor, Self-Protection for the practitioner is also at issue. The difference from most other malpractice suits is that it is concerned with protecting the public from the actions of clients, rather than protecting clients from acts of their therapists.

Practitioners can take two basic attitudes toward *Tarasoff*—as an imposition on their practice or as an opportunity to learn. As with the previous chapter on malpractice, the assumption in this chapter is that the deliberations of the courts can be instructive, and what is learned may well contribute to ethical practice. In this case it is necessary to become familiar with the central case and its subsequent ramifications, as well as with the controversies that it has engendered. This chapter will first provide a description of the case and its immediate legal aftermath. Then it will consider the doctrine of "special relationships" that was the background rationale for this case and the legal duty that it expanded. The arguments, pro and con the ruling will be examined with special attention to corresponding ethical implications. This will be followed by sections on the extension of *Tarasoff* in subsequent rulings, and an analysis of why such rulings do and might well continue to vary from state to state. The final three sections will speculate on the extrapolation of *Tarasoff* to other areas such as AIDS and sexual assault, the attempts to provide practitioners with some clear legal guidelines through legislation, and recommendations for responding to situations in which clients appear to pose a threat to others.

TARASOFF: THE CASE

One of many interesting facets of this case is that everyone knows about it and can recall some of the more pertinent details, but few realize that what they "know" may be seriously inaccurate. The reason for this is that the case was settled out of court before it came to trial; hence the "facts" of the case were never determined in a court of law where both sides present their versions of what happened. Thus commentators have had to rely on the alleged sequence of events in the complaint filed by the plaintiff's attorney. These statements are assumed to be true for purposes of determining whether there are grounds for the suit (Peter Swanson, law professor, personal communication, April 3, 1988).

Another anomaly, a very rare occurrence, is that the Supreme Court of California reviewed the case twice, each time deciding that there were grounds for action, but modifying its decision the second time. Those decisions have led to a long and continuing debate over their merit and have resulted in a rich legacy of subsequent judgments. Before reviewing this debate and the legacy, I will piece together what seems to be the course of events that started it all and the subsequent legal processes, as described primarily by Alan Stone (1976), and other sources as noted.

The Events Leading to the Murder

Prorosenjit Poddar, a native of India studying naval architecture at the University of California at Berkeley, was enamored of Tatiana Tarasoff. She did not respond in kind and it is presumed that this rejection led to his going to the student health facility at the University of California at Berkeley. The psychiatrist who evaluated him referred him to a psychologist for treatment. The psychologist subsequently decided that Mr. Podder was dangerous, based on his pathological attachment to Ms. Tarasoff and his intent to purchase a gun. After consultation with two psychiatrists, the staff decided to request the campus police to take custody of Mr. Poddar pending civil commitment.

The police questioned Mr. Poddar at length, decided he was not dangerous, and released him. A contributing factor was that Ms. Tarasoff was in Brazil and wasn't expected back for some time. The psychiatrist who was director of the clinic and who had been away reviewed the case when he came back, and perhaps noting that Mr. Poddar had no known history of violence, decided that the staff had overreacted, requested that the police return the written information the staff had sent them, and ordered this and all other case records destroyed. He also directed that no further action be taken to commit or detain Mr. Poddar, who had broken off therapy following his detention and questioning by the police (Knapp, 1980; Mappes, Robb, & Engels, 1985).

Two months later Mr. Poddar went to Ms. Tarasoff's home and during a protracted chase shot her repeatedly with a pellet gun and then stabbed her to death.

Legal Aftermath

Ms. Tarasoff's parents filed a suit against the Regents of the University of California, the involved professional staff of the health center, and the police. The trial court dismissed the complaint, which dismissal was sustained upon appeal. The case was then appealed to the California Supreme Court. It was argued that the defendant had a duty to warn the Tarasoffs of Mr. Poddar's threat and to initiate commitment proceedings against him.

The supreme court reversed, finding that the special relationship between therapists and clients gives them the legal duty to warn those members of the public who are potential victims of the clients.

Upon petition by the defendants abetted by several *amici curiae,* including one from the American Psychiatric Association, the court granted a rehearing, a very unusual event. Susequently, the court confirmed its original decision but modified it by removing the police from the list of those who could be held liable. It also broadened the duty of the therapists as follows:

> When a therapist determines, or pursuant to the standards of his profession would determine, that his patient presents a serious danger of violence to another, he incurs an obligation to use reasonable care to protect the intended victim against such danger. The discharge of this duty may require the therapist to take one or more of various steps, depending on the nature of the case. Thus it may call for him to warn the intended victim or others likely to apprise the victim of the danger, to notify the police, or to take whatever other steps are reasonably necessary under the circumstances. (*Tarasoff v. Regents of University of California,* 17 Cal. 3d at 431, 1976)

As for Mr. Poddar, he was convicted of voluntary manslaughter. He has since been released from prison, returned to India, and reports being happily married.

THE LEGAL BASIS FOR THE DECISION

In order to understand the *Tarasoff* decision, it is necessary to place it in its legal context by first noting its position in law; next examining the meaning of the concept of "special relationship" and how it gives rise to an expanded duty for psychotherapists; and then examining the arguments regarding its value. Following that is a review of *Tarasoff's* application in the past, present, and anticipated future.

Tarasoff is an instance of malpractice law. In *Hedlund v. Superior Court* (cited in Melton, 1983, December) the California Supreme Court ruled that injury resulting from therapists' neglect to warn potential victims is "professional negligence" rather than "ordinary negligence"; thus California's 3-year statute of limitations applies rather than the 1-year statute for ordinary negligence, and *Tarasoff* is formally considered as an instance of professional malpractice.

Doctrine of "Special Relationship"

The duty to warn (and thus protect) potential victims was found by the court to stem from the "special relationship" that psychotherapists have with their patients. Schopp and Quattrocchi (1984) have critically examined this concept at some length. They note that "while the court definitely asserts that the psychotherapeutic relationship is such a special relationship, it does not indicate exactly what makes a relationship special in this sense or what it is about psychotherapy that renders it such a relationship" (p. 15). They note that under common law one person usually has no obligation to control the conduct of a second person; thus the court created an exception in certain instances. After reviewing the precedents that the court cited, including several in which physicians have been found negligent for failure to warn others of the dangers emanating from the illnesses of their patients, they advanced the following formulation of the court's position:

A professional (P) has a duty to conduct his professional relationship with a third [second] person (B) in such a manner as to exercise reasonable care to prevent harm to others potentially caused by B just in case the nature of this relationship is such that: (1) the practice of P's profession provides him with some special ability to decrease the probability of harm potentially caused by B; (2) P knows or should know that he has this ability; and (3) P knows or should know of the necessity and opportunity for influencing the harm threatened by B. (p. 21)

Thus the doctrine of special relationships is an extension of the general principle of negligence: Assuming P's profession provides "a special capacity to influence harm, then he violates the ordinary competence provision if he lacks this capacity; if he possesses it but fails to exercise it, then he falls short of the reasonable care requirement" (p. 21). Schopp and Quattrocchi go on to point out that warning victims does not constitute a special ability; it only presupposes certain capacities. This duty is well established for physicians whose patients have diseases that threaten others. The duty to warn arises from the physician's special knowledge of these diseases, which provides a special capacity to prevent harm by communication of this knowledge.

Special relationships that give rise to a duty to protect have been recognized in many other areas of tort law. Melella, Travin, & Cullen (1987) point out that a number of courts have agreed that landlords must take reasonable measures to protect tenants from foreseeable risk of crime; that business proprietors are obligated to protect their patrons from foreseeable assaults; that innkeepers are required to protect their guests from harm; and that common carriers (such as buses and trains) also have such a responsibility.

The Nature of the Duty

In the original court's decision the duty was limited to the duty to warn; in the final decision the duty was defined as the duty to protect the public, which may include warning potential victims. As will be seen later, this general duty to protect the public is not new, but is well established in law; however, the specific instance of it—warning potential victims of clients of psychotherapists—is new. Greenberg (1984) points out that in *Tarasoff* the duty to warn is owed to the specifically identified victim and to those foreseeably harmed by injury to her. This was clarified in a subsequent case, *Hedlund v. Superior Court* (1983), in which the Supreme Court of California found that a psychotherapist may be liable for the injury that a young child incurred during a violent assault upon the child's mother by a patient of the psychotherapist.

In *Cole v. Taylor* (1981) the Supreme Court of Iowa refused a rather presumptuous extension of this reasoning when it found against a psychiatrist's patient who had sued the psychiatrist for failing to warn her husband of her intentions to kill him, which, indeed, she did. The court argued that the duty was owed the victim, not the patient. It also barred the patient's new husband from suing for loss of consortium during his wife's imprisonment for murder.

The duty to protect in other ways becomes salient when the victim is not specifically identifiable and thus cannot be warned. Perhaps the patient can be confined through commitment proceedings, or not released if already in an institution, or, as Greenberg (1984) suggests, it may be possible to warn others who can take steps to prevent the threatened danger (such as warning the police in case of a bomb threat in a public building). Schopp and Quattrocchi (1984) also suggest that the most effective thing the therapist can do is to keep the client in therapy and do a good job with him or her.

ARGUMENTS PRO AND CON THE *TARASOFF* RULING

At the time and ever since, there has been considerable debate over the merits of the *Tarasoff* ruling. This debate is far from moot; it influences future rulings in other suits based on common law and the nature of future legislation in this area.

Arguments Pro

Historically, perhaps the most important argument was made in an article by two law professors, Fleming and Maximov (1974), which was published at the time the California Supreme Court reviewed the *Tarasoff* case. Fleming and Maximov advocated adoption of the principle of "the least restrictive option." In most cases where clients are considered dangerous to others, proceedings are instituted to confine them through civil commitment. However, such commitment effectively deprives psychiatric patients of liberty, stigmatizes them, and destroys their will to resist; therefore it should be invoked only as a last resort. Moreover, commitment is a faulty process: It may not be enacted in a timely fashion, and it has uncertain results. For these reasons other, less restrictive means should be considered first, such as warning intended victims.

The basic argument is that the life and physical well-being of others is more important than the observance of confidentiality stemming from the therapist–client relationship. The analogy here is to the physician's duty to report venereal disease, tuberculosis, or gunshot wounds to the proper authorities.

From a philosophical viewpoint the claim is that Nonmaleficence toward the public has priority over infringing on the Autonomy of the client. Fidelity may also be involved if the client was not told beforehand that confidentiality did not extend to disclosures indicative of harm to others. The validity of this claim is supported in a number of different ways. It is recognized in the ethical codes of the various psychotherapy professions, which stipulate that confidentiality can be broken in situations of "clear danger" to the client or to others. Surveys of psychotherapists demonstrate that they agree with this guideline (Baird & Rupert, 1987; Beck, 1985; Haas et al., 1988; Medella et al., 1987; Pope, Tabachnick, & Keith-Spiegel, 1987). Finally, the general public concurs: A recent telephone survey (Rubanowitz, 1987) found that respondents "felt that confidentiality should be broken when a client reveals the occurrence of . . . murder [planned or confessed], suicide plans, child abuse, major theft, and treason/sabotage against the U.S." (p. 616).

It will be argued in the following section that psychotherapists are unable to predict dangerousness with any accuracy; therefore it makes no sense to require them to warn or otherwise protect the public against the possible actions of their clients. However, it should be noted that, able to or not, psychotherapists have been willingly and unwillingly used by the courts and other legal authorities to offer such predictions for many years. Commitment proceedings, for example, often require just such prognostications.

Arguments Con

Most of the arguments here are concerned with the specific action of warning victims, perhaps because this is the new, additional legal duty for therapists to observe, whereas instituting commitment procedures has been an accepted practice by psychotherapists as a means of protecting the public for many years. Yet even this new duty was, according to one survey of California psychotherapists that was taken shortly after the *Tarasoff* decision, practiced by some therapists (Wise, 1978).

The arguments fall into two basic camps: (1) Disclosure of such threats without the permission of the client will not really act to protect the public; and (2) such breaches will adversely affect the client–therapist relationship and hence actually work against the public's welfare.

In general, it can be argued that unless therapists have custody control of their clients, they should not have any special duty to protect the public, because it is only when they have such control that they can effectively inhibit their clients from certain actions (Greenberg, 1984; Schopp & Quattrocchi, 1984). As Fleming and Maximov (1974) pointed out, for instance, instituting commitment proceedings may take too long to be timely or may result in release of dangerous subjects. However, warning potential victims has many pitfalls also. For one thing the allegedly "dangerous" party is still at liberty; for another, warned parties may act in such a way as actually to increase the danger to themselves. As Schopp and Quattrocchi assert, there is "the serious possibility that warnings may increase rather than decrease the overall likelihood of violence" (p. 31). Klein and Glover (1983) concur and add that "such warnings entail risks to the patient who might lose a job or harm a family relationship disrupted thereby" (p. 154). Thus, warning potential victims also threatens the Principle of Nonmaleficence to the patient.

Another reason that disclosure of potential danger is ill-advised is that psychotherapists have no special abiilty to make such judgments. This was argued in the *amici curiae* briefs that the defendants presented in the *Tarasoff* decision and could very well be true even though the court and society and the professions themselves will at other times, and in other places, claim such ability for psychotherapists. Schopp and Quattrocchi (1984) state that this claim is the basis for the duty to protect the public and that it is basically flawed.

The second set of reasons concerns the negative effect that such a legal duty has on the practice of psychotherapy. First of all, it is claimed that therapists will be less apt to accept clients whom they perceive to be "dangerous" or potentially dangerous to others (Klein & Glover, 1983). And to the extent that this is true, society will actually be less protected because such individuals will be less likely to change in the direction of self-control. How true this assertion is has yet to be determined. A national Institute of Mental Health (NIMH) survey in 1980 indicated that *Tarasoff* had not had this sort of impact, but the Committee on Legal Issues of the APA has had anecdotal evidence to the contrary since that time (Fisher, 1985).

Excluding angry, jealous, or vindictive clients from psychotherapy can also be seen as a violation of the Principle of Justice because there is no basis for believing that they would be less able to benefit from psychotherapy than other classes of clients.

Another argument is that therapists will overpredict dangerousness in order to to protect themselves from possible legal suits (Klein & Glover, 1983; Stone, 1976). Because, as will be shown, they already tend to do so (American Psychological Association Committee on Legal Issues, 1985; Knapp & Vandecreek, 1982), this leads to even more inaccuracy in such judgments and more unfair discrimination in the handling of such clients. Thus the Principles of Justice, Autonomy, and Nonmaleficence in the treatment of these clients give way to the Principle of Self-Interest.

The other arguments pertain to the deleterious effect that unauthorized disclosure, or the knowledge of its likelihood, can be presumed to have on the therapeutic relationship. First, it is argued that if, as Fleming and Maximov (1974) suggest, therapists avoid breaching confidentiality by informing clients in advance that it does not extend to instances where others might be endangered, clients will be less likely to disclose their harmful impulses or intentions toward others. Yet unless they disclose such material, it may be impossible to do therapy with them (Greenberg, 1984). Moreover, whether preadvised or not, clients will be more apt to discontinue therapy should the therapist contact legal authorities or potential victims without permission to do so from their clients. Thus the Principle of Beneficence is threatened, insofar as it may be presumed that therapy would be beneficial with such clients.

It is also argued that warning potential victims, although the "least restrictive option," is apt to be more disruptive to ongoing therapy or to resumption of the therapeutic relationship at a later point than either informing the police or instituting commitment (Schopp & Quattrocchi, 1984; Stone, 1976). This is because the other parties (the court, the police) are more apt to be seen by clients as neutral third parties who are appointed by society to take on such tasks, whereas therapists are supposed to represent and protect their clients' interests. When therapists take personal action contrary to a client's wishes, the action is apt to be perceived as a betrayal.

LEGAL DEVELOPMENTS

It is not my intention to do a full, original review of all the cases engendered by *Tarasoff*. However, I will refer to a number of other reviews that have been done and will provide, where available, the legal citations for the cases cited in these reviews. I will cover some of the more pertinent developments including the institution of statutory law to handle *Tarasoff*-like situations. I warn the reader beforehand that *any legal review will be inconclusive because of the "home rule" aspect of the U.S. Constitution, which gives states considerable sovereignty in lawmaking.* Lack of appreciation of this fact alone has led to much misinterpretation and inappropriate extrapolation of the *Tarasoff* ruling, which as Slovenko (1975) has pointed out, was based on a very unusual set of circumstances.

Variables Affecting State Laws

The following variables come into play in the likelihood that any particular state will adopt the *Tarasoff* precedence:

1. *The Strictness and Extensiveness of the Confidentiality Statutes in the State.* For example, in *Hopewell v. Adebimpe* (cited in Greenberg, 1984, p. 322) a Pennsylvania court held that the confidentiality of the patient–psychotherapist relationship is absolute. Subsequently a Pennsylvania trial court held that a psychotherapist may not disclose privileged communications without written consent even if the client is thought to present a serious danger of violence to a third party. In Illinois, on the other hand, a privileged communication act specifically allows psychotherapists to breach confidentiality when the lives of others are endangered (Knapp & Vandecreek, 1982).

2. *The Strictness of the Mental Health Commitment Statutes in the State.* The harder it is to get allegedly potentially dangerous clients committed, the more proof required, the more likelihood there is that warning the victim will be seen as the appropriate action. For example, some states require proof that the client has a severe mental illness and/or has performed an overt act demonstrating violent tendencies (Knapp & Vandecreek, 1982). This will have an indeterminate effect on the willingness of therapists to act and on third parties to sue. *Tarasoff* might never have occurred in a state with less strict commitment statutes than California's.

3. *The Presence of Other Laws Pertaining to "Dangerous" Clients or Patients.* For example, in Oregon the supreme court recently refused to decide if there was basis for a common law civil action in a *Tarasoff*-like case, because the perpetrator was under the authority of the state's psychiatric security review board at the time due to a previous incident. The treatment facility that had contracted with the state to provide psychiatric care was found already liable under the state law giving such facilities responsibility for their patients (Goodwin, 1987).

4. *The Presence of Statutes Directly Inspired by the* Tarasoff *Case.* For example, the state of Washington has recently enacted a statute stipulating that therapists are not required to sound a warning unless an actual threat of physical violence is made against a reasonably identifiable victim or victims (Landers, 1987). Such statutes take precedence over common law.

5. *The State Psychological "Climate."* Underlying the laws of various states is the nature of the people populating that state; what they consider important and unimportant, frightening or safe, not to be tolerated or more interesting than threatening. It is clear how these attitudes affect laws in certain areas, such as gambling, death penalty for murder, and abortion. It can be expected that they might also affect laws in almost all areas, although less clearly, more ambiguously. One might suspect that barns might be more important in rural states than more urban states, for example, as in the following *Tarasoff* progeny case in Vermont.

John Peck had told his primary psychotherapist, who had an MA in educational counseling and a certificate as a psychological counselor, that he was thinking of burning down his father's barn in retribution for his father's unkind words to him in a heated argument. The therapist got John to promise not to do so; nevertheless he did burn down the barn some 6 days later. The parents sued the counseling service for the property loss, and the trial court was inclined to grant their suit. However, they first forwarded the case to the Vermont Supreme Court to create the legal duty that would have required the defendants to give warning. The court did so, but tied it to the risk of danger that the burning barn created to the parents, whose home was some 130 feet distant: "Arson is a violent act and represents a lethal threat to human beings who may be in the vicinity of the conflagration" (cited in Stone, 1986, p. 354).

New Hampshire has gone a step further. They have passed a statute that requires warning or other means of protecting not only when people are endangered but when there is "a serious threat of substantial damage to real property" (Herlihy & Sheeley, 1988).

POSSIBLE EXTENSIONS AND CLARIFICATIONS OF *TARASOFF*

What implications do the cases that have followed *Tarasoff* and which have used it as a precedent have for the practice of psychotherapy today? This question is difficult to answer in view of the differences between states, but a short summary of the rulings is potentially instructive.

How Identifiable Does the Victim Have to Be?

In *Tarasoff* it was clear who the intended victim was, but in many subsequent cases it has not been so clear. It may be better to ask the question: How effectively can the therapist's actions protect the victims, whoever they may be? This seems to be the logic behind several cases reviewed by Greenberg (1984): In Washington, D.C., mental hospitals were ruled as potentially liable for negligently permitting the escape or release of dangerous patients who subsequently attack random victims (*Semler v. Psychiatric Inst. of Washington, D.C.*); in California the supreme court ruled that a psychotherapist may be liable for injury to a young child who was present when the child's mother, the intended victim, was assaulted (*Hedlund v. Superior Court*); and an appeals court in California found a physician's failure to warn a patient not to drive in an uncontrolled diabetic condition was actionable because the likelihood was that the patient would have complied (*Myers v. Quesenberry*, 1983). Also in California basis for suit was found against a Kaiser Foundation Hospital psychiatrist whose client did not mention his parents but who did cause them multiple injuries (*Mavroudis v. Superior Court,* 1980), cited in Slimak & Berkowitz, 1983). The court thought the psychiatrist could have readily found out who the potential victims were.

Since Greenberg's review a Veterans Administration Hospital in Nebraska was held liable when a former patient, who had been discharged against medical advice 40 days earlier, fired a shotgun into a crowded dining room. Also in *Davis v. Lhim* (1982) a patient released to go to a relative in Detroit actually went to his mother's home in Tennessee and shot her. The Michigan state appeals court ruled that the therapist should have known he would do so based on a statement he had made some 3 years earlier, as recorded in a case note. (Both cases are cited in Fisher, 1985.) However, since that time the Michigan supreme court has overturned the ruling (Bales, 1988, July).

Note that in many of the preceding cases the patient had been in institutional custody, thus, theoretically at least, more information about the patient was available and more control measures could be enacted than is possible with nonremanded outpatients. Actually courts have ruled since at least 1949 that mental hospitals have a duty to protect the public from their dangerous patients, but until *Tarasoff* this duty did not include a duty to warn the public, nor was this duty applied to outpatient clinics. (See APA Committee on Legal Issues, 1985, for summary of suits against mental health care providers for the violent acts of patients. Also Fulero, 1988, gives an annotated list of cases involving duty to protect or warn up to June 1987).

Conversely, in Pennsylvania a federal district court ruled that a hospital was not liable for warning the plaintiffs of the patient's dangerousness because the plaintiffs were not the type of readily identifiable victims to whom the duty was owed (*Leedy v. Harnett,* 1981). The patient had beaten the people with whom he resided. Also in *Thompson v. County of Alameda* (1980) the Supreme Court of California ruled against the plaintiffs who claimed that the local police and the parents of neighborhood children should have been warned when a juvenile delinquent was released who had threatened at one time to take the life of some young child at random and did indeed kill a 5-year-old boy in his neighborhood. The court found such warning to be impracticable. However, dissenting justices thought that at least the delinquent's mother should have been apprised of this threat. They further noted that "whether the victim was identifiable was not relevant to the existence of a duty of care but only to whether a warning was a reasonable means of exercising that duty" (Greenberg, 1984, p. 327).

Also in this collection of cases where identifiability of potential victims is questionable is the case of *Brady v. Hopper* (1983, cited in Melton, 1983, December). Brady, President Reagan's press secretary at the time, was injured in Hinckley's attack on President Reagan. His suit against Hinckley's psychiatrist was not found actionable by the Colorado District Court on the basis that the duty to protect third parties is not "owed to the world at large."

Does Duty to Warn Extend to Suicide? Property Damage? Victims of Clients in Group Counseling?

In *Bellah v. Greenson* (1977) the parents of an outpatient brought suit against their daughter's psychotherapist 2 years after her suicide on the basis that the therapist ought to have warned them of her suicidal tendencies. The California court found that although Dr. Greenson was statutorily permitted to divulge this information, he was not required to do so.

> We conclude that *Tarasoff* . . . requires only that a therapist disclose the contents of a confidential communication where the risk to be prevented thereby is the danger of violent assault, and not where risk of harm is self-inflicted harm or mere property damage. (cited in Greenberg, 1984, p. 325)

One could argue that the Vermont barn-burner case cited previously does extend *Tarasoff* to property damage, at least in Vermont, but the Vermont court was careful to point out that arson is a "lethal" activity. However, as noted earlier, New Hampshire has recently enacted a statute that "requires psychologists to warn or protect when there is 'a serious threat of substantial damage to real property' as well as to persons" (Herlihy & Sheeley, 1988, p. 210).

Does Duty to Warn Extend to Potential Victims of Clients Who Are in Group Counseling or Group Therapy?

In *Shaw v. Glickman* (1980, cited in Knapp & Vandecreek, 1982) a Maryland court ruled not. The case itself was weak in that the violent act was not readily foreseeable, but the court gratuitously added the observation that Maryland's privileged communication law does not allow for breach of confidence even when the lives of others may be endangered. Thus the matter is far from settled for other states whose laws are not so written, and even in Maryland it may be possible that the privilege statute would prove insufficient protection in a clear-cut case of obvious real threat and an identified victim. As noted earlier, Pennsylvania has a similar privilege statute, yet in *Leedy v. Harnett* (1981) a federal district court said, "When ... a particular victim can be identified, there is good reason to impose upon psychotherapists or custodians a duty to warn the intended victim of the danger posed by the person under their care" (cited in Greenberg, 1984, p. 322).

Does Duty to Warn Extend to Partners of Clients with AIDS?

Perhaps the most recent potential issue is whether the specific duty to warn will be extended to therapists with sexually active clients who are infected with the acquired immune deficiency syndrome (AIDS) virus. Will they be required to warn their clients' sexual partners if they have reason to believe that their clients have not done so and proper precautions are not being taken? The need for guidelines in this area is pressing (Bales, 1988, January).

A recent article has taken the stance that "a sexually active, seropositive individual places an uninformed sexual partner (or partners) at peril, and the situation therefore falls under the legal spirit of the *Tarasoff* case and the ethical tenets of 'clear and imminent danger'" (Gray & Harding, 1988, p. 221). The authors argue that *Tarasoff* would apply once three factual conditions are met: "a special relationship, a reasonable prediction of conduct that constitutes a threat, and a foreseeable victim" (p. 220). They then advise counselors who have clients with AIDS to request such clients to inform their sex partners. If they are unable to persuade them to do so, then it is up to the counselors to directly inform such partners themselves. If the partners are anonymous, the state public health officer and the appropriate professional or civil authority should be informed.

In a rejoinder article Kain (1988) substantially concurs but adds several pertinent observations. He points out that those who contract AIDS from sexual partners are unlike victims of assault in that they can avoid risk by saying no. This point is also made by Russ Newman, director of professional affairs and director of legal and regulatory affairs for the APA's Practice Directorate (cited in Landers, 1988). Newman adds that such victims should be aware of the risk and how to reduce it.

Kain also points out that it may be insufficient for the counselor merely to inform potential victims, but that the counselor then incurs an accompanying ethical responsibility for supplying support and reassurance to the recipient of the bad news. This is an interesting observation because in some cases it would seem to apply as well to warning potential victims of physical assaults. Stephen Morin, a member of the APA task force on AIDS, states that the task force will advise that therapists who do decide to report should do so to public health officials and not directly to victims because they are better qualified to give advice in such matters (cited in Landers, 1988).

Finally, Kain warns that AIDS clients might be loath to disclose their condition if they thought this would lead to mandatory disclosure of it to their sexual partners and/or public officials. Considering that many of today's carriers are on the fringe of society in important respects, this would seem to be a most likely occurrence, and, if so, would undermine the potential benefit counseling could provide such people. In this connection Posey (1988), in another rejoinder article, states that in her experience as a facilitator of a support group for people who have AIDS, AIDS-related complex (ARC) or test positive for the human immune deficiency virus (HIV): "Group members who have been in a relationship for a significant period of time have not shown serious reluctance to inform their partners of their AIDS-related condition" (p. 226).

A final caution from Stephen Morin of the APA task force is that therapists should not consider breaking confidentiality unless they have gotten a very detailed, specific history confirming that the individual is truly a risk to others.

The American Psychiatric Association has taken a more aggressive stand. In its annual meeting the 420-member House of Delegates voted to pursue legislation to require public health officials to "solicit, identify, and notify" partners of AIDS patients and virus carriers (cited in "AMA: Warn Partners of AIDS Victims," 1988, p. 3a). It also urged its members to try to persuade patients infected with the virus to inform their sexual partners, and, failing that, to try to have the public health officials do it, and, if all other means failed, the doctor "should notify and counsel the endangered third party" (p. 3a).

Will *Tarasoff* Be Extended to Sexual Assault?

One more area that has recently emerged, at least for purposes of speculation, as a possible extension of *Tarasoff* is sexual assault. This possibility was extensively treated in the article by Melella et al. (1987). They review rape, incest, and other sex offenses. With respect to rape they conclude:

> Although no specific cases to date have been found holding a psychotherapist liable for rape committed by his patient, it can be inferred generally from the case law. Since courts and juries have been willing to conclude that the burden of preventing rape should be shared by landlords, businesses, hotels, common carriers, employers, parents, and governmental

custodians, it appears to be a short logical step to ascribe this same liability to psychotherapists—especially in cases where the victims were known or foreseeable. (p. 108)

They also believe the third-party *Tarasoff* liability potential is high in incest cases, especially because the victim is almost always clearly identifiable. However, if the victim is a child, then most legal jurisdictions already require reporting under child abuse laws. They question the value of such reporting in that it does not always lead to a better result. In fact, "It may have a devastating impact on the treatment, the victim, and the family ... in view of the way child protective agencies manage these cases" (p. 109). Thus the therapist's ethical responsibility may conflict with legal requirements. They also note that insofar as reporting undermines any trust necessary to continue with psychotherapy, this would also apply to pedophiles and rapists.

Psychotherapists who treat sex offenders need to be concerned about paraphiliacs, and of the paraphiliacs, especially those whose acts involve physical or psychological harm to others. Melella et al. (1987) argue that the mere diagnosis of pedophilia, if properly applied, indicates that the patient poses a serious danger of violence to others because the deviant behavior pattern involves coerced, forced, or violent sex with a child. Such diagnoses must often be made from sources other than the patient because the self-reports of sex offenders are not to be trusted. They recommend the use of a plethysmograph in order to determine whether deviant sexual fantasies lead to arousal.

Whether *Tarasoff* might apply would be dependent on the degree of harm that was inflicted. If the victims were violently assaulted and physically injured or killed, then they believe that *Tarasoff* would logically apply. However, mental distress and emotional damage often take years to appear in a clear manner, by which time the tort statute of limitations may have expired in some states.

Who Are Included as Liable Practitioners under *Tarasoff?*

Another issue is the broadness of the definition of the class of practitioners who have the obligation to protect the public; that is, who are deemed, under the law, to be "psychotherapists." This would clearly be a matter of state statute, because each state determines who is to be licensed or certified as having expertise in psychotherapy. As was described earlier, in Vermont a master's degree in education, if coupled with certification as a psychological counselor and employment in a county counseling service, provides sufficient credentials. In Oregon a state law would seem to extend the liability even further, to anyone who a client had reason to believe was a psychotherapist (Oregon Revised Statutes, 1985, 40.230:1c).

LEGISLATIVE RESPONSES TO *TARASOFF*

One way to clarify a confusing set of precedences in common law is to enact a statutory law that then takes precedence over previous rulings. The Committee on Legal Issues of the American Psychological Association has suggested just this course of action in a white paper that it released in 1985. Part of this white paper consists of a model bill whose main provisions are as follows:

1. No liability exists for "failing to predict, warn of, or take precautions to provide protection from violent behavior" except if the patient has communicated "an actual threat of physical violence against a clearly identified or reasonably identifiable victim or victims."

2. The duty is discharged "if reasonable efforts are made [to communicate the threat to the victim or victims] or [to seek civil commitment of the patient . . .] or [to notify the police department closest to the patient's (or the victim's) residence of the threat of violence]." (brackets in the original)

3. No liability exists for breach of confidence if such duty is discharged.

The American Psychiatric Association also has a proposed model law to be used as a guide for state legislatures. The duty to protect would extend only to reasonably identifiable victims and only then if there is an actual threat of serious bodily harm and the means to carry it out (Fulero, 1988).

It appears that mental health practitioners have decided they can't return to former times when they had no legal obligation to warn potential victims of their clients and rather than be subject to the vicissitudes of common law they have actively campaigned for statutory law with clear-cut limits to their legal duties.

Such legislation has already passed in 11 states—California, Colorado, Indiana, Kentucky, Louisiana, Minnesota, Montana, New Hampshire, Ohio, Utah, and Washington—and is proposed in several others (Landers, 1987; Fulero, 1988; Bales, 1988, June).

RECOMMENDATIONS

Given the preceding review of cases and laws and their various implications, what can prudent psychotherapists do to protect themselves against liability suits and still continue to see those who can profit from their services? A number of recommendations have been issued by various writers, some of which would seem to adversely affect the therapy itself. I consider the following ones important in any case involving life-threatening situations:

1. Prospective clients should receive a simply written, not overlong description of what to expect regarding the services they will receive, fees, and complaint procedures. This is for them to keep so they can refer to it later. Included in this document will be a statement informing them that in cases of clear danger to themselves or to others, the therapist reserves the right to inform others as necessary to protect the lives and well-being of the endangered individual(s). This document, as well as any embellishments that apply only to a given client or a small subset of clients of which this person is a member, should be gone over orally early on to be sure the client understands it.

2. If it appears that an instance of clear danger is in the offing during the course of therapy, the therapist will consult with appropriate others about the proper course of action and document the results of this consultation, any decisions that are made, the reasoning behind the decisions, and any actions that are taken. It is especially important to document any facts that bear on the decision, such as in the case of a homicidal patient whether he or she has ready access to and knows how to use a gun. This detailed documentation should continue until such time as the crisis appears to have passed (Knapp & Vandecreek, 1982; Thompson, 1983).

3. If it seems necessary to inform outside third parties (authorities, potential victims) of the danger the client appears to pose, the therapist should then inform the client of such intentions and invite the client to participate in the process if this seems at all therapeutically possible. This may preserve the therapeutic relationship and precipitate the resolution of the issue between the client and other concerned parties (Mappes et al., 1985).

ISSUES

Which ethical principles are pitted against each other in *Tarasoff?*

Is *Tarasoff* an imposition on clinicians or an opportunity?

Why have the basic facts of the case never been ascertained?

On what basis (doctrine) did the California Supreme Court base its decision?

Is it clear what is "special" about the "special relationship" of psychotherapists with their clients that creates a duty to warn and to protect third parties?

What is the relationship between the duty to warn and the duty to protect the public? What is new about the duty to warn?

Why is warning potential victims considered ethically superior to committing clients who are deemed dangerous to others?

Do psychotherapists concur with the courts that disclosure should be made in *Tarasoff*-like cases?

Does warning potential victims actually protect them, or does it lead to increased likelihood of harm?

Should psychotherapists be in the business of predicting violence?

How might *Tarasoff* impact negatively on the practice of psychotherapy and the way it protects the public?

Why may a legal precedent in one case not apply to another state?

Is the duty to warn limited to identifiable potential victims, or is it better to consider it the duty to protect by warning when practicable, regardless of the identifiability of any particular potential victim?

Does the duty to warn extend to warning family members of the potential suicide of a client?

Does it extend to property damage? To victims of group clients?

Should the duty to warn extend to the sexual partners of those clients who carry the AIDS virus?

Should it extend to potential victims of sexual offenders? of paraphiliacs?

Are mental health counselors also legally liable under *Tarasoff*?

Why have both the American Psychiatric Association and the American Psychological Association proposed legislation in this area, and what conditions do they suggest must be present for a duty to exist?

What recommendations for dealing with potentially violent clients in an ethical manner also provide some protection from legal liability?

CHAPTER 13

Child Abuse

DILEMMAS OF CHILD ABUSE

Child abuse is one of the foremost concerns in our society. In recent years it has reached such a crescendo that some observers claim that hysteria has set in and abuse is being "discovered" where none exists; that care givers of children have had their businesses and reputations destroyed by false accusations from children who have been inadvertently coached and encouraged to make such accusations. Others insist that this is only the tip of the iceberg of real abuse, that much needs to be done to educate the public, train parents, and prosecute the offenders. As with any other complex situation all these claims may well be true. Unquestionably this is an emotionally laden topic. Few people, including psychotherapists, are able to keep their emotions in check if they believe that a helpless, innocent child is being cruelly treated or molested by a powerful adult. Yet unless some people with the authority to investigate and affect the situation do so in an objective fashion, hysteria will take over and no one will benefit.

Three ethical dilemmas are apt to be invoked in any case of child abuse that comes to the fore during counseling and psychotherapy:

1. Disclosure of the abuse without the permission of the abuser and/or the abusee versus prevention of further abuse (Autonomy and Fidelity to the client versus Nonmaleficence to the abusee)
2. Harm to the abusee if no report is made and the state does not intervene versus harm to the abuser, the abusee, and the structure of the family if the state does intervene (Nonmaleficence versus Nonmaleficence)
3. Legal risks that the therapist occurs by reporting versus not reporting (Self-Protection versus Self-Protection. This will be considered under Legal Aspects, near the end of the chapter.)

Under ideal situations child abusers would voluntarily disclose the abuse during the course of therapy and request help in dealing with it.

The therapist and the abuser would then examine the nature of the abuse, the current ability of the abuser to control the abuse, and the options available for enhancing such control. They would then arrive at a joint decision as to the course of action to pursue, which might or might not involve requesting state intervention in order to obtain the aid of state resources and programs for the abuser, the abusee, and the family involved.

Such is not always the case, especially if the abusee is the client rather than the abuser. This does not mean that the therapist cannot attempt to bring about the ideal situation, perhaps by talking with the abuser, assuming it is a family member, and encouraging the abuser to seek out treatment for this behavior. If it appears that the abuser will not voluntarily take steps to stop the abuse, and it is continuing, then forceful intervention may be appropriate, depending on other factors mentioned in the following paragraphs. In such cases professional ethical codes, as well as the presumption that Nonmaleficence takes precedence over Fidelity and Autonomy in matters of clear physical or psychological damage, make clear that it is permissible for the therapist to report the abuse to the authorities. In fact, most psychotherapists believe that breach of confidentiality is ethically required in such instances, as judged by a recent survey (Pope, Tabachnick, & Keith-Spiegel, 1987). A telephone survey of the general public (Rubanowitz, 1987) found that over 80% of respondents thought that therapists *should* notify the police if a client admits to child abuse.

A complicating factor is that not all interventions may be helpful; in fact some may produce more harm than good. Almost any intervention will disrupt the current integrity of the household if the abuser is a member of it. The abusee may be seen as the cause of the disruption, and although one form of abuse may cease, especially physical abuse, other more psychological forms may increase. If the abuser has to leave the household, then financial problems may become a major factor because the family income is not likely to increase in order to pay for the additional lodging. These problems, in turn, may cause other stresses, other difficulties. Also there is no guarantee that the intervention, in the long run, will effectively reduce the abuse that triggered the intervention. A study in 1977 by the Berkeley Planning Associates was selected by Starr (1979) as the best that had been done in measuring treatment. It evaluated 11 demonstration treatment programs for child abuse. A reduced propensity for abuse or neglect was found in 42% of 1208 families; however, there was a severe recurrence of abuse or neglect in 30% of the families *during treatment*. One wonders what follow-up would discover.

Melella et al. (1987) note the negative aspects of reporting sexual abuse:

Although few would dispute the importance of protecting children from sexual abuse, it may have a devastating impact on the treatment, the victim, and the family in that it will result, more often than not, in separating the father from the family and lead to his arrest or an order of protection from a family court denying his parental right to custody and perhaps even visitation rights. . . . Many pediatricians and child psychiatrists think that the results of reporting will be more traumatic to the child than the sexual abuse. (p. 109)

Melton and Davidson (1987) are especially concerned about intervention in the case of "psychological abuse" and make several recommendations based on their review of this area:

In view of the substantial difficulty in defining psychological maltreatment in a way that will minimize arbitrary or harmful intervention in family life, states should require specific findings before intervention is permitted on the ground of psychological maltreatment alone. Intervention should be predicated on actual or reasonably foreseeable injury that is likely to result in protracted difficulties for the child if untreated. The nature of the "injury" . . . should be defined in specific behaviors capable of reliable assessment. . . . Even if these criteria are met, states should not permit involuntary intervention unless the risk of harm from such intervention is significantly less than the benefit that is likely to accrue to the child. (p. 173)

This last statement could as well apply to intervention for reasons of physical abuse or molestation also. Therapists need to weigh, as best they can, the potential value of forced intervention against its potential harm both in terms of disruption to the family and interference with the ongoing therapy with the abuser or the abusee. Thus they need to acquaint themselves with the various treatment programs available to offenders and their families within their area of practice, and the criteria which are employed, to determine who receives which. Another role therapists may take is that of advocate for prevention programs as is suggested by Starr (1979):

On a most basic level, our overburdened and fragmented system for providing services to abusive families must be modified. Caseworkers do not have time to provide effective therapy, and implementation of such effective interventions as parent aides and Parents Anonymous is limited. Although services must be provided to identified families, the key to the elimination of child abuse is primary prevention. (p. 877)

Melton and Davidson (1987) came to a similar conclusion in their review of this issue:

In the end, whether the focus is on the family or an institution and the authority is the state or a professional ethics committee, perhaps policy-makers should reconceptualize the effort as *promotion* of children's well-being, not *protection* from maltreatment. For children, harm may come from failure to provide the environment and resources necessary for healthy development. (p. 174)

LEGAL ASPECTS

Child abuse has been recognized by both the United States Congress and all 50 state legislatures as a matter of legal concern. The Child Abuse Prevention and Treatment Act, enacted in 1974 and last amended in 1986, provides modest funding for state and local child protection efforts, contingent upon, among other things, the state's substantial agreement with the federal definition of child abuse and neglect, which now includes the concept of "mental injury." As a result almost all the states have included mental or emotional injury in their definitions of abuse, but with varying specificity (Melton & Davidson, 1987). Following is a somewhat abbreviated set of definitions of child abuse and neglect that is representative of statutes that provide specific rather than general descriptions of abuse (Child Protective Services Program, 1985, pp. 13–16):

Physical Abuse

Abuse constitutes any physical injury to a child which has been caused by other than accidental means, including any injury which appears to be at variance with the explanation given for the injury. Non-accidental physical injuries may appear as bruises, burns, fractures, bites, cuts, sprains, internal injuries, auditory, dental, ocular or brain damage.

Neglect

Neglect is negligent treatment or maltreatment of a child which causes actual harm or substantial risk of harm to a child's health, welfare, and safety. Neglect includes but is not limited to:

Failure to provide adequate supervision such that a child is endangered; an act of reckless behavior which places the child at risk; an act of exploitation such as requiring a child to be involved in criminal activity; failure to provide life necessities such as food, clothing, shelter, hygiene, nurturance; "medical neglect," failure to provide necessary medical care, including the withholding of medically indicated treatment from disabled infants with life-threatening conditions; abandonment or desertion of a child; and "emotional neglect," failure to provide the emotional nurturing, physical, and cognitive stimulation needed to prevent serious development deficits.

Mental Injury or Emotional Abuse

A child who has been mentally injured is one who has been the victim of cruelty which has resulted in observable and substantial impairment of the child's intellectual, psychological or emotional capacities.

Mental injury results from parental behavior which has a harmful effect on a child which can be observed. A mental injury to a child is long lasting and constitutes a handicap to the child's ability to function as a normal human being—to think, to learn and to feel.

Acts of parents which can cause mental injury include, but are not limited to, habitual scapegoating, ridicule, denigration, threats to health/safety, physical and sexual abuse, torture, and confinement.

Sexual Abuse and Sexual Exploitation

Sexual abuse includes a wide range of sexual offenses. . . . Sexual abuse is any incident of forcible sexual assault involving a victim under age 18; or sexual contact between a child and another youth or adult in which threats, bribery, or similar methods are used to get the child to participate; and any sexual contact between a child and a person of power or authority. Examples of sexual abuse include but are not limited to rape, sodomy, penetration, sexual molestation or fondling, voyeurism, and sexual harassment/intimidation.

All states require physicians to report suspected cases of child abuse, and most states have extended this requirement to other professionals who work with children, such as nurses, schoolteachers, social workers and psychotherapists (Schwitzgebel & Schwitzgebel, 1980; Mappes et al., 1985). Also according to the Schwitzgebels:

> Every state provides some form of immunity for the reporter against possible defamation of character, invasions of privacy and breach of confidence, although, even without such statutes, a person acting in good faith and without malice would probably have a successful defense. (p. 167)

On the other hand penalties for failure to report, when the law requires it, are provided in most states. "Violation of the reporting statute may, in itself, constitute negligence and therefore support a civil suit against the professional" (Schwitzgebel & Schwitzgebel, 1980, p. 167). The overall effect, then, is to encourage reporting, and although theoretically possible, it seems unlikely that suits claiming breach of confidentiality in this area would receive a favorable response in the courts. Such suits would have even less basis if confidentiality was not initially promised in such matters.

CLARIFYING QUESTIONS

The following questions may prove helpful in determining what to do in cases of child abuse (cf. Thompson, 1983, p. 87).

1. Is the abusee currently being abused and/or likely to be abused in the near future? If the abuse appears to be wholly a matter of the past, then no clear danger is involved and there is no ethical obligation and possibly no legal obligation to report it, depending on your state's statutes.

2. Is it reasonably clear what happened? If not, can you determine it within your office by questions or simple procedures? For example, one way to check to see if sexual molestation has occurred with very young children is to ask them to place their hands on the parts of the body where they were touched. Any thorough investigation is properly the responsibility of the duly authorized authorities.

3. Is the "abuse" definitely physically or psychologically damaging, or is it more a matter of interpretation and context? Cultural and religious practices of minority groups may appear to be abusive to outsiders, but they may be normal, perhaps even essential, to the group's beliefs about child rearing.

4. Do you know what constitutes child abuse in your state? Do you know when or if you are legally required to report child abuse or testify in court regarding it? Ask for a copy of the exact legislation from your local authorities, probably the Children's Services Division.

5. Do you know what treatment programs are available with and without reporting? What is likely to happen to various kinds of abusers if they are reported? Your local Children's Services Division can be helpful in these matters, as can colleagues and other practitioners who have experience in this area.

6. Have you recourse to medical and to peer consultation? If not, develop such contacts.

If you have gathered all the information required to affirmatively answer the preceding questions, you are now in the position to weigh the pros and cons of reporting any given abuse and to make an ethically informed decision.

ISSUES

What ethical principles are violated when disclosure of child abuse is made to the authorities without the client's permission? Which are promoted?

Is Nonmaleficence apt to be violated regardless of what is done? Why?

What legal risks do psychotherapists incur by disclosure? By nondisclosure?

What types of harm are apt to result from disclosure?

Why do some writers believe that most ethical course of action is not to *protect* children from maltreatment but rather to *promote* their well-being—that is, to promote Beneficence rather than Nonmaleficence?

What are the various kinds of legally defined child abuse?

Is there actually much legal risk of breach of confidence suits for practitioners who report child abuse?

What information clarifies the issues in deciding what to do in a case that seems to involve child abuse?

CHAPTER 14

Suicide

INTERVENTIONS IN SUICIDE

Nothing is more demoralizing to counselors or psychotherapists than to have a client commit suicide, especially one with whom they have worked for some time, trying desperately to help the person find or create an existence that diminishes self-destructive impulses. Clinicians take such events as personal failures and as personal losses. It seems, then, "cruel and unusual punishment" for therapists not only to suffer such losses, but also to have to fear legal consequences from their clients' actions. However, such is the case, and indeed there may be some instances where these consequences are appropriate. In any case, this chapter treats the potential for malpractice suits in this area as an educative endeavor and not as something that will go away if ignored.

The central ethical issue is respect for client autonomy versus protection of the client from harm—that is Autonomy versus Nonmaleficence. The clinician's task is to decide at what point the client's ability to reason is so impaired that the therapist must override the inclination to commit suicide by any available means, including police intervention and involuntary commitment.

Fortunately most clients already in psychotherapy want help in dealing with their self-destructive tendencies and impulses, so there is no conflict between the goals of the therapists and the clients. Conflicts are most apt to arise when clients adopt an either-or attitude: Either their lives turn around in the very near future in some specific or general way or they will elect to terminate their suffering. For example, clients may come for help in finding a mate or in becoming successful in their vocational endeavors, and they consider suicide to be an acceptable alternative if it appears that their goals are not being realized.

Probably the most common type of counseling that involves suicide prevention is crisis intervention counseling. This type of counseling is typically initiated by the client, who, by virtue of having come in or having made the telephone call, has implicitly asked for help in dealing with his or her suicidal ideation. The risk is that the oral interaction between the client and the counselor will not be effective, and the client will decide to act on the suicidal impulse. It is the responsibility of the counselor to judge whether this is the case, and, if possible, to intervene in intrusive ways that physically restrain the client from acting on self-destructive urges, such as asking the police to hold the individual until such time as the danger is past or the person is secured in a treatment setting.

Other, less intrusive types of intervention require the client's cooperation. If it is apparent to both counselor and client that counseling sessions, in and of themselves, provide inadequate impact on the client's mood and ideation, then the client may be persuaded to seek treatment voluntarily in an inpatient facility. Sometimes it is possible to arrange monitoring and emotional support from friends or family within the client's residence or to have the client temporarily change residence to that of family members or friends who agree to provide such care. Sometimes medication may sufficiently reduce the destructive impulses.

Deciding what to do when with whom is often an extremely difficult task, requiring a good deal of training and experience. Ironically, most crisis intervention of this sort is done by amateurs, individuals who have a desire to help out in such cases but have no professional background in any of the fields of psychotherapy. They staff the crisis "hot lines" that operate day and night in most of the major communities across the United States. They receive training from professionals in this narrow area of crisis intervention, but may never have taken so much as a regular practicum or graduate level course in counseling or psychotherapy. However, they provide a service that would not otherwise be available. Because of the difficulties with doing conclusive research in this area it is not clear and probably will never be clear whether, in fact, such persons actually prevent suicide, but anecdotal evidence is supportive. Also it is clear that having such a resource helps relieve professional counselors from onerous and often impossible demands on their personal lives.

The primary focus in this chapter is on the professional counselors and psychotherapists in ongoing relations with clients who appear to be in danger of taking their own lives. Unless one takes an extreme view and decries all paternalism, it is clear that the ethical obligation of such professionals is to try to prevent suicide that, in their judgment, is based on irrational ideation. This then obligates them to intervene, as necessary, to protect clients from acting out such ideation.

But what about those clients whose ideation is not clearly irrational? What about clients, for example, who suffer from a deteriorative, incurable physical illness who choose not to continue their increasingly helpless, increasingly painful existence? Should psychotherapists attempt to persuade them not to take their own lives? Here it would seem that this would serve neither Nonmaleficence or Autonomy, at least insofar as these principles apply to the client. However, it can be argued that it would be maleficent to our society as a whole not to intervene in such cases, or that it would be maleficent to friends and relatives of the client who would be upset by the client's action or "untimely" death. These arguments will be reviewed shortly under "Involuntary Psychiatric Commitment."

A related issue is that of euthanasia: Is it ethical for psychotherapists or counselors actually to abet a client who is contemplating suicide? At first glance this issue might appear to be irrelevant to psychotherapists, qua psychotherapists and not physicians. If a therapist, however, contracts with terminally ill clients, such as AIDS clients, to help cope with their distress or has other clients who, during the course of therapy, discover they have a terminal disease, such clients may inform their therapist of contemplation of suicide to escape future pain and dependency. Should the counselor treat this as an irrational idea to be eradicated, or as an acceptable option under certain conditions? The counselor who fails to argue against this option implicitly endorses the idea. As a result some clients may end up taking their own lives who might not otherwise have done so.

This type of abetting has not been, and may never be, legally regulated, but it is not beyond the realm of possibility that someday a relative of a client who committed suicide will bring suit against a therapist for encouraging the client in this action. Unfortunately, as will be seen later, there is no security against such malpractice suits in today's legal arena; thus it is up to individual practitioners to decide whether they are going to let their practices be shaped by fear of such suits—that is, whether Self-Protection is to take precedence over what they otherwise would consider best for their clients.

LEGAL ASPECTS

Two main types of legal procedures concern psychotherapists and counselors of potentially suicidal clients: involuntary psychiatric commitment and malpractice suits. The first is initiated by the therapist or others as a means of preventing suicide; the second is initiated against the therapist by those who claim to be adversely affected by the suicide or the consequences of the suicide attempt.

Involuntary Psychiatric Commitment

David Greenberg (1982) has critically analyzed mental health professionals' use of involuntary psychiatric commitment for handling clients who
are considered suicidal. Because much of what he says bears on the ethical
issues that are involved, I have summarized his remarks here.

By way of introduction Greenberg points out that suicide and suicide
attempts are, in themselves, criminal offenses in a few states. However,
they are seldom enforced, perhaps because the serious suicide attempter
is more to be pitied than blamed. What does enjoy widespread use is the
civil commitment procedure of involuntary hospitalization. Data regarding
the exact number of people committed in each state on an annual basis,
the length of their stay, or other details are not available.

The early rationales for coercive protective care were religious or political: rejecting God's gift of life or depriving the state of its property.
Three more contemporary grounds are prevention of harm to others,
particularly survivors; prevention of harm to the suicide attempter; and
suicide as a product of a mental illness that needs treatment.

Prevention of Harm to Others

Suicide can result in emotional suffering in others, such as experiencing
guilt over failure to treat the suicide attempter or victim properly, or
fearing that others may blame them for the suicide. Swenson (1986) pos-
tulates that one of the major reasons for malpractice suits is to shift such
blame onto the therapist. As Greenberg points out in such cases, "We
have no reason to assume that they [posthumous accusations] are necessarily undeserved or so serious in their consequences as to justify coercive state intervention" (p. 285). Suicide can also cause financial loss,
such as occurs when the survivors inherit legally contracted debt. Finally,
the loss of those with some special talent may be felt by society as a
whole.

Yet the attempts to prevent suicide, even when an injury to others can
be clearly identified, may result in extreme invasion of privacy and regulation of the lives of those considered at risk and of those associated
with them. Other personal costs to the person kept alive should also be
taken into consideration, such as long-term deprivation of freedom.

Greenberg concludes:

> The case for coercion to prevent injury to others from a suicide clearly is
> weak. . . . Exceptions might be made only in the very rare case when a
> suicide would result in extremely serious injury to others. For example, if

the potential suicide is the only witness to an alibi for a defendant on trial for a serious crime. (pp. 285–286)

Prevention of Harm to the Client

Greenberg states that this claim must be rejected. For one thing no one knows what happens after death, and secondly, it is possible that death is the lesser evil in some situations, such as when it is an escape from an excruciating terminal illness.

Even in the cases where the cause for the distress seems minor to observers, such as guilt over some societally accepted sexual practice, that this would not distress the observer does not reduce the sufferer's anguish. To permit interference in such cases is to violate the right to die when one wishes, "which would seem to be a necessary part of the right to live with dignity and privacy. . . . This right would mean little if it could be exercised only when consistent with others' view of what is reasonable or appropriate" (p. 286).

Suicide as the Product of Mental Illness

The law recognizes implicitly the preceding argument in that most commitment statutes require not only that defendants be considered dangerous to themselves, but that they also suffer from a mental illness. It is sometimes also specified that the suicidal ideation be a consequence of the mental illness and not simply be coterminus. Greenberg points out that this is difficult to prove in view of the inexactitude of the diagnosis of mental illness, and, in any case, "It is safe to assume that these fine points are ignored in present commitment practice" (p. 287). Lay notions of mental health and psychiatric classifications or the judge's own moral judgments often prevail in the absence of vigorous legal representation of the defendant. It is often assumed, for example, that anyone who is suicidal must be psychotically depressed or schizophrenic. Yet, as Greenberg points out: "To plan and carry through a suicide attempt may require more ability to think coherently and to act in a realistic, organized fashion than a patient with delusions or obsessions possesses" (p. 288).

Greenberg's Proposal

Greenberg grants that suicide may, indeed, arise out of a temporary period of distress and irrationality which, if survived, may never again occur. Therapists would want to prevent such cases. However, it may also be the reasoned choice of those who have thoughtfully considered the alternatives over an extended period of time. Such persons should be allowed to exercise their autonomous right to die. He also suggests that any intervention "not be excessively painful, unpleasant or protracted, for, if it were, the human costs of prevention might well be thought to exceed its benefits" (p. 291).

With that in mind Greenberg proposes first that the state intervene for a period of time not to exceed 24 hours in the case of suicide attempts in progress or about to begin. Such "minimal interventions" would include giving whatever medical assistance was necessary, such as giving artificial respiration to someone found unconscious from gas inhalation or lavaging the stomachs of those who have overdosed on various medications. He claims: "There is abundant testimony from psychiatrists experienced in the treatment of suicide attempters that survivors of an attempt rarely pose a danger of immediate suicide, even when opportunities for further attempts are not lacking" (p. 292).

Secondly, Greenberg proposes:

> The state might even accommodate determined attempters by granting immunity from any interference to those who register their intention to commit suicide in advance, or by providing resources for painless suicide following a short waiting period so as to be confident that only those who wish to die kill themselves. (p. 293)

Unfortunately, he does not make any proposals for intervention by the state for those who are contemplating suicide or have apparently even decided to do so but have as yet not acted. These individuals pose the most difficulty for the practicing psychotherapist.

MALPRACTICE SUITS

All of the states have what are referred to as "wrongful death" statutes, which provide for a civil cause of action if the death of an individual is brought about wrongfully (Cohen, 1979). Professional malpractice suits in this area appear to be increasing both in absolute and in relative frequency. Bellamy (cited in Swenson, 1986) reports that of 18 suits (nationwide) that reached appellate courts from 1946 to 1961, only one involved a patient's suicide. However, such suits had become among the most common in the mid-1970s. Also Pope's (1987) review of the APA Insurance Trust data revealed that the death of the patient was involved in almost 10% of malpractice suits.

The vast majority of reported cases involving alleged negligence of psychotherapists in preventing suicide occur when the client is already under protective custody, as in a mental hospital. Only one case that reached the appellate court level involved a never-hospitalized patient. In *Bellah v. Greenson* (1977) the court found that a therapist could be held liable for an outpatient's suicide if it was foreseeable and appropriate preventative measures were not taken. A *Tarasoff*-type warning to the parents was not, however, required (cited in Swenson, 1986).

The questions inevitably asked in court are: "Had this person previously attempted suicide or expressed suicidal ideation?" and "What evidence was there that this person was suicidal?" (Cohen, 1979, p. 213).

Many suits are unsuccessful. Among other things honest errors in judgment are insufficient grounds for negligence, and there has to be a clear causal connection between the therapist's actions, negligent or not, and the resultant death. Also government institutions and employees may enjoy immunity from such liability (Cohen, 1979).

Swenson (1986) reviews two ways in which psychotherapists may be liable: if they were found to have *caused* the suicide and if they *did not take steps to prevent reasonably foreseeable suicide*. She points out that even if the therapist mistreated the client according to the professional standard of care, this in itself could not be said to cause the client's suicide or suicide attempt as long as there was basis for believing that the client's decision to do so was still a voluntary decision. She states:

> To be liable, the therapist's negligent act must bring about insanity in the patient which prevents him from realizing the nature and risk of the act, or which creates an irresistible impulse, thus rendering the patient irresponsible. Implicit here is the notion that the suicide must be irrational or involuntary for there cannot be negligence liability for voluntary suicide. (p. 419)

This seems like an extremely difficult claim for a plaintiff to substantiate, and indeed it might be; however, Swenson later adds:

> Psychiatrists have been found liable for severe emotional distress resulting from gross breach of privacy and beating the patient. Both of these practices are certainly below the standards of the profession and clear ethical violations. It is reasonable to assume that if these practices had caused a suicidal state of mind resulting in suicide, the therapist would have been liable. (p. 423)

Slovenko (1981) also believes that psychotherapy can precipitate or contribute to a suicide:

> Suppose, for example, the therapists [*sic*] dwells on homosexuality in a way that upsets the patient and he is unable to deal with it, and becomes in-

creasingly upset. Other examples in the outpatient setting where it might be said that suicide is the fault of the therapist is where the patient is abandoned, or a confidentiality is breached causing the patient great humiliation. Clearly, returning a gun to a suicidal patient would be hard to explain to a jury. (pp. 20–21)

In actuality, Besharov and Besharov (1987) refer to a case where the husband of a client successfully sued a psychiatrist who had told the client he would divorce his wife and marry her and did not do so, thus presumably causing the client's suicide.

The more likely basis for malpractice suits will be negligence for not preventing suicide or suicide attempts. As pointed out, this is far more likely to be a factor in inpatient institutions where it can be assumed that the institution has the monitoring capacity and the control measures readily available for such prevention. This does not mean that all patients who are depressed or who have expressed suicidal ideation must be kept locked up in self-damage secure rooms or constantly monitored. Doing so would substantially interfere with treatment. In *Baker v. United States* (1964), for example, the court acknowledged that therapy requires risks and these were probably worthwhile (cited in Swenson, 1986). The degree of the risk has to be balanced against its promised utility and the value of the life of the patient.

RECOMMENDATIONS

Given the foregoing ethical and legal considerations, I offer some "flow chart" procedures that identify the crucial judgments involved in adequately fulfilling ethical obligations to potentially suicidal clients. Any one of these judgments may be extremely difficult to make. The general recommendation in all such cases is to seek out consultation in making the judgment; then record the fact of that consultation, the nature of it, and the rationale for your decision. All relevant actions and rationale should be recorded for legal protection. Include documentation of the steps taken to assess the risk, the options considered for prevention, and the pros and cons of possible treatments (Soisson, VandeCreek, & Knapp, 1987).

Assessment of suicide is an art in itself, and in one respect it is bound to fail because any predictive system will overpredict, even one that is 99% accurate. The reason is that the base rate of suicide in the general population is so low—about 10 to 12 per 100,000 ("Suicide—Part I," 1986)—that most persons identified as "suicidal" will not, in fact, deserve that appellation. Nevertheless therapists must do what they can. The

Harvard Medical School Newsletter ("Suicide—Part I," 1986, February; "Suicide—Part II," 1986, March) perhaps provides the best review of suicide factors that should be taken into consideration. Explicit threat, history of past attempts, plan and means to execute plan are all important factors, along with various diagnostic and demographic variables.

Flow Chart

1. Is the threat of suicide real?
2. If so, is the suicidal thinking clearly irrational?
3. If so, have persuasive methods been tried without apparent effect (the basic rationale being that continuance of life is a necessary condition for finding new meaning in it)?
4. If so, is the client already in a place where others can serve as monitors and provide emotional support for continuance of life?
5. If so, will the client agree to informing them as necessary and getting their cooperation to do so?
6. If not, will the client agree to move to an environment where informed others can provide such monitoring and support, such as returning to the family home or seeking admission to a psychiatric ward?
7. If not, consider taking action without the consent of the client but with the client's knowledge (if at all possible or feasible). Such action might involve requesting the police to institute a hold (especially in situations of immediate danger), starting involuntary commitment procedures, and informing roommates, relatives, or friends and soliciting their assistance.

ISSUES

What is the central ethical issue raised by taking steps to prevent suicide of clients? When is it not an issue?

What is the role of crisis counselors in terms of responsibilities and services?

What does the presumed rationality or irrationality of the client have to do with the clinician's ethical duties?

Could it be ethical to abet a client's suicide?

How might clinicians do this implicitly?

What are the legal grounds, historical and contemporary, for involuntary psychiatric commitment for potential suicides?

Can prevention of suicide be justified on the basis of harm that the suicide might cause others?

Is it presumptuous to judge that humiliation or other painful psychological experiences are insufficient reasons for committing suicide?

Is the case for suicide as a product of mental illness a sound one?

Why is short-term restraint qualitatively better, from an ethical perspective, than long-term?

Which two questions are always asked therapist defendants in professional malpractice suits involving wrongful death?

How might therapists "cause" their clients to commit suicide?

How might therapists be deemed negligent in preventing suicide?

What procedures promise to reduce the likelihood of malpractice suits?

PART SIX

Self-Interest

This final section describes the Principle of Self-Interest and its applications to psychotherapy and psychological counseling. Without this principle our set could not be complete, for there can be no doubt that self-interest has a profound influence on whether we conduct ourselves ethically in our dealings with our fellow humans. If we do not accord this basic motivation the status it inevitably usurps, we will be less than clear in our ethical analyses of situations, and what is left implicit may impact on our subsequent actions in unknown and unwanted ways.

CHAPTER 15

The Principle of Self-Interest

CONSIDERATION OF SELF-INTEREST AS
AN ETHICAL PRINCIPLE

It seems almost a moral affront to claim that Self-Interest is a legitimate ethical principle on a par with the other principles in determining ethical courses of action. Yet, as has been demonstrated again and again throughout the book, many of the actions that are recommended and, in fact, are even guidelines in ethical codes, have self-interest as their implicit ethical justification, most typically, the self-protection of the profession or the professional. Perhaps discomfort over that fact causes professional codes to be largely inexpressive regarding their underlying rationale. It is my contention that it is time to come out of the closet in this area and overtly claim moral right to pursue that which will protect and benefit individual practitioners of psychotherapy and counseling, and to specify limits for such protection and benefits.

As mentioned in the Introduction, there is some precedence for this position. Kant provides the major impetus in this area, as he does in many other aspects of philosophy. In his exposition of the categorical imperative (1929, pp. 277–278) he admitted that the state of being of the individual who is morally obligated to follow the imperative is a relevant consideration. He stated that one has an "indirect" duty to secure one's own happiness "for discomfort with one's condition . . . might easily become *a great temptation to transgression of duty* [italics in original]." Ross (1930) specifically mentioned Self-Improvement, which he saw as Beneficence applied to oneself, as one of the *prima facie* duties. More recently philosophy professor John Thomas (1987) placed self-preservation among the moral duties which we have to ourselves: "In fact we do have moral duties to ourselves, so prudence is important" (p. 20).

In the abstract of his presidential address to the American Psychological Association, Robert Perloff (1987) took a Kantian perspective and pointed out the inevitable connection between doing right to others and to oneself:

> Although self-interest is recognized as a powerful force underlying the behavior of animals and humankind, its ubiquity and influence on performance in and adjustment to all aspects of life are frequently underestimated and discredited because self-interest is, mistakenly, equated with mean-spirited selfishness and viewed as an inhibitor of the commonweal. In this article several positive and beneficial consequences of self-interest are presented, along with the proposition that personal responsibility, in the service of self-interest, is an effective tool for enhancing personal well-being and, hence, for contributing to the public good. (p. 3)

I would add the observation that in terms of a lifetime the only person who is or can be primarily responsible for one's personal welfare is oneself. To rely on others to watch out for oneself, even when one is willing to try to do so reciprocally for them, is unwise and ultimately infeasible. Only the individual has direct access to his or her own interests, hurts, wants, goals, and knowledge of the behavior that has helped/not helped, worked/not worked in the past. Not to assume responsibility for oneself is actually an act of irresponsibility with respect to others, making it burdensome for them to do what is right for that person. Whereas only those who are self-responsible are in the position to be consistently helpful to others.

Does this provide one with *carte blanche* to pursue his or her own interests without regard to others? Obviously not: As Kant and Perloff point out, there is an essential connection between exercising one's self-interest and acting ethically toward others. How then can one ensure that this connection is honored? I suggest the following criterion:

> An act is to be judged *selfish* or *ethically unjustified* when it is clear that it works primarily to one's own benefit at the cost of the benefit of others, albeit some others may benefit incidentally, or in some other very restricted sense.

That is, it is ethically permissible to pursue one's own interests when doing so can also be expected to promote the interests of others. If, on the contrary, it is clear that one's profit will cause the interests of others to suffer, by and large, then the act is clearly unethical.

The application of this criterion may at times be difficult: One problem is that it is hard to imagine a situation in which only one person benefits. Even committing a crime may be said to benefit the members of the police and the judicial system in that their employment is contingent upon the presence of crime. However, this may be seen as an incidental or very restricted benefit and is clearly and directly detrimental to the victims of the crime. One could erect a criterion that depended on the motive or intent of the actor, but motive and intent are clearly subjective phenomena and lead rather quickly into very murky depths indeed. So here, as elsewhere, one is left with applying common sense to any given situation in order to make a judicious decision. The following sections will demonstrate whether application of the criterion helps clarify the boundary between selfishness and ethical behavior. The same order of principles will be followed as in the preceding parts of the book.

SELF-AUTONOMY (PROFESSIONAL AUTONOMY)

"Self-Autonomy" is obviously redundant: The meaning here is that individuals have a duty to preserve and promote their own autonomous functioning. Individuals who have, by virtue of training and education, earned the right to be called "professionals" can expect that this duty will be recognized within their place of employment. Given the boundaries of the mission of the agency, clinic, or institution within which the therapist or counselor works, and the needs of the clientele that it serves, the professional employees should have the latitude to establish their own hours of work, to schedule clients when they see fit, and to have a significant voice in the selection and execution of tasks that are assigned to them.

Professional therapists and counselors should also be able to reject working with clients whom they feel incompetent to treat or who evoke negative biases in them, as long as such preferences can be accommodated without distortion of the overall employment framework.

The granting of such prerogatives is both ethically permissible and desirable, because it enhances the possibility that the practitioners will do good work. Clinicians who feel their needs are being ignored for arbitrary or mean-spirited reasons, or merely because accommodating them would cause some minor inconvenience, will find it difficult to focus on the tasks on hand and may perform them grudgingly. On the other hand, those who receive maximum autonomy, given the legitimate confines of the agency's mission, are more apt to be committed and competent in their performance.

Such matters are seldom at issue for private practitioners but can be extremely troublesome for those who work within agency and institutional settings. It may also be essential for these individuals to have a significant role in determining the overall responsibilities and goals of the agency or institution.

Professional autonomy has found its way into several codes of the mental health professions. Standard 1 of the *NASW Standards for the*

Practice of Clinical Social Work (1984) states: "All social workers have a fourfold responsibility to clients, to the profession, to *self* [italics added], and to society." Standard 11 adds: "Clinical social workers shall have the right to establish a separate independent practice as a form of secondary employment or after leaving a place of employment."

The ethical code for psychiatrists (American Psychiatric Association, 1986) states: "A physician shall, in the provision of appropriate patient care, except in emergencies, be free to choose whom to serve, with whom to associate, and the environment in which to provide medical services" (Section 6, Preamble). In the text itself, a provision has been added that was not in the 1981 code: "An ethical psychiatrist may refuse to provide psychiatric treatment to a person who, in the psychiatrist's opinion, cannot be diagnosed as having a mental illness amenable to psychiatric treatment" (Section 6:2).

The *General Guidelines for Providers of Psychological Services* of the American Psychological Association (1987b) also has some relevant directives. Section 3.2 states: "Psychologists pursue their activities as members of the independent, autonomous profession of psychology." The final sentence in the "Illustrative Statement" that follows clarifies: "Psychologists are responsible for defining and developing their profession, consistent with the general canons of science and with the public welfare." The footnote to this sentence adds, "The APA is prepared to cooperate with any responsible professional psychological organization in opposing any unreasonable limitations on the professional functions of the members of that organization."

SELF-FIDELITY

Self-Fidelity seems almost like a nonsensical concept—how can one be faithful to oneself? Being faithful or fidelious is always in context of the relationship to others, is it not? Yet people do talk of keeping promises to themselves. They also talk of being true to themselves. Both ways of speaking have some substance and merit some attention. People also are capable of assuming an observatory role with respect to their actions, feelings, and even thought processes, and, equally important, they typically evaluate themselves when assuming this observatory role. Insight-oriented psychotherapy teaches clients to take on this role deliberately and then to use it constructively, as opposed to acting blindly and automatically condemning themselves for certain feelings and actions.

People may make many kinds of promises to themselves—some serious, some playful, some hopeful, some in desperation, some trivial, some of great importance. They may, for example, promise themselves a vacation, or they may promise themselves to lose 10 pounds or to quit smoking by some set time in the future. If they do not keep these promises, especially the ones oriented toward self-improvement, then they are apt to think less of themselves, perhaps even to despair at ever being a worthwhile or a lovable individual.

When people promise to be true to themselves, they usually have in mind acting more in accordance with their convictions when interacting with certain others in certain situations where fears or guilt have controlled them in the past—that is, they promise to drop pleasing, subservient roles and assert instead their own wants and opinions. If such individuals fail to follow through on these promises, they are apt to denigrate themselves even more.

It seems clear that enactment of those promises that result in self-improvement or better feelings about oneself is not apt to work against any ethical duties to others, and, in fact, the contrary would seem to be the case. The only exception would be that others could be upset by changes in a person's behavior brought about by keeping such promises, but even so, such distress might well be only temporary, leading to improved relationships later. If not, it is highly questionable that the old relationships were of the nature that deserved perpetuation in any case.

However, promises to act destructively toward others, such as promises to "get even," or perhaps even promises to harm oneself, such as committing suicide if things are not better by such and such a date, are of a different ethical genre. They are more apt to lead to long-term disruption of the lives of others.

Vindictive acts toward others can also conceivably benefit those whose lives are affected by the recipient of the retribution, if this individual acts in hurtful ways toward such people. For example, if "getting even" results in imprisoning a criminal, then Justice may be seen as being served. However, harboring such thoughts is apt to act in negative ways on the life of the revenge seeker.

The relationship of Self-Fidelity to therapist–client relationships is probably tangential in most instances. Most promises that therapists might make to themselves would not involve their clients. Some would, however, such as a promise to learn about another culture in order to better serve clients with such a cultural background. Obviously keeping such a promise would benefit the affected clients. It seems highly unlikely that therapists would make vindictive, retributive promises that might affect their clients, or promise to cease being intimidated by them.

SELF-JUSTICE

Most humans seem especially endowed with a sense of justice as it applies to themselves. This is evident among brothers and sisters at an early age or among children at play: "It's my turn!" "How come she gets to go and I don't?" "All my friends have pets, why not me?" As children get older, they are able to see the humor in the claim by the comedian Tom Smothers, "Mom always liked him [his brother Dick] best," but they may be no less sensitive to injustices they experience in their place of work, or even in their social life. Nothing arouses ire more than feeling maltreated.

Professional psychological care givers are not immune to this sensitivity, and like other professionals they have learned to band together to fight for what they consider their fair share of the available benefits. These benefits include status, with the privileges and opportunities that derive therefrom, and a good income. Status is achieved by official recognition of the value of one's services, which in our society is usually signified by licensure by the state. A good secure income is obtained by governmental and private funding of agencies that offer psychological services, and by persuading governments, and thus in turn insurance carriers, that psychological services are vital benefits to include in insurance coverage. Without this official support it is unlikely that private practitioners can, by and large, persuade the public to compensate their services highly.

However, there is large diversity in the professions that offer psychotherapy and psychological counseling. Psychiatrists, for example, are grounded in the study and treatment of physical ailments before studying psychological (psychiatric) ones. Social workers are educated regarding the social care system as a whole and how to apply various resources to various clients. Psychologists study intensively and extensively both "normal" and "abnormal" psychological functioning and specialize in the development and use of instruments that diagnose and assess such functioning. Thus each has a special claim for access to society's benefit distribution system. Yet members of each profession, plus a number of less formally educated, but not necessarily less competent, counselors of various types practice psychotherapy, albeit they may not be allowed by law to call it that.

Because the resources of society are not limitless and much of society remains unpersuaded and skeptical about the value of psychotherapy, the various mental health professions have not often banded together to try to make a common case to governmental bodies. Instead each profession has tried to persuade such bodies that it is especially deserving of whatever benefits are to be distributed. The next section briefly describes the resulting situation and the ethical problems that arise thereform.

Turf Battles between Mental Health Professions

As of now only physicians, and thus psychiatrists, have full status as providers of mental health services, including psychotherapy. Almost without exception all insurance policies that offer such coverage, whether by regular insurance carriers or by special healthcare organizations such as health maintenance organizations (HMOs) or professional provider organizations (PPOs), recognize psychiatrists as first-line providers—that is, as eligible recipients of insurance monies. Such designated providers may or may not refer to other professionals as they see fit. The reason is at least partially historical in that the original psychotherapists, at least in the developed societies of Western Europe, were almost exclusively physicians who trained themselves and then trained others in various psychological treatments. Freud was such a physician. He first studied under Bleur and then learned the use of catharsis and hypnosis under Charcot before developing psychoanalysis (Hall, 1954). There were some "lay analysts" without a medical degree, but not many. Nowadays there are several hundred different theories of therapy, many of which have been developed by nonphysicians, and all of them are practiced by a full range of professions. Nevertheless, the tradition has continued that to be *really* competent at psychotherapy one needs to have a medical degree.

Among the good arguments for this tradition is that one cannot and should not separate the physical from the psychological aspects of humans; both are inextricably intertwined in any "psychiatric disorder." Thus only those who are trained in both physical and mental illness are competent to see the whole picture and judiciously decide on the course of treatment. Also many such disorders are directly traceable to physiological disruptions, such as chemical imbalances, and are only or best treated by physical means, such as drugs. Accordingly, psychiatrists should be the arbiters of the preferable treatment or treatment combination, and others should play a secondary, assigned role. Even ordinary physicians are considered to have considerable competence in this area, because they, at least, should be able to rule out physical causes of psychological disruptions.

As noted earlier, however, other professions believe they have equally important, if different, competences to offer. They argue that their training offers them sufficient medical knowledge to enable knowing when it is appropriate to refer clients for evaluation of physical causes and physical treatment.

To the extent that such arguments are successful, legislators and other decision makers are then open to the arguments that pertain to increasing the competent provider base, thus enabling the general populace to have more service providers and more services available, and at a more affordable price because the service is no longer so hard to get.

Psychologists have been the most successful of the "competing" professions in persuading legislators to include them as eligible providers in legislation creating national mental health coverage for certain groups, as in Medicaid, and in writing state insurance regulations ensuring that they are among the professional psychotherapists that policyholders are free to choose without first obtaining a physician's referral. Clinical social workers have been somewhat less successful; marriage and family therapists are licensed and recognized as providers for some services in some states; and various kinds of "mental health counselors" are beginning to make some headway in this struggle.

Unfortunately, it is largely a political battle, and as such it has some ethically questionable aspects as is evident from the following quote from a recent issue of the *APA Monitor* (Buie, 1987a):

> Professional psychology made some valuable political inroads at this year's convention here, showing up in record numbers for meeting with political allies, helping to fill the campaign coffers of several national leaders, and strengthening its network of activists around the country.

> While most activists agreed the profession still has a long way to go to develop real political muscle, they said all of these activities should help advance psychologists' political agenda, such as increasing the mental health benefits for Medicare patients, recognizing psychologists as independent providers in Medicare, protecting state-managed mental health benefits and preserving quality mental health care in health maintenance organizations (HMOs) and preferred provider organizations (PPOs). (p. 5)

The article goes on to describe how the APA's convention held a $1,000-a-plate dinner for the chairman of the Senate Finance Committee's Health Subcommittee and raised $40,000 for his campaign coffers, thus demonstrating the "profession's sophistication about the very real necessity and urgency of these things" (p. 5).

The obvious justification for the practice of buying access to influential politicians is that it is necessary to do so, even though ethically repugnant, in order to achieve a good end. Such an ethical analysis may be acceptable to consequentialists, who separate means from ends, but it is more difficult to accept from the perspective that has dominated this book, namely that of W.D. Ross (1930). Nevertheless it is possible to cast this situation in terms of an ethical dilemma.

On the one side would be the increased benefit to consumers of having access to a greater number and variety of qualified psychotherapists (Beneficence to consumers). The difficulty here is how to decide who is "qualified" or "competent" and on what grounds. Assuming that the aspirant profession does meet the resultant criteria and the criteria are valid, then the profession is in the position to claim that it is only just for members to have the full benefits of this status (Justice for the profession).

On the other side is the perpetuation and promotion of a bribery system of gaining political influence, which is also a matter of Justice. Why should certain politicians, namely incumbent members and chairs of certain committees, receive special treatment that tends to ensure their position and increase their status? Is this fair either to other politicians or to would-be politicians (Justice to politicians)? More important, does such a system of government work to the benefit of the citizenry, or only to those who are rich and powerful enough to be willing and able to bribe their officials in pursuit of their own interests (Justice to the citizenry)? Does not this very system of determining which professions are truly qualified promote subjectivity and bias rather than objective, dispassionate analysis (Justice to the aspirant professions and to the citizenry)?

Does this mean that one shouldn't give to the politician of one's choice? Because there is no meaningful public financing of political campaigns, except for the presidential race, this would be an unwarranted limitation of individual autonomy. However, such contributions need to be limited; otherwise the contributions of a few wealthy individuals can dwarf those of most others, rendering the exercise of their autonomous choices almost meaningless.

Organizations can promote their members' individual autonomy by providing accurate information about the stances of various politicians and political candidates on issues of common concern, thus enabling informed choices as to whom to support and whom to lobby. Ironically, however, organizations inadvertently distort by omission when they limit the information about politicians to such issues, for other stances of the politicians may be of greater concern to individual members.

Organizations arguably overstep ethical bounds when they orchestrate the collection of campaign contributions and funnel them to chosen politicians. When they do so, they distort the promotion of the members' individual autonomy because the decisions as to how much money goes to whom and when, as well as communication of these decisions, are all part of a political process that interprets rather than directly manifests the wishes of members. Also the size of the contribution instead of the justice of the cause threatens to become the salient factor.

Most disturbing about the present trend is that it is an accelerating process—each political success is apt to be attributed to the shrewd dispersal of funds to the right politicians. It then follows that ever more funds are needed—both to hire more lobbying time from high-priced, "effective" lobbyists, and to put more in the campaign coffers of selected politicians. From an ethical perspective, unless the now enjoined battle between the professions for pieces of the public pie can be stopped, and they can somehow make peace together, the future is bleak in this arena.

Indigenous Clients

The other area in which the Principle of Self-Justice is prominent is in the handling of clients who cannot pay for the services they seek. This has already been discussed at some length in Chapter 6, which considered the justice of turning away such clients. Associated with that problem is the situation created by clients who are apparently able to pay when they start therapy but later lose their jobs or otherwise find themselves in reduced circumstances. Abandoning such clients would be unjust and also could lead to a lawsuit so it is prudent to make other arrangements, including being prepared to write off the fees in such a case, if necessary. This was also touched upon in Chapter 11, Malpractice.

Another problem occurs when clients are referred for evaluation or therapy and the funds provided are insufficient to do a good job at the usual rates. Self-Justice would argue for nonacceptance of such referrals, but Justice for the clients would argue for acceptance and willingness to work for less, otherwise the clients would suffer unfair discrimination. Some compromise would seem to be in order, along with lobbying for increase in such funding.

SELF-BENEFICENCE

Self-Improvement was seen by Ross (1930) as a *prima facie* duty; that is, rational, mature individuals upon reflection would see that they have a duty to work for their own improvement. Kant (1929) suggested that more than just self-improvement might be involved: To have the will to act ethically toward others, it is important to alleviate one's discontent. Using these wider criteria, a number of kinds of activities and pursuits suggest themselves, such as working to improve one's status, one's income, one's living conditions; pursuing hobbies; continuing education in one's field;

taking "mental health" breaks; and taking vacations. All these also fall under the "pursuit of happiness," which is considered a fundamental human right in our society.

Again, however, the ethical limits of such activities and pursuits would be defined by whether they conflict with or interfere with the well-being of others, and for professional psychotherapists, clients are the special group of others that cause concern. As seen in Chapter 7, supervised training and continuing education that directly relate to improvement of services to present or future clients present no problem. The same cannot be said for frequent, long, or unexpected absences that might interrupt and adversely affect the progress of some clients. Judiciously planned vacations can well refresh the clinician, however, and result in better service to clients.

Improving one's status by seeking licensure is of problematic value to the consumer. Insofar as the process of taking the requisite courses, getting the requisite degrees and training, and studying for and passing the exams truly improves the clinician's quality and scope of service, then licensure also benefits the consumer and there is no ethical problem. However, insofar as the coursework, the degrees, the training, and/or the exams create artificially high barriers that shut out competent practitioners from effectively competing in the marketplace, and thus restrict the offerings of service to the consumer, then it is difficult ethically to justify this requirement.

SELF-PROTECTION (NONMALEFICENCE TO SELF)

The legitimacy of the claim to be a moral duty may be questionable for some of the other principles when applied to oneself, but this is clearly not the case for Nonmaleficence to Self, more commonly referred to as Self-Protection. Self-Protection, at least when it comes to a question of survival, is not only an important right, it is often seen as the most important right, so much so that the taking of the lives of others is legal under the law in most situations when it is deemed necessary to do so in order to save one's own life. If it is permissible to take someone else's life, to do the ultimate harm to someone else and thus completely override the moral duty to Nonmaleficence, then surely the principle that makes it permissible can also be considered a moral duty. That laws permit this ultimate harm does not, in itself, make self-protection a duty, however; it is rather that the laws reflect society's basic conviction that survival is the ultimate "law" for any individual.

Nevertheless, it is seldom that one's own life or death is at issue in the practice of psychotherapy and counseling; thus the issue of when Self-Protection should have precedence over ethical duties to others is still a very viable one. How far does, should, Self-Protection extend? At what point does Self-Protection become Self-Gratification at the expense of others—such as in overcharging clients to "protect" one's high standard of living? A way of exploring this concern is to review the various situations in which Self-Protection has been invoked as an ethical justification in the preceding parts of this book.

Under Part One, Autonomy, it was pointed out that the process of obtaining informed consent from clients and from participants in research projects is, in part, regulated by ethical codes and by law; thus it is a matter of Self-Protection that counselors, therapists, and researchers observe such regulations, even though it may often be dubious that clients want, understand, or profit from all the information they receive.

It was also pointed out that, at least in the case of the Federal Trade Commission's stance on advertising, ethical injunctions and the law are at variance. The provisions of codes that were intended to prevent misleading advertising, for example, were by and large considered inhibiting of open competition by the FTC, with the result that the professions involved may have to permit unethical practices or violate the law.

Under Part Two, Fidelity, it was pointed out that having sexual relations with clients endangers the therapist's continued professional existence in several ways: It can result in malpractice suits, in loss of insurance coverage, loss of license, and loss of clientele. Therefore to enter into such relationships, especially with ongoing and recently terminated clients, is not only unethical but is self-destructive.

The risk of retribution from therapists who may believe their clients have been stolen by another therapist was noted in the analysis of the ethical issues involved in accepting other therapists' clients. In the chapter on confidentiality the legal ins and outs of privilege statutes and of responding to subpoenas were discussed with obvious implications for Self-Protection.

There were no instances of Self-Protection noted in part Three, Justice.

Under Part Four, Beneficence, it was recommended that in certain cases, such as those involving risks of suicide or homicide, the therapist should keep especially extensive records as a protection against malpractice suits. Another recommendation was that official guidelines, whether federal, state, or agencywide, be followed with regard to record retention, also as a means of protection against legal action.

Part Five, Nonmaleficence, contained a slew of instances where Self-Protection is relevant. Chapter 9, Regulation by Professional Associations, noted the various sanctions that professional associations could impose on errant members, ranging from reprimand to publicized expulsion. Also it was noted that both clients and therapists are protected from incompetent and unethical behavior and its consequences when therapists take an active role in peer supervision groups and when there are treatment programs available for impaired therapists. The sanctions available to licensing boards were listed in Chapter 10, again directed primarily against those practitioners who have been found incompetent or unethical in other ways. Chapter 11, Malpractice, and Chapter 12, The *Tarasoff* Case, were concerned with the grounds for legal actions that might be brought against clinicians. In Chapter 13, Child Abuse, the possible legal repercussions of reporting or not reporting were explored. Finally, Chapter 14 specified the grounds for legal liability for the suicide of one's client.

It is obvious from the above résumé that the major area of Self-Protection for therapists and counselors is that of protection against legal action. There is a definite hazard to client welfare if the therapist reacts to the fear of legal reprisal in a hysterical or otherwise rigid manner. Not taking any risks with clients for fear that they, or their relatives, will later sue distorts treatment of them, with the result that the therapy is less effective, or perhaps even of negative value. In some extreme cases attempting always to remain on the good side of the clients will result in failure to confront their erroneous conceptions, or self-destructive actions. With other clients who seem the least bit dangerous to others, fear of a *Tarasoff*-like case may result in rejecting them as clients, in precipitously trying to commit them, or in warning possible victims, with the result that the clients never work through their violent tendencies in therapy.

On a more mundane but more pervasive level, clinicians may be so concerned with appearing, on paper, to have performed competently, that they will write excessively extensive case notes, engage in unnecessary consultation, and have clients read, talk over, and sign long, largely incomprehensible overinclusive "informed consent" forms. This forces the initial stage of therapy into a safe-for-the therapist but not-helpful-to-the-client format, and it reduces the number of clients who can be handled.

On the grand scale the risk is that ethics will take a back seat to law, rather than providing a corrective and independent perspective. This is evidenced even now in the ethical codes, which in the interest of prudently protecting the professions, instruct members to be aware of and duly observant of the relevant laws. This is not subservience to the law but threatens to be the case when professional codes of ethics are designed to conform to the law, or to its interpretation by some agency of the government, such as seems to be the case with the Federal Trade Commission's stance on advertising.

Burnout

One area that has not been mentioned is that of protecting oneself from burnout. This phenomenon often occurs in oversubscribed public agencies that offer psychotherapy and counseling. To a large extent burnout can be avoided by granting professionals sufficient autonomy over when, who, and how many clients they see, as well as over any other required tasks. This would work to the detriment of clients to the extent that professionals over-protect themselves. In general such self-protection seems to be both in the interests of the therapists and of the clients they serve. The American Psychological Association's *General Guidelines for Providers of Psychological Services* (APA, 1987b, Section 2.1.2) indirectly addresses this issue by stating: "If necessary, the director appropriately modifies the scope or workload of the unit to maintain the quality of the services, and, at the same time, makes continued efforts to devise alternative systems for delivery of services."

Burnout can also occur to practitioners in private practice. Freudenberger (1984) has treated at least 50 therapists over an 8-year period for symptoms of burnout and offers a number of "personal strategies for prevention of burnout" (p. 226). These include shifting or varying jobs, joining a peer supervision support group, taking minivacations, saying no if requests for service become excessive, scheduling time for relaxation during the day, and seeking personal counseling or therapy if symptoms persist.

Protection from Angry Clients

A final area is that of protecting oneself from retaliation by disgruntled clients, especially if they are physically dangerous, or by disgruntled, jealous spouses of clients. Total security from such retaliation is not realistic, but certainly it is possible to establish and rehearse office procedures for handling situations that involve clients and other individuals who appear to be dangerous, both in the reception area and in the interview rooms. This concern finds voice in the code of the National Association of Social Workers (1984, Standard 8), which notes: "Steps should be taken to assure the client's and the social worker's personal security."

CLOSING REMARKS: HANDLING OF ETHICAL DILEMMAS

As should be abundantly manifest at this point, many, if not most, situations that arise in the course of psychotherapy, beginning with obtaining the client's informed consent, are ethically complex. It is not unusual for one or more principles to be pitted against each other with no clear "weight" on one side or the other. It was not the hope or the purpose of this book to *eliminate* such situations, but only to *illuminate* them by casting them in terms of a set of philosophical ethical principles. Once there is sufficient illumination, it then becomes feasible, in any given situation, to devise a course of action that does the least damage or promises the most benefits. What is needed is close attention to the nuances and possibilities that obtain in that particular situation. But whatever the situation, the *will* to act ethically must also be present, as Kant noted; hence the importance of adding the principle of Self-Interest. It is my hope that this book might, in some small way, promote this will in the ethical practice of psychotherapy.

ISSUES

What role might "discomfort with one's condition" have in ethical functioning?

How can one distinguish between "selfish" acts and ethically justified acts, even though they work to one's personal advantage?

How might Self-Autonomy be applied to one's professional life?

Do professional ethical codes promote professional autonomy?

What sorts of promises do people make to themselves that are important in terms of overall ethical functioning?

What kinds of promises are best left unmade?

In what way has concern over Self-Justice become a major issue dividing the various mental health professions?

What ethically suspect practices are associated with this "turf battle"?

What special problems do indigenous clients pose in terms of Self-Justice and malpractice?

When does Self-Beneficence dovetail with ethical treatment of clients? When does it not?

In what dramatic way does society recognize Nonmaleficence to Self as a valid principle?

In what area does Self-Protection become a major concern for practitioners?

In what ways does fear of violation of the law work against or otherwise subtract from the provision of services to clients?

When does Self-Protection obviously work toward improving services to clients?

If the application of philosophical ethical principles doesn't eliminate ethical dilemmas, what good are such principles?

How might observance of Self-Interest promote overall ethical functioning?

Sample Analyses of Cases

The 12 sample situations in this section contain ethically problematic actions. Each situation is followed by an analysis, using those of the six principles in the book that are relevant to the situation. These analyses are not intended to be presentations of the "truth," but rather informed efforts to identify the major ethical components of each situation. To gain practice in making such analyses, readers might consider covering over my analyses until such time as they have made their own.

Situations 3, 4, 5, and 9 have been taken from the *Ethical Standards Casebook* (1982) of the then American Personnel and Guidance Association, now American Association for Counseling and Development (AACD). Situations 8, 10, and 11 have come from cases found in the *Casebook on Ethical Principles of Psychologists* put out by the American Psychological Association (APA) in 1987. Situation 6 was presented orally by Ken Pope, chair of the APA Ethics Committee, in a workshop on ethics he conducted in Portland, Oregon, during the summer of 1988. The other situations are of my own invention.

SITUATION 1. A CASE OF MISREPRESENTATION

Zenna Carlson sets herself up in private practice. Her newspaper ads and fliers state that she specializes in leading groups in Gestalt therapy, Bioenergetics, and Rebirthing. She claims to "have worked with" a number of leading exponents of these therapies, mentioning several by name. She also states that she has a master's degree in psychology. The truth of the matter is that she has never received formal training in any of these therapies but has only been a member of workshops and groups for lay people led by the experts. Also her master's is in educational psychology.

Analysis

Assuming that Zenna is not a member of any professional group of counselors, because she would not meet their membership requirements, she is not breaking any official ethical codes. Nevertheless her ads and fliers are misleading potential clients to assume that she has had formal education and training in the areas in which she is offering services. Thus they are not in a position to choose intelligently whether to be her clients. If any of them are damaged by the group exeriences, they may seek legal action against her on the grounds of misrepresentation.

What Is Owed Whom?

Autonomy to Potential Clients. Without accurate and adequate information about the therapist and the therapies, they are not in a position to exercise their autonomy.

Beneficence and Nonmaleficence to Clients. The fulfillment of these principles is problematic given the therapist's lack of qualifications.

Self-Protection to the Therapist. The actions of the therapist may provoke potential reprisal by clients who believe themselves damaged by her services.

SITUATION 2. GETTING IN TOUCH WITH ANGER

Dr. John is the leader of a therapy group that was advertised as helping participants to get in touch with their emotions. One of the group exercises requires them to pound a pillow while imaging something or someone who arises anger in them. Several members seem to be making halfhearted efforts; they claim difficulty in finding a good image. Sally, in particular, complains that she finds the exercise causes her distress and she wishes to withdraw from it. The group leader exhorts all of them to pound hard, even without an image, and see if one comes to focus. He tells Sally that it is especially important that she participate—otherwise she will continue to "run away" from whatever is bothering her. She tries, ends up sobbing, and despite the efforts of the group and the leader, she is unable to articulate her feelings or thoughts. She calms down somewhat by the end of the group and puts on a brave smile when they break up and leave. The group leader assures her she will feel fine by next time.

Analysis

Dr. John is obviously imposing his standard of "therapeutic behavior" on the group in this exercise. He provides no option for withdrawal and pressures reluctant members to participate against their will. He may have triggered a response in Sally that could contribute to severe depression, suicide, or psychosis.

What Is Owed Whom?

Autonomy to the Group Members. Their own judgment as to what exercises are helpful or hurtful is not respected, much less promoted.

Nonmaleficence to the Group Members, in Particular, Sally. Once her distress is apparent, the leader should take steps to assess the extent of the distress and to reduce it. This would involve inviting her to stay after the group and also checking on her before the next group meeting.

Beneficence to the Group Members. It is doubtful that the group will be helpful if members are not allowed to withdraw from exercises that may be inappropriate for them.

Self-Protection to the Leader. He may incur ethical and legal sanctions for his risk-taking behavior.

SITUATION 3. HELPING OUT A FRIEND*

A counselor receives a frantic phone call from a personal friend whose wife has been working with another counselor for 18 months. This woman's counselor has been out of town on vacation for almost three weeks. During that time the client has become increasingly troubled and has spent the last 2 days refusing to get out of bed. The friend is frightened and asks the counselor to come talk with her just this once. Her counselor will be back next week, but the friend indicates he is afraid to wait that long. The counselor agrees to see her on an interim basis until her counselor returns.

Analysis

It appears that the counselor overlooked two aspects of this situation before acting: what the wife wants, and whether her counselor had given her the name of someone to contact in case of emergency during his 3-week vacation. He has also either not considered or has rejected the option of referring the wife to some other counselor whom he trusts and who would not be personally involved with the family. As it is, the counselor risks intervening where he is not wanted (by the wife). In addition, he cannot be effective if the wife is feeling estranged from her husband

*From *Ethical Standards Casebook,* Incident B.11 (b+), p. 47. Copyright 1982 by the American Association for Counseling and Development. Used by permission.

and sees the counselor as taking her husband's side. Also he risks his relationship with his friend if he tries to intervene and the intervention seems to make matters only worse from his friend's perspective.

What Is Owed Whom?

Autonomy to the Wife, the Prospective Client. She should at least be consulted before any intervention takes place.

Nonmaleficence to the Wife. How best to achieve this is difficult to determine without investigating what she is willing to accept voluntarily and whom to refer her to. Her regular therapist should have provided her referral for backup emergency counseling.

Fidelity to the Wife's Therapist. Referral would generally be made to whomever she or he has picked as backup.

Fidelity to His Friend. This friendship can be served by having someone else be the wife's replacement therapist, and such action would be less likely to jeopardize the relationship the counselor has with his friend.

Self-Interest to the Therapist. Operating in a manner consistent with the preceding principles would also act to protect the therapist.

SITUATION 4. BIZARRE HOMEWORK*

A high school counselor is contacted by three different teachers in regard to a student. All three report that his behavior in class is normal but that his written material reflects bizarre thinking and a preoccupation with death. He is seen by the counselor who feels that he is very disturbed. The counselor senses the uncertainty of the student to pursue counseling and so leaves any decision as to further help to the client to consider. The client says he will think it over. The counselor decides not to consult with anyone pending further word from the client and not to involve the parents or school officials.

Analysis

As described, there seems a strong possibility that the student is engaging in psychotic thinking and may have suicidal or homicidal tendencies. To do a competent job, the counselor will need to assess these possibilities carefully. He should ask for copies of the student's homework and show

---

*From *Ethical Standards Casebook*, Incident B.4 (c−), p. 32. Copyright 1982 by the American Association for Counseling and Development. Used by permission.

or describe them, along with the student's interview behavior, to a psychological expert whose judgment the counselor trusts. The consultant can also advise how best to proceed from this point with the client—in fact it would have been better to contact the consultant before meeting with the student. It may well be that the counselor will have to contact the parents as well as appropriate school officials, even if the student does agree to come in for counseling. This is because these parties are in the best position to monitor or arrange for monitoring the student's behavior both in and out of school and prevent harm to the student or to others. If there is to be involvement of the parents or others, the student should be informed of this fact, and of the reasons for it, so he can better understand what is being done that may impinge on him, and why.

What Is Owed Whom?

Nonmaleficence to the Student and Potential Others. This is accomplished by taking steps to prevent harm to the student and to others.

Fidelity to the School and the Concerned Teachers. The counselor discharges this duty by doing a competent job of assessment and follow-through. This would also represent Fidelity of the school to the public, in particular the parents of the students in the school.

Autonomy to the Student. The counselor provides this by informing the student of the actions that are to be taken that concern him and the reasons for these actions.

Self-Protection to the Counselor. He risks legal and other sanctions if found at fault for not preventing harm.

SITUATION 5. OVER MY HEAD—WHAT CAN I DO?*

A counselor has had three interviews with a client. Over the course of these interviews it becomes evident that the client's problems are more extensive than those with which the counselor feels competent to work. After careful consideration, the counselor decides that the client would benefit from long-term, intensive therapy, which the counselor does not feel qualified to provide. The counselor informs the client of this decision and offers to refer the client to a qualified therapist. The client refuses to accept the suggested referral. The counselor explains that it is necessary to terminate the relationship and does so.

*From *Ethical Standards Casebook,* Incident B.10 (a+), p. 44. Copyright 1982 by the American Association for Counseling and Development. Used by permission.

Analysis

Apparently the client holds the opinion that continuing with the present counselor would be more helpful than changing to another. The counselor cannot be sure, but must trust her own judgment of her own limitations and exercise her own autonomy by refusing to continue to do what she believes will be an inadequate job. The counselor watches out for the well-being of the client by offering to make an appropriate referral, which the client refuses, at least for now, as is the client's prerogative. The client's choice is limited, but not obviated.

What Is Owed Whom?

Self-Autonomy and Self-Protection to the Counselor. This is achieved by exercising her professional judgment to treat only those clients who fall within the field of her expertise.

Nonmaleficence and Beneficence to the Client. In the counselor's judgment, the client would not be helped and might be harmed by continuing with the present counselor.

Autonomy to the Client. This is provided by the provision of referral to another therapist, along with the reasons for transfer.

SITUATION 6. HARMLESS (?) JOKES*

Dr. Strong has just been hired as a psychotherapist in a large medical-social clinic. Her first day on the job she is invited to sit down for lunch at a table with some of the core administrative and therapy staff. They begin to tell jokes, apparently a favorite pastime for them. In three of the jokes a minority person is portrayed in stereotypic ways: A Jew is depicted as sly and avaricious; an Afro-American as dumb and strong; and a Lesbian as burly and masculine. Dr. Strong is disturbed by these jokes and wonders what she should do. Unable to think of anything at the moment, she silently endures the lunch hour.

Analysis

Such jokes continue characterizations of minority groups that are unfair to the groups and could prove detrimental to the individuals of the groups. These attitudes are inappropriate for help-giving professionals and may well indicate that they, consciously or unconsciously, demean or other-

*From Ken Pope (Workshop in Portland, Oregon, Summer 1988). Used with permission.

wise provide poor service to clientele who represent minority groups. Because they tell the jokes in a semipublic forum, these key staff members set the tone for the entire clinic, which could mean that staff members who don't concur in such opinions are discouraged from continuing their clinic employment or are not hired in the first place. In either case there may well be an adverse effect on both present and potential clientele.

Should Dr. Strong keep silent about her objections to this demeaning of minority group members, she risks feeling badly about herself and her employment. Should she choose to take action, two complementary courses of action are available to her. She can return to the luncheon group, or individuals thereof, and express her dismay at their jokes and her concerns over the implications that such jokes have for the fair treatment of minority group clientele. She can also seek out appropriate administrative personnel and express these concerns. Given a favorable response, she could suggest that the clinic hold in-sevice training in this area.

What Is Owed Whom?

Justice to Clientele of the Clinic. They may be members of minority groups. It is also owed to present and potential staff who may be members of such groups.

Self-Protection to Dr. Strong. She can invoke this principle by attempting to rectify the situation.

Self-Fidelity to Dr. Strong. She can remain true to her own sense of justice toward minorities and feel good about herself by attempting to rectify the situation.

SITUATION 7. THE TROUBLESOME TEENAGER

Mrs. Lovely, a single parent, has been seeing Dr. P for some time for a variety of problems associated with the stresses of going to college, parenting two children, aged 10 and 13, making ends meet, and dealing with occasional conflicts with her ex-husband. Her headaches have reduced, her anxiety level has lowered, and she is gaining confidence that she will reach her goals. However, she has had increasing difficulty with her 13-year-old son. He is missing from home for long periods of time, which absences he explains, if pressed, in vague terms. Also the school calls and informs her that he is often truant and his homework is of erratic quality.

Mrs. Lovely asks Dr. P if she has grounds for worry and what she should do. In particular she asks if he would see her son. Dr. P has had no training in treating adolescents; however, he has three teenage children of his own whom he believes he has done a good job in raising. He agrees to an initial interview.

On the basis of this interview Dr. P dismisses the mother's concerns as the usual hysterical reaction of single-parent mothers to teenage displays of independence and tells her that her son is just going through a "phase." Some weeks later the son is in a coma in a hospital as a result of drug overdose. His friends, who first reported his collapse, admit that they had been experimenting with drugs for some time.

Analysis

Obviously Dr. P stepped out of his area of competency in agreeing to see and then diagnose his client's teenage son. His defense is that he was only trying to help his client, but this could have been better done by referral to therapists who are qualified to diagnose and work with adolescents.

What Is Owed Whom?

Fidelity to Dr. P's Client, the Mother. This is best discharged by recommending an appropriate referral for her son.

Beneficence and Nonmaleficence to the Client's Son. This is also served by an appropriate referral.

Self-Protection to Dr. P. He risks sanctions by his professional association and/or licensure board, as well as a malpractice suit by his client for practicing outside his area of competency.

SITUATION 8. NATIVE AMERICANS NEED NOT APPLY*

A psychologist is employed by a satellite community health agency in Montana. After a while it becomes apparent to a nurse in the agency that he refuses to do psychotherapy with Native Americans in the region who come to the agency for such help. When asked, he replies that he "prefers not to work with Native Americans." He has, however, served a clinical internship in which he provided psychotherapy to Native Americans in the southwestern United States.

Analysis

It would appear that the psychologist's previous internship qualifies him for working with Native Americans as thoroughly as, if not more than,

*From *Casebook on Ethical Principles of Psychologists,* Case 3.c.2, pp. 47–48. Copyright 1987 by the American Psychological Association. Adapted by permission of the publisher.

most clinicians. However, it also appears that this experience persuaded him that he was either incapable of helping them or that he disliked dealing with them. In any case he has decided not to work with them. However, the clinic's area of responsibility includes this population, and it would seem unlikely that the clinic hired him with the clear understanding that he would not have to see such clients; in fact, his clinical internship may have been a factor in his being hired for his job. Certainly the Native Americans are entitled to clinic services comparable to those received by other populations in the area served by the clinic.

What Is Owed Whom?

Justice to Native Americans.

Self-Autonomy to the Clinician. In this case his choice not to serve Native Americans would be better enacted in another employment setting, unless he has arranged with the clinic to have some other qualified therapist provide such services.

SITUATION 9. MY PROFESSOR, MY THERAPIST*

Two professors in a small graduate program in counseling psychology have a private practice. Graduate students in the department often request to see them for help in identification of their blind spots and for therapy in their private practice. The professors tell them of the free services available at the university's counseling center, but accept the students as clients if they continue to request it, provided that the students are not their advisees. However, due to the size of the program, it is quite likely that the students will have the professors on dissertation committees or for teachers in their classes.

Analysis

It would seem that the students have the right to choose whom they will as their therapists, but that choice may, in this case, be a restricted one in that only the counseling center is suggested as an alternative. They may believe, with reason, that the counseling center will not provide the particular kind of service they want. However, there are surely other private practitioners in the communitiy who can provide such service. If the students are not looking so much for specialized diagnosis or didactic

*From *Ethical Standards Casebook,* Incident A, pp. 115–116. Copyright 1982 by the American Association for Counseling and Development. Used by permission.

therapy, but rather for some special relationship with their professors, then that rationale is not one the professors, qua professors, can accept without risking injustice to other students who are not their clients. The professors' acceptance of graduate students from their department as clients when there are alternatives places the students and the professors in dual relationships in which it would be difficult to keep priorities straight.

What Is Owed Whom?

Fidelity to Clients. This would be jeopardized if the clients are also students whose work is evaluated by the therapists as professors.

Autonomy and Beneficence to Potential Clients. These principles are protected by giving students a choice of appropriate, suitable referral to other therapists.

Justice to All Students in the Department. The professors, by not establishing special, nonacademic relationships with some students, would provide justice for all of them.

SITUATION 10. A CASE OF BLACKMAIL*

Psychologist A has a sexual relationship with his client, Mrs. Y. She accuses him of seducing her, and then inducing her to continue the sexual relationship by waiving fees and promising to testify for her in child custody hearings. She further claims the relationship was the final blow to her marriage, caused her emotional trauma, and that she is now in therapy from another therapist for the trauma.

Psychologist A has another version. He claims Mrs. Y seduced him after repeated propositions, and she subsequently threatened him with public exposure if he didn't continue the relationship, which would then wreck his marriage and his career. She even threatened to kill him at one point. As a result he has a bleeding ulcer, is in therapy for himself, and has put his practice under the supervision of another therapist.

Analysis

Regardless of which version one believes, it is clear that the therapy was not successful, and both parties suffered from the inclusion of the sexual relationship. Moreover the therapist did not fulfill his obligation to the

*From *Casebook on Ethical Principles of Psychologists,* Case 6.a.1, p. 80. Copyright 1987 by the American Psychological Association. Adapted by permission of the publisher.

client to terminate and transfer the client whenever it became obvious that the treatment was not working out.

What Is Owed Whom?

Fidelity to the Client. This requires not entering into a dual relationship in the first place, and not continuing it once started.

Beneficence and Nonmaleficence to the Client. Transferring her to another therapist is required as soon as it becomes clear that the present therapy is not beneficial and might prove harmful to her.

Self-Protection to the Therapist. In the short run it might appear to require submitting to her alleged demands, but in the long run, as with almost any form of blackmail, the situation is only apt to get worse.

SITUATION 11. A CLIENT WITH TWO THERAPISTS*

A psychologist is approached by a potential client for individual therapy. He states that he is a member of a group led by a psychiatrist, one of the rules of the group being that no one would receive outside therapy. However, after a year in the group he was feeling the need for additional help. He did not plan to inform the psychiatrist of this step and insisted that the psychologist not do so either.

After 6 months of dual therapy, both of which were apparently going well, the client inadvertently comments about his individual therapy in the group. The psychiatrist immediately files a complaint with the Ethics Committee of the American Psychological Association.

Analysis

By accepting the psychiatrist's client for individual therapy under such conditions, the psychologist implicitly endorsed a model of interpersonal relationships that permits deceit in such situations. The frequent result of such deceit is eventual discovery and disruption of the relationship. In this case whatever mutual respect and collegiality that existed or might have existed between the two therapists was destroyed, and it is likely that the psychiatrist's attitude toward psychologists in general was soured. Also the therapeutic relationship between the psychiatrist and the client was threatened.

*From *Casebook on Ethical Principles of Psychologists,* Case 7.b.2, p. 98. Copyright 1987 by the American Psychological Association. Adapted by permission of the publisher.

What Is Owed Whom?

Fidelity to the Psychiatrist by the Psychologist. This is owed at least to the extent of not deliberately abetting defiance of the group rules the psychiatrist considers essential for his therapy groups. Also the psychologist owes *Fidelity* to other psychologists who may suffer an adverse effect insofar as his action is considered representative of the profession's attitude.

Beneficence and Nonmaleficence to the Client. The psychologist has a responsibility to promote an open, honest model of relationships that does not contain in it the seeds of eventual disruption.

Autonomy to the Client. This can be served by pointing out to the client that he can ask the psychiatrist for an exception to his rule, and, if not granted, he can seek another group therapist.

Self-Protection to the Psychologist. Respecting the ground rules of the psychiatrist protects the psychologist from retaliation by other therapists for interfering with the practice of one of their colleagues.

SITUATION 12. THE INCOMPETENT PRACTICUM STUDENT

A practicum student claims that one of her clients does not wish his sessions to be recorded. The agency does not require the recording of clients of counselors in training but only asks that the students identify their status to their clients and explain that recordings are helpful to their supervision. The supervisor accepts the situation with provisions. The provisions are that the student give full reports regarding the progress of this client and that she check with the client after a few sessions about recording the sessions.

However, the student's reports are sparse and general; she identifies no particular problem with the client except some "resistance." One day the client walks into the supervisor's office and complains that his counselor is incompetent, that she does not seem to understand his problems, and that she alternates between being silent and sporadically asking nonsensical questions. He claims that he asked to be referred, but she kept postponing any action until she could find someone appropriate. He denies that he had refused permission to be recorded and claims that on the contrary they did record the first couple of sessions.

The supervisor subsequently confronts the practicum student who admits that the client's assertions are essentially correct.

Analysis

Apparently the practicum counselor was taking advantage of the lenient policy on recording to cover up her incompetency. As a result she was able to continue with the client in the hopes she could get on top of things, albeit without informed supervision, until the client asserted his right to a competent counselor. This brings into question the wisdom of the recording policy and points out the need for special vigilance by supervisors in cases where recordings are not available.

What Is Owed Whom?

Beneficence and Autonomy to the Client. He should have had the opportunity for competent counseling and for referral when, in his judgment, he was not receiving it.

Fidelity to the Counselor. It was the supervisor's job to ensure, as best as possible, that the counselor received the supervision and help she needed to become competent, or at least to find out if that was realistic.

Self-Interest to the Counselor and to the Supervisor. The counselor thought she was acting in her self-interest by covering her incompetency, but in the long run she was only avoiding the supervisory help she needed to become competent. The supervisor must be aware that the actions of her supervisees reflect on her, and in fact she can be held responsible for such actions, insofar as she is in a position to control them, both by her professional organization and by the law.

References

Adair, J. G., Dushenko, T. W., & Lindsay, R. C. L. (1985). Ethical regulations and their impact on research practice. *American Psychologist, 40,* 59–72.

Adams, S., & Orgel, M. (1975). *Through the mental health haze: A consumer's guide to finding a psychotherapist, including a sample consumer/therapist contract.* Washington DC: Public Citizen: Health Research Group.

American Association for Counseling and Development (AACD). (1982). *Ethical Standards Casebook.* Alexandria, VA: Author.

American Association for Counseling and Development (AACD). (1988). *Ethical Standards.* Alexandria, VA: Author.

American Association for Marriage and Family Therapy. (1982). *Code of ethical principles for family therapists.* Upland, CA: Author.

American Educational Research Association, American Psychological Association, & the National Council on Measurement in Education. (1985). *Standards for educational and psychological testing.* Washington, DC: American Psychological Association.

AMA: Warn partners of AIDS victims. (1988, July 1). *Register-Guard,* Eugene, OR, p. 3a.

American Psychiatric Association. (1986). *The principles of medical ethics with annotations especially applicable to psychiatry.* Washington, DC: Author.

American Psychiatric Association. (1987). *Diagnostic and statistical manual of mental disorders* (DSM-III-R; 3rd ed.-rev.). Washington DC: Author.

American Psychological Association (APA). (1973). *Guidelines for psychologists conducting growth groups.* Washington DC: Author.

American Psychological Association (APA). (1981a). Ethical principles of psychologists (rev. ed.). *American Psychologist, 36,* 633–638.

American Psychological Association (APA). (1981b). Specialty guidelines for the delivery of services by clinical psychologists. *American Psychologist, 36,* 639–686.

American Psychological Association (APA). (1982). *Ethical principles in the conduct of research with human participants.* Washington DC: Author.

American Psychological Association (APA). (1987a). *Casebook on ethical principles of psychologists.* Washington, DC: Author.

American Psychological Association (APA). (1987b). *General guidelines for providers of psychological services.* Washington DC: Author.

American Psychological Association (APA). (1987c). *Model act for state licensure of psychologists*. Washington DC: Author.

American Psychological Association Committee on Legal Issues. (1985). White paper on duty to protect. Washington, DC: Author.

American Psychological Association Training Committee. (1987, December). *Resolutions from the National Conference on Graduate Education and Training, June 13–18, 1987*. Washington DC: Author.

American Psychological Association, American Educational Research Association, & the National Council on Measurement in Education. (1974). *Standards for educational & psychological tests*. Washington, DC: American Psychological Association.

Baird, K. A., & Rupert, P. A. (1987). Clinical management of confidentiality: A survey of psychologists in seven states. *Professional Psychology: Research and Practice, 18,* 347–352.

Baker v. United States, 226 F. Supp. 129 (D.C. Iowa 1964).

Bales, J. (1985, July). Single fund could aid mentally ill. *APA Monitor,* p. 14.

Bales, J. (1988, January). Psychiatrist not liable for decision to release. *APA Monitor,* p. 35.

Bales, J. (1988, March). FTC demands end to ad, fee-splitting restrictions. *APA Monitor,* p. 19.

Bales, J. (1988, June). New laws limiting duty to protect. *APA Monitor,* p. 18.

Bales, J. (1988, July). Duty-to-protect issue pressing for guidelines. *APA Monitor,* p. 15.

Baumrind, D. (1985). Research using intentional deception: Ethical issues revisited. *American Psychologist, 40,* 165–174.

Beauchamp, T. L., & Childress, J. F. (1983). *Principles of biomedical ethics* (2nd ed.). New York: Oxford University Press.

Beck, E. S. (1983, March). Counseling colleagues (Letter to the editor). *APA Monitor,* p. 6.

Beck, J. C. (1985). Violent patients and the *Tarasoff* duty in private psychiatric practice. *Journal of Psychiatry and Law, 13,* 361–375.

Bellah v. Greenson, Cal. App. 3d, 141 Cal. Rptr. 92 (1977).

Belter, R. W., & Grisso, T. (1984). Children's recognition of rights violations in counseling. *Professional Psychology: Research and Practice, 15,* 899–910.

Benn, S. I. (1967). Justice. In P. Edwards (Ed.), *The encyclopedia of philosophy* (Vol. 4, pp. 298–302). New York: Macmillan.

Bentham, J. (1970). *The collected works of Jeremy Bentham: An introduction to the principles of morals and legislation*. J. H. Burns & L. A. Hart (Eds.). London: Athlone Press.

Bergin, A. E. (1971). Carl Rogers' contribution to a fully functioning psychology. In A. R. Mahrer & L. Pearson (Eds.), *Creative developments in psychotherapy* (Vol. 1). Cleveland, Ohio: Case Western University Press.

Bergin, A. E. (1980). Psychotherapy and religious values. *Journal of Consulting and Clinical Psychology, 48,* 95–105.

Bernard, J. L., & Jara, C. S. (1986). The failure of clinical psychology graduates to apply understood ethical principles. *Professional Psychology: Research and Practice, 17,* 313–315.

Bernard, J. L., Murphy, M., & Little, M. (1987). The failure of clinical psychologists to apply understood ethical principles. *Professional Psychology: Research and Practice, 18,* 489–491.

Besharov, D. J., & Besharov, S. H. (1987). Teaching about liability. *Social Work, 32*(6), 517–522.

Bouhoutsos, J. (1985). Therapist-client sexual involvement: A challenge for mental health professionals and educators. *American Journal of Orthopsychiatry, 55*(2), 177–182.

Bouhoutsos, J., Holroyd, J., Lerman, H., Forer, B., & Greenberg, M. (1983). Sexual intimacy between psychotherapists and patients. *Professional Psychology: Research and Practice, 14,* 185–196.

Brady v. Hopper, 570 F. Supp. 1333 (D.C. Colo. 1983).

Braithwaite, R. B. (1950). Moral principles and inductive policies. *Proceedings of the British Academy of 1950.* London: Oxford University Press.

Brown, J. E., & Slee, P. T. (1986). Paradoxical strategies: The ethics of intervention. *Professional psychology: Research and Practice, 17,* 487–491.

Buie, J. (1987a, November). Field forging valuable political ties. *APA Monitor,* p. 5.

Buie, J. (1987b, November). Survey spots areas with care shortages. *APA Monitor,* p. 4.

Buie, J. (1987c, November). 12-step program can boost therapy. *APA Monitor,* p. 12.

Buie, J. (1987, December). Trust liability premiums stable for third year. *APA Monitor,* p. 27.

Canadian Psychological Association. (1986). *A Canadian code of ethics for psychologists.* Quebec: Author.

Child Protective Services Program. (1985). *Recognizing and reporting child abuse & neglect: An explanation of Oregon's mandatory reporting law.* Salem, OR: Children's Services Division, Department of Human Resources, State of Oregon.

Cleary, E. W. (Ed.). (1984). *McCormick on evidence* (3rd ed.). St. Paul, MN: West.

Cohen, R. J. (1979). *Malpractice: A guide for mental health professionals.* New York: Free Press.

Cole v. Taylor, 301 N.W.2d 766 (Iowa 1981).

Committee for the Protection of Human Subjects/Institutional Review Board, University of Oregon (1982). *Policy and procedures governing the protection of human subjects*. Eugene: University of Oregon Graduate School, Office of Research Administration.

Corey, M. S., & Corey, G. (1987). *Groups: Process and practice* (3rd ed.). Monterey, CA: Brooks/Cole.

Craddick, R. A. (1975). Sharing oneself in the assessment procedure. *Professional Psychology, 6,* 279–281.

Croghan, L. M. (1974). Encounter groups and the necessity for ethical guidelines. *Journal of Clinical Psychology, 30,* 430–445.

Cummings, N. A., & Sobel, S. S. (1985, Summer). Malpractice insurance: Update on sex claims. *Psychotherapy, 22,* 186–188.

Danish, S. J., & Symer, M. A. (1981). Unintended consequences of requiring a license to help. *American Psychologist, 36,* 13–21.

Davis v. Lhim, 335 N.W. 481 (Mich. App. 1983).

Davis, K. L. (1982). Is confidentiality in group counseling realistic? *Personnel and Guidance Journal, 59,* 197–201.

Deardorff, W. W., Cross, H. J., & Hupprich, W. R. (1984). Malpractice liability in psychotherapy: Client and practitioner perspectives. *Professional Psychology: Research and Practice, 15,* 590–600.

DeKraai, M. B., & Sales, B. D. (1982). Privileged communications of psychologists. *Professional Psychology: Research and Practice, 13,* 372–388.

DeKraai, M. B., & Sales, B. D. (1984). Confidential communications of psychotherapists. *Psychotherapy, 21,* 293–318.

Department of Health and Human Services. (1983). Additional protections for children involved as subjects in research. *Federal Register, 40,* 9814–9820.

Department of Health and Human Services. (January 21, 1986). Final regulations amending basic HHS policy for the protection of human research subjects. *Federal Register, 46,* 8366–8392.

Duncan, J. A. (1976). Ethical considerations in peer group work. *Elementary School Guidance and Counseling, 11,* 59–60.

Edel, A. (1973). Right and good. In P. P. Wiener (Ed.-in-chief), *Dictionary of the History of Ideas* (pp. 173–187). New York: Charles Scribner's Sons.

Ethics Committee of the American Psychological Association. (1986). Report of the ethics committee: 1985. *American Psychologist, 41,* 694–697.

Ethics Committee of the American Psychological Association. (1988). Trends in ethics cases, common pitfalls, and published resources. *American Psychologist, 43,* 564–572.

Ethics statement issued. (1984, May). *APA Monitor,* p. 36.

Farrely, F., & Brandsma, J. (1974). *Provocative therapy.* San Francisco: Shield.

Fisher, K. (1985, May). Charges catch clinicians in cycle of shame, slip-ups. *APA Monitor,* pp. 6–7.

Fleming, J. G., & Maximov, B. (1974). The patient or his victim. *California Law Review, 62,* 1025–1068.

Flexner, A. (1910). *Medical education in the United States and Canada.* New York: Carnegie Foundation.

Foltz, D. (1979, January). CHAMPUS peer review set to begin shortly. *APA Monitor,* pp. 1, 9.

Foltz, D. (1981, August–September). California charges bias in psychology licensing exam. *APA Monitor,* pp. 4, 50.

Freedman, R. J. (1976). The effects of extra-group socializing and alternate sessions on group psychotherapy outcome. *Dissertation Abstracts International, 37*(4-B) 1896–1897.

Freudenberger, H. J. (1984). Impaired clinicians: Coping with "burnout." In P. A. Keller & L. G. Ritt (Eds.), *Innovations in clinical practice: A source book* (Vol. 3., pp. 221–228). Sarasota, FL: Professional Resource Exchange.

Frey, J. (1988, February). From the president. *National Association of Social Workers Newsletter, 10,* pp. 1, 2, 20.

Fulero, S. M. (1988). *Tarasoff:* 10 years later. *Professional Psychology: Research and Practice, 19,* 184–190.

Galinsky, M. J., & Schopler, J. H. (1977). Warning: Groups may be dangerous. *Social Work, 22*(2), 89–94.

Gartrell, N., Herman, J., Olarte, S., Feldstein, M., & Localio, R. (1986). Psychiatrist-patient sexual contact: Results of a national survey, I. Prevalence. *American Journal of Psychiatry, 143*(9), 1126–1131.

Gaza, G. M., Duncan, J. A., & Sisson, P. J. (1971). Professional issues in group work. *Personnel and Guidance Journal, 49,* 637–643.

Gelwick, R., & Gelwick, B. P. (1986, October). *Ethical theories and counseling center decisions: An introduction.* Paper presented at the 35th annual conference of the Association of University and College Center Directors, San Diego, CA.

Goodwin, D. (1987). *Legislative update:* Tarasoff *revisited.* Portland, OR: Oregon Psychological Association.

Gray, L. A., & Harding, A. K. (1988). Confidentiality limits with clients who have the AIDS virus. *Journal of Counseling and Development, 66,* 219–223.

Greenberg, D. F. (1982). Involuntary psychiatric commitments to prevent suicide. In R. B. Edwards (Ed.), *Psychiatry and ethics* (pp. 283–298). Buffalo, NY: Prometheus Books.

Greenberg, L. T. (1984). The evolution of *Tarasoff:* Recent developments in the psychiatrist's duties to warn potential victims, protect the public, and predict dangerousness. *Journal of Psychiatry and Law, 12,* 315–348.

Gross, M. L. (1978). *The psychological society.* New York: Random House.

Gustafson, K. E., & McNamara, J. R. (1987). Confidentiality with minor clients: Issues and guidelines for therapists. *Professional Psychology: Research and Practice, 18,* 503–508.

Haas, L. J., Malouf, J. L., & Mayerson, N. L. (1986). Ethical dilemmas in psychological practice: Results of a national survey. *Professional Psychology: Research and Practice, 17,* 316–321.

Haley, J. (1970). *Uncommon therapy.* New York: W. W. Norton.

Hall, C. S. (1954). *A primer of Freudian psychology.* Cleveland: World.

Hall, J. E., & Hare-Mustin, R. T. (1983). Sanctions and the diversity of ethical complaints against psychologists. *American Psychologist, 38,* 714–729.

Handelsman, M. M., & Galvin, M. D. (1988). Facilitating informed consent for outpatient psychotherapy: A suggested written format. *Professional Psychology: Research and Practice, 19,* 223–225.

Handelsman, M. M., Kemper, M. B., Kesson-Craig, P., McLain, J., & Johnsrud, C. (1986). Use, content, and readability of written informed consent forms for treatment. *Professional Psychology: Research and Practice, 17,* 514–518.

Hare-Mustin, R. T., & Hall, J. E. (1981). Procedures for responding to ethics complaints against psychologists. *American Psychologist, 36,* 1494–1505.

Hare-Mustin, R. T., Marecek, J., Kaplan, A. G., & Liss-Levinson, N. (1979). Rights of clients, responsibilities of therapists. *American Psychologist, 35,* 3–16.

Hargrove, D. S. (1986). Ethical issues in rural mental health practice. *Professional Psychology: Research and Practice, 17,* 20–23.

Hedlund v. Superior Court, 34 Cal. 3d 695, 194 Cal. Rptr. 805 (1983).

Herbert, W. (1979, February). New York Medicaid inquiry tests psychologist–client privilege. *APA Monitor,* p. 40.

Herlihy, B., & Sheeley, U. L. (1988). Counselor liability and the duty to warn: Selected cases, statutory trends, and implications for practice. *Counseling Education and Supervision, 28,* 203–215.

Hogan, D. B. (1979). *The regulation of psychotherapists* (Vols. 1, 3). Cambridge: Ballinger.

Hopewell v. Adebimpe, Pa. Ct. Common Pleas (1981).

Howard, A. (1983). Work samples and simulations in competency evaluation. *Professional Psychology: Research and Practice, 14,* 780–796.

Imber, S. D., Glanz, L. M., Elkin, I., Sotsky, S. M., Boyer, J. L., & Leber, W. R. (1986). Ethical issues in psychotherapy research. *American Psychologist, 41,* 137–146.

Insurance no longer covers sexual misconduct. (1985, February 25). *The Register-Guard,* Eugene, OR, p. 8a.

Jensen, J. P., & Bergin, A. E. (1988). Mental health values of professional therapists: A national interdisciplinary survey. *Professional Psychology: Research and Practice, 19,* 290–297.

Kain, C. D. (1988). To breach or not to breach. Is that the question? A response to Gray and Harding. *Journal of Counseling and Development, 66,* 224–225.

Kanfer, F. H., & Goldstein, A. P. (Eds.). (1980). *Helping people change.* New York: Pergamon Press.

Kant, I. (1886). *The metaphysic of ethics* (J. W. Semple, Trans., H. Calderwood, Ed.). Edinburgh: T. T. Clark.

Kant, I. (1929). *Kant selections.* (T. K. Abbott, Trans., T. M. Green, Ed.). New York: Charles Scribner's Sons.

Katz, N. W. (1979). Behavioral hypnotic inductions. *Journal of Consulting and Clinical Psychology, 47,* 119–127.

Keith-Spiegel, P. (1977). Violations of ethical principles due to ignorance or poor professional judgment versus willful disregard. *Professional Psychology, 8,* 288–296.

Keith-Spiegel, P. (1986, June). *Limits of confidentiality between mate or family members in couples/family therapy: Client waiver form.* Form distributed at the Fall 1987 conference of the Oregon Psychological Association, Portland.

Keith-Spiegel, P., & Koocher, G. P. (1985). *Ethics in psychology: Professional standards and cases.* New York: Random House.

Kelley, P., & Alexander, P. (1985). Part-time private practice: Practical and ethical considerations. *Social Work, 30*(3), 254–258.

Kilburg, R. R., Nathan, P. E., & Thoreson, R. R. (Eds.). (1986). *Professionals in distress: Issues, syndromes, and solutions in psychology.* Washington, DC: American Psychological Association.

Kitchener, K. S. (1984). Intuition, critical evaluation and ethical principles: The foundation for ethical decisions in counseling psychology. *Counseling Psychologist, 12,* 43–55.

Klein, J. I., & Glover, S. I. (1983). Psychiatric malpractice. *International Journal of Law and Psychiatry, 6,* 131–157.

Knapp, S. (1980). A primer on malpractice for psychologists. *Professional Psychology, 11,* 606–612.

Knapp, S., & VandeCreek, L. (1981). Behavioral medicine: Its malpractice risks for psychologists. *Professional Psychology, 12,* 677–683.

Knapp, S., & VandeCreek, L. (1982). *Tarasoff:* Five years later. *Professional Psychology, 13,* 511–516.

Knapp, S., & VandeCreek, L. (1987). *Privileged communications in the mental health professions.* New York: Van Nostrand Reinhold.

Lakin, M. (1986). Ethical challenges of group and dyadic psychotherapies: A comparative approach. *Professional Psychology: Research and Practice, 17,* 454–461.

Landers, S. (1987, July). WA: Livable standard. *APA Monitor,* p. 16.

Landers, S. (1988, January). Practitioners and AIDS: Face-to-face with pain. *APA Monitor,* p. 1.

Leedy v. Harnett, 510 F. Supp. 1125 (M.D. Pa. 1981).

Lieberman, M. A., Yalom, I. D., & Miles, M. B. (1973). *Encounter groups: First facts.* New York: Basic Books.

London, P. (1964). *The modes and morals of psychotherapy.* New York: Holt, Rinehart & Winston.

London, M., & Bray, D. W. (1980). Ethical issues in testing and evaluation for personnel decisions. *American Psychologist, 35,* 890–901.

Lowe, M. C. (1969). *Value Orientations in Counseling and Psychotherapy.* San Francisco: Chandler.

Mahoney, M. J. (1974). *Cognition and behavior modification.* Cambridge, MA: Ballinger.

Mahoney, M. J. (1977). Publication prejudices: An experimental study of confirmatory bias in the peer review system. *Cognitive Therapy and Research, 1,* 161–175.

Mappes, D. C., Robb, G. P., & Engels, D. W. (1985). Conflicts between ethics and law in counseling and psychotherapy. *Journal of Counseling and Development, 64,* 246–252.

Mavroudis v. Superior Court for County of San Mateo, 162 Cal. Rptr. 724 (Ct. App. 1980).

Mead, M. (1932). *Coming of age in Samoa: A psychological study of primitive youth for Western civilization.* New York: Blue Ribbon Books.

Melella, J. T., Travin, S., & Cullen, K. (1987). The psychotherapist's third-party liability for sexual assaults committed by his patient. *Journal of Psychiatry and Law, 15,* 83–116.

Melton, G. B. (1983, December). Progeny of *Tarasoff. APA Monitor,* p. 6.

Melton, G. B. (1983). Toward "personhood" for adolescents. *American Psychologist, 39,* 99–103.

Melton, G. B., & Davidson, H. A. (1987). Child protection and society: When should the state intervene? *American Psychologist, 42,* 172–175.

Mental and Developmental Disabilities Confidentiality Act. (1979, January). *III. Stat. Ann., CA 91 1/2,* §801 et. seq.

Menustik, C. (1986, Fall). Pending business: Ethics committee update. *Oregon Psychology, 33,* 7–9.

Mistrial in Peoples Temple case. (1981, October 9). *Facts on File, Inc.,* pp. 733–734.

Molien v. Kaiser Foundation Hospitals. 167 Cal. Rptr. 831, 616 P.2d 813 (1980).

Moore, R. A. (1985). Ethics in the practice of psychiatry: Update on the results of enforcement of the code. *American Journal of Psychiatry, 142*(9), 1043–1045.

Morris, W. (Ed.) (1981). *The American heritage dictionary of the English language.* Boston: Houghton Mifflin.

Myers v. Quesenberry, 144 Cal. App. 888, 193 Cal. Rptr. 733 (1983).

Narveson, J. (1967). *Morality and utility.* Baltimore: The Johns Hopkins Press.

National Association of Social Workers, Inc. (NASW). (1980). *Code of Ethics.* Washington, DC: Author.

National Association of Social Workers, Inc. (NASW) (1984). *NASW standards for the practice of clinical social work.* Washington, DC: Author.

National Board for Certified Counselors (NBCC). (1987). *Code of ethics* (rev. ed.). Alexandria, VA: Author.

National Board for Certified Counselors (NBCC). (1988). *National counselor certification: Information and application, 1988.* Alexandria, VA: Author.

Noll, J. O. (1981). Material risks and informed consent to therapy. *American Psychologist, 36,* 915–916.

Oklahoma Psychological Association Insurance Committee. (1981, April). A code of ethics for insurance procedures. *APA Monitor,* p. 16.

Oregon Legislative Assembly. (1987). Salem, OR: Committee of the Legislative Assembly, State of Oregon.

Oregon Revised Statutes. (1985). Salem, OR: Legislative Counsel: Committee of the Legislative Assembly, State of Oregon.

Patterson, C. H. (1972). Ethical standards for groups. *The Counseling Psychologist, 3,* 93–101.

Perloff, R. (1987). Self-interest and personal responsibility redux. *American Psychologist, 42,* 3–11.

Peters, J. J. (1973). Do encounter groups hurt people? *Psychotherapy: Theory and Practice, 10,* 33–35.

Plamentatz, J. (1958). *The English utilitarians.* Oxford: Basil Blackwell.

Plotkin, R. (1978, December). The malpractice blues. *APA Monitor,* p. 10.

Pope, K. S. (1987). New trends in malpractice cases and changes in APA liability insurance. *Oregon Psychology, 33*(3), 20–27.

Pope, K. S., Tabachnick, B. G., & Keith-Spiegel, P. (1987). Ethics of practice: The beliefs and behaviors of psychologists as therapists. *American Psychologist, 42,* 993–1006.

Posey, E. C. (1988). Confidentiality in an AIDS support group. *Journal of Counseling and Development, 66,* 226–227.

Prosser, W. L. (1971). *Law of torts* (4th ed.). St. Paul, MN: West.

Rawls, J. (1971). *A theory of justice.* Cambridge, MA: Harvard University Press.

Reaves, R. P. (1982). *Survey of cut-off scores for EPPP.* Printed reference material for the Legal Issues Workshop at the 1982 national conference of the American Psychological Association, Washington, DC.

Redd, W. H., Andresen, G. U., & Minagawa, R. Y. (1982). Hypnotic control of anticipatory emesis in patients receiving cancer chemotherapy. *Journal of Consulting and Clinical Psychology, 30,* 14–19.

Reese, H. W., & Fremouw, W. J. (1984). Normal and normative ethics in behavioral sciences. *American Psychologist, 39,* 863–876.

Reilley, R. R., Dupree, J., Rodolfe, E., & Kraft, W. (1987). Attitudes toward the ethical use of hypnosis: An interdisciplinary study. *American Journal of Clinical Hypnosis, 30,* 132–138.

Roberts, A. L. (1982). Ethical guidelines for group leaders. *Journal for Specialists in Group Work, 7,* 174–181.

Rogler, L. H., Malgady, R. G., Costantino, G., & Blumenthal R. (1987). What do culturally sensitive mental health services mean? The case of Hispanics. *American Psychologist, 42,* 565–570.

Roskam, P. (1979, March). First-person review: CHAMPUS hit on confidentiality. *APA Monitor,* pp. 3, 18.

Ross, W. D. (1930). *The right and the good.* Oxford: Clarendon Press.

Rubanowitz, D. E. (1987). Public attitudes toward psychotherapist–client confidentiality. *Professional Psychology: Research and Practice, 18*, 613–618.

Schopp, R. F., & Quattrocchi, M. R. (1984). *Tarasoff*, the doctrine of special relationships, and the psychotherapist's duty to warn. *Journal of Psychiatry and Law, 12*, 13–37.

Schwitzgebel, R. L., & Schwitzgebel, R. K. (1980). *Law and Psychological Practice*. New York: Wiley.

Semler v. Psychiatric Inst. of Washington, D. C., 538 F.2d 121 (4th Cir. 1976).

Shaw v. Glickman, 415 A.2d 625 (Md. Ct. Spec. App. 1980).

Sieber, J. E., & Stanley, B. (1988). Ethical and professional dimensions of socially sensitive research. *American Psychologist, 43*, 49–55.

Silverstein, C. (1984). *The ethical and moral implications of sexual classification: A commentary*. Unpublished monograph.

Singer, J. L. (1980). The scientific basis of psychotherapeutic practice: A question of values and ethics. *Psychotherapy Theory, Research and Practice, 17*, 372–383.

Slimak, R. E., & Berkowitz, S. R. (1983). The university and college counseling center and malpractice suits. *Personnel and Guidance Journal, 62*, 291–294.

Slovenko, R. (1975). Psychotherapy and confidentiality. *Cleveland State Law Review, 24*, 375–396.

Slovenko, R. (1977). Group psychotherapy: Privileged communication and confidentiality. *Journal of Psychiatry and Law, 5*(3), 405–466.

Slovenko, R. (1981). Malpractice in psychiatry and related fields. *Journal of Psychiatry and Law, 9*, 5–35.

Smith, M. L., & Glass, G. V. (1977). Meta-analysis of psychotherapy outcome studies. *American Psychologist, 32*, 752–760.

Soble, A. (1978). Deception in social science research: Is informed consent possible? *Hasting Center Report, 8*, 40–46.

Soisson, E. L., VandeCreek, L., & Knapp, S. (1987). Thorough record keeping: A good defense in a litigious era. *Professional Psychology: Research and Practice, 18*, 498–502.

Stadler, H. A., Willing, K. L., Eberhage, M. G., & Ward, W. H. (1988). Impairment: Implications for the counseling profession. *Journal of Counseling and Development, 66*, 258–260.

Starr, R. H. (1979). Child Abuse. *American Psychologist, 34*, 872–878.

Steininger, M., Newell, J. D., & Garcia, L. T. (1984). *Ethical issues in psychology*. Homewood, IL: Dorsey Press.

Stone, A. A. (1976). The *Tarasoff* decisions: Suing psychotherapists to safeguard society. *Harvard Law Review, 90*, 358–378.

Stone, A. A. (1986). Vermont adopts *Tarasoff*: A real barn-burner. *American Journal of Psychiatry, 143*(3), 352–355.

Stone, A. S. (1983). Sexual misconduct by psychiatrists: The ethical and clinical dilemma of confidentiality. *American Journal of Psychiatry, 140*(2), 195–197.

Sue, S. (1988). Psychotherapeutic services for ethnic minorities: Two decades of research findings. *American Psychologist, 43,* 301–308.

Suicide—Part I. (1986, February). *The Harvard Medical School Mental Health Letter,* pp. 1–4.

Suicide—Part II. (1986, March). *The Harvard Medical School Mental Health Letter,* pp. 1–4.

Suinn, R. M. (1987, March). Minority issues cut across courses. *APA Monitor,* p. 30.

Swenson, E. V. (1986). Legal liability for a patient's suicide. *Journal of Psychiatry and Law, 14,* 409–444.

Szasz, T. S. (1960). The myth of mental illness. *American Psychologist, 15,* 113–118.

Tarasoff v. Regents of the University of California, 118 Cal. Rptr. 129, 529 P.2d 533 (1974) (*Tarasoff* I).

Tarasoff v. Regents of the University of California, 17 Cal. 3d 425, 551 P.2d 334 (1976) (*Tarasoff* II).

Temerlin, M. K., & Temerlin, J. W. (1982). Psychotherapy cults: An iatrogenic perversion. *Psychotherapy: Theory, Research and Practice, 19,* 131–141.

Thomas, J. (1987, November 23). *The professional and the moral life.* An address given at the annual meeting of the Western Association of Counselor Educators and Supervisors, Portland, OR.

Thompson v. County of Alameda, 614 P.2d 728 (Cal. 1980).

Thompson, A. (1983). *Ethical concerns in psychotherapy and their legal ramifications.* Lanham, MD: University Press of America.

Thompson, A. (1987). Ethical perspectives of some Swiss psychotherapists. *Brennpunkt, 32,* 56–62.

Turkington, C. (1986, May). Setting limits on marketing. *APA Monitor,* pp. 32–33.

Turkington, C. (1986, June). Arizona sues over ad ethics. *APA Monitor,* p. 36.

Turkington, C. (1986, November). Suit data show no need to panic. *APA Monitor,* p. 9.

Tymchuk, A. J., Drapkin, R., Major-Kingsley, S., Ackerman A. B., Coffman, E. W., & Baum, M. S. (1982). Ethical decision making and psychologists' attitudes toward training in ethics. *Professional Psychology, 13,* 412–421.

Tyron, W. W. (1976). Behavior modification therapy and the law. *Professional Psychology, 7,* 468–475.

Vinson, J. S. (1987). Use of complaint procedures in cases of therapist–patient sexual contact. *Professional Psychology: Research and Practice, 18,* 159–164.

Wade, T. C., & Baker, T. B. (1977). Opinions and use of psychological tests: A survey of clinical psychologists. *American Psychologist, 33,* 874–882.

Wand, B., & Weaver, S. J. (1983, December). AASPB on EPPP. *APA Monitor,* p. 6.

Wendorf, D. J., & Wendorf, R. J. (1985). A systemic view of family therapy ethics. *Family Process, 24,* 443–453.

Wiens, A. N., & Menne, J. W. (1981). On disposing of "straw people." *American Psychologist, 36,* 390–395.

Wilson, S. (1984). Privileged communication. In P. A. Keller & L. G. Ritt (Eds.), *Innovations in clinical practice: A source book* (Vol. 3, pp. 391–405). Sarasota, FL: Professional Resource Exchange.

Wise, T. P. (1978). Where the public peril begins: A survey of psychotherapists to determine the effects of *Tarasoff. Stanford Law Review, 31,* 165–190.

Woody, R. H. (1983). Avoiding malpractice in psychotherapy. In P. A. Keller & L. G. Ritt (Eds.), *Innovations in clinical practice: A source book* (Vol. 2, pp. 205–216). Sarasota, FL: Professional Resource Exchange.

Wright, R. H. (1981a). Psychologists and professional liability (malpractice) insurance: A retrospective review. *American Psychologist, 36,* 1485–1493.

Wright, R. H. (1981b). What to do until the malpractice lawyer comes. *American Psychologist, 36,* 1535–1541.

Yalom, I. D. (1980). *Existential psychotherapy.* New York: Basic Books.

Zimpfer, D. G. (1971). Needed: Professional ethics for working with groups. *Personnel and Guidance Journal, 50,* 280–287.

Author Index

Ackerman, A., 133
Adair, J. G., 52
Adams, S., 19, 22, 134
Alexander, P., 26, 61
American Association for
 Counseling and
 Development, 36–37, 38,
 41, 57, 58, 59, 73, 105,
 127, 130, 223
American Association for
 Marriage and Family
 Therapy, 62, 71, 130
American Educational
 Research Association, 44
American Psychiatric
 Association, 58, 71, 77,
 93, 113, 130, 182, 184,
 210
American Psychological
 Association, 25, 26, 29,
 38, 41, 44, 45, 47, 50, 51,
 57, 58, 59, 62, 64, 68, 74,
 84, 98, 106, 108, 110,
 112, 114, 123, 127, 129,
 140–141, 150, 184, 210,
 220, 223
American Psychological
 Association Committee
 on Legal Issues, 175, 179
American Psychological
 Association Training
 Committee, 100
Andressen, G. V., 33

Baird, K. A., 174
Baker, T. B., 44
Bales, J., 29, 62, 98
Baum, M. S., 133
Baumrind, D., 50

Beauchamp, T. L., 2, 4, 6,
 21, 89, 93, 105, 121
Beck, E. S., 137
Beck, J. C., 174
Belter, R. W., 24, 76
Benn, S. I., 89
Bentham, J., 4
Bergin, A. E., 22, 121, 122
Berkowitz, S. R., 157, 165,
 166, 179
Bernard, J. L., 134
Besharov, D. J., 155, 157,
 165, 166, 201
Besharov, S. H., 155, 157,
 165, 166, 201
Blumenthal, R., 100
Bouhoutsos, J. C., 57, 150,
 164
Boyer, J. L., 49
Braithwaite, R. B., 2, 4
Brandsma, J., 37
Bray, D. W., 44
Brown, J. E., 36
Buie, J., 91, 155, 214

Canadian Psychological
 Association, 57, 71, 98,
 106
Child Protective Services
 Program, 190–191
Childress, J. F., 2, 4, 6, 21,
 89, 93, 105, 121
Cleary, E. W., 81
Coffman, E. W., 133
Cohen, R. J., 154, 155,
 159, 160, 161, 199, 200
Committee for the
 Protection of Human
 Subjects/Institutional

Review Board,
 University of Oregon,
 48–49
Corey, G., 42, 128
Corey, M. S., 42, 128
Costantino, G., 100
Craddick, R. A., 8, 45–46,
 165
Croghan, L. M., 127
Cross, H. J., 154
Cullen, K., 172, 174,
 182–183, 188–189
Cummings, N. A., 157, 159

Danish, S. J., 95, 122
Davidson, H. A., 189–190
Davis, K. L., 72
Deardorff, W. W., 154, 166
DeKraai, M. B., 78, 80, 81,
 84
Department of Health and
 Human Services, 47–48,
 78
Drapkin, R., 133
Duncan, J. A., 127
Dupree, J., 122
Dushenko, T. W., 52

Eberhage, M. G., 137
Edel, A., 2
Elkin, I., 49
Engels, D. W., 28, 170,
 185, 191
Ethics Committee of the
 American Psychological
 Association, 29, 57, 58,
 96, 133

Farrely, F., 37
Feldstein, M., 58

Fisher, K., 175, 179
Fleming, J. G., 173, 174, 176
Flexner, A., 146
Foltz, D., 97, 148
Forer, B., 57
Freedman, R. J., 125
Fremouw, W. J., 49
Freudenberger, H. J., 220
Frey, J., 155
Fulero, S. M., 179, 184

Galinsky, M. J., 124
Galvin, M. D., 23, 24
Garcia, L. T., 4
Gartrell, N., 58
Gaza, G. M., 127
Gelwick, B. P., 4
Gelwick, R., 4
Glanz, L. M., 49
Glass, G. V., 90
Glover, S. I., 155, 157, 175
Goldstein, A. P., 20
Goodwin, D., 177
Gray, L. A., 181
Greenberg, D. F., 197–199
Greenberg, L. T., 172, 173, 174, 176, 177, 178, 179, 180, 181
Greenberg, M., 57
Grisso, T., 24, 76
Gross, M. L., 17, 31, 90
Gustafson, K. E., 76, 77, 78

Haas, L. J., 132, 174
Haley, J., 35
Hall, C. S., 213
Hall, J. E., 131
Handelsman, M. M., 23, 24
Harding, A. K., 181
Hare-Mustin, R. T., 21, 22, 33, 37, 122, 131
Hargrove, D. S., 60
Herbert, W., 97
Herlihy, B., 178, 180
Herman, J., 58
Hogan, D. B., 9, 139, 144–146, 149, 153–154, 157, 158

Holroyd, J., 57
Howard, A., 147
Hupprich, W. R., 154

Imber, S. D., 49

Jara, C. S., 134
Jensen, J. P., 22, 122
Johnsrud, C., 23

Kain, C. D., 181, 182
Kanfer, F. H., 20
Kant, I., 3, 6, 207, 208, 216
Kaplan, A. G., 21, 22, 33, 37, 122
Katz, N. W., 33
Keith-Spiegel, P., 57, 72, 132, 134, 136, 174, 188
Kelley, P., 26, 61
Kemper, M. B., 23
Kesson-Craig, P., 23
Kilburg, R. R., 137
Kitchener, K. S., 6, 122
Klein, J. I., 155, 157, 175
Knapp, S., 81, 82, 83, 109, 110, 111, 158, 166, 170, 175, 177, 180, 185, 201
Koocher, G. P., 57
Kraft, W., 122

Lakin, M., 42, 43, 124, 128
Landers, S., 177, 181, 182, 184
Leber, W. R., 49
Lerman, H., 57
Lieberman, M. A., 121, 126, 127
Lindsay, R. C. L., 52
Liss-Levinson, N., 21, 22, 33, 37, 122
Little, M., 134
Localio, R., 58
London, P., 16, 44
Lowe, M. C., 15

Mahoney, M. J., 34, 37, 38, 91
Major-Kingsley, S., 133
Malgady, R. G., 100
Malouf, J. L., 132, 174

Mappes, D. C., 28, 170, 185, 191
Marecek, J., 21, 22, 33, 37, 122
Maximov, B., 173, 174, 176
Mayerson, N. L., 132, 174
McLain, J., 23
McNamara, J. R., 76, 77, 78
Mead, M., 1
Melella, J. T., 172, 174, 182–183, 188–189
Melton, G. B., 24, 26, 171, 180, 189–190
Menne, J. W., 147, 150
Menustik, C., 136
Miles, M. B., 121, 126, 127
Moore, R. A., 133–134
Morris, W., 3
Murphy, M., 134

Narveson, J., 2
Nathan, P. E., 137
National Association of Social Workers, Inc., 58, 59, 64–65, 71, 130, 209–210, 220
National Board for Certified Counselors, 58, 64, 150
National Council on Measurement in Education, 44
Newell, J. D., 4
Noll, J. O., 68

Oklahoma Psychological Association Insurance Committee, 96
Olarte, S., 58
Oregon Legislative Assembly, 142
Oregon Revised Statutes, 79, 141, 184
Orgel, M., 19, 22, 134

Patterson, C. H., 126, 127
Perloff, R., 7, 207–208
Peters, J. J., 127
Plamentatz, J., 4

Plotkin, R., 113, 158, 165
Pope, K. S., 134, 136, 154, 156–157, 174, 188, 199, 223
Posey, E. C., 182
Prosser, W. L., 163

Quattrocchi, M. R., 171–172, 173, 174, 175, 176

Rawls, J., 89, 94
Reaves, R. P., 148
Redd, W. H., 33
Reese, H. W., 49
Reilley, R. R., 122
Robb, G. P., 28, 170, 185, 191
Roberts, A. L., 41, 42, 71, 73, 116, 126, 128
Rodolfe, E., 123
Rogler, L. H., 100, 101
Roskam, P., 97
Ross, W. D., 5, 105, 121, 207, 215, 216
Rubanowitz, D. E., 174, 188
Rupert, P. A., 174

Sales, B. D., 78, 80, 81, 84
Schopler, J. H., 124
Schopp, R. F., 171–172, 173, 174, 175, 176
Schwitzgebel, R. K., 36, 68, 72, 79, 83, 112, 191

Schwitzgebel, R. L., 36, 68, 72, 79, 83, 112, 191
Sieber, J. E., 50
Silverstein, C., 16, 17
Singer, J. L., 47
Sisson, P. J., 127
Slee, P. T., 36
Slimak, R. E., 157, 165, 166, 179
Slovenko, R., 72, 82, 90, 176, 200–201
Smith, M. L., 90
Sobel, S. S., 157, 159
Soble, A., 51
Soisson, E. L., 109, 110, 111, 201
Sotsky, S. M., 49
Stadler, H. A., 137
Stanley, B., 50
Starr, R. H., 188, 189
Steininger, M., 4
Stone, A. A., 169, 175, 176, 178
Stone, A. S., 132
Sue, S., 101
Suinn, R. M., 99, 100
Swenson, E. V., 197, 199, 200, 201
Symer, M. A., 95, 122
Szasz, T. S., 17, 18

Tabachnick, B. G., 134, 136, 174, 188
Temerlin, J. W., 38, 43, 125
Temerlin, M. K., 38, 43, 125

Thomas, J., 7, 207
Thompson, A., 32, 37, 108, 116, 122, 128, 159, 161, 185, 192
Thoreson, R. R., 137
Travin, S., 172, 174, 182–183, 188–189
Turkington, C., 26, 27, 28, 154, 155
Tymchuk, A. J., 133
Tyron, W. W., 158

VandeCreek, L., 81, 82, 83, 109, 110, 111, 158, 175, 177, 180, 185, 201
Vinson, J. S., 135

Wade, T. C., 44
Wand, B., 144
Ward, W. H., 137
Weaver, S. J., 149
Wendorf, D. J., 35, 72
Wendorf, R. J., 35, 72
Wiens, A. N., 147, 150
Willing, K. L., 137
Wilson, S., 80
Wise, T. P., 174
Woody, R. H., 162, 165
Wright, R. H., 154, 165, 166–167

Yalom, I. D., 91, 121, 126, 127

Zimper, D. G., 116, 127

Subject Index

Adolescents, 23–24, 75–79. *See also*
  Children
Advertising, 27–29, 41, 218, 219
Advocacy, 18, 23–24, 32, 35, 132, 189
Assent of children, 49, 78
Assessment of clients, 43–46, 73, 77, 99,
  114, 140, 142, 156, 189, 201
Autonomy, 13, 61, 73, 90, 95, 103, 111,
  115, 165, 166, 174, 187, 188, 194, 196

Beneficence, 37, 41, 42, 44, 51, 59, 72, 81,
  103, 119, 166, 176, 190, 215, 218
Burnout of therapists, 220

Causation, legal, 163, 200
Certification, 139, 141, 151
Child abuse, 17, 23, 81, 123, 174, 182–183,
  219
Children, 17, 20, 36, 43, 46, 49, 76–79,
  172, 174, 178, 179, 182–183, 212
Coercion of clients or research
  participants, 18, 21, 25, 41, 42, 50, 69,
  123, 127, 157
Commitment, psychiatric, 155, 157, 169,
  170, 173–174, 176, 194, 196, 197–198,
  202
Competency:
  of clients, 22, 23–24, 79, 95, 194
  of counselors, 28, 45, 61, 69, 72, 75, 83,
    108, 113–115, 119, 121, 122, 130, 133,
    137, 139, 143, 144, 146–149, 164, 172,
    209, 213–216, 217, 219
  of parents, 74, 76, 79
  of trainees, 39, 70
Complaints against therapists, 57–59, 64,
  130, 132, 133–134, 139, 143, 149–150,
  170, 185
Confidentiality, 22, 23, 24, 44, 48, 96, 108,
  109, 111–113, 132, 154, 156, 157, 173,
  174, 176, 180, 182, 184, 188, 192, 201,
  218

Consulting, 22, 37, 63, 71–72, 82, 83,
  113–115, 128, 132, 140, 157, 165–166,
  169, 185, 192, 201, 219
Continuing education, 100, 113, 139, 216,
  217
Couples, 60, 67, 71–72, 82, 83, 96
Crime, 17, 81, 82, 109, 146, 159, 160, 174,
  198, 208, 211
Crises, 24, 93, 106, 109, 166, 185, 195
Cults of psychotherapists, 38–39, 43, 125

Deception, 26, 28, 47, 50–52, 61
Dependency, 13, 75, 107, 116, 125, 158,
  196
Diagnosis
  and confidentiality, 67, 68, 69, 74, 79,
    81, 82
  of dangerousness, 183, 198, 202
  impact of, 16–18, 43–46, 90, 92, 95–97,
    109, 110, 111, 122, 210, 212
  and licensure, 140, 142
  and malpractice, 156, 157, 165
Dual relationships, 35, 56–59, 122. *See
  also* Sexual relationships

Employee Assistance Programs, 73
Ethical theory, 35
Ethnic and cultural minorities, 44, 99–101,
  148, 192
Expert witnesses, 21, 162–163
Expertise of clients, 19
Expertise of therapists, 19, 23, 31, 34,
  55–56, 122–123, 142, 162, 183

Family, 23, 25, 51, 60, 69, 70, 71, 72,
  75–78, 82, 83, 90, 92, 95, 100, 112,
  114–115, 139, 140, 142, 175, 183, 185,
  188, 189, 190, 191, 195, 202
Fees:
  of clients, 23, 28, 31, 61, 166, 185, 216
  legal, 160, 163

licensure, 143, 146, 149
Fidelity, 43–44, 53, 96, 97, 103, 106, 174, 187, 188. *See also* Dual relationships; Sexual relationships
Files, *see* Records
Friendship, 25, 32, 35, 49, 51, 56–57, 59, 69, 75–76, 95, 115, 195, 202

Gifts from clients, 60
Groups:
    of clients, 41–43, 60, 67, 71–73, 82–83, 91, 92, 99, 104, 115–116, 123–128, 180, 182
    of therapists, 38–39, 165, 219, 220
Guardians, 51, 75–79

Homicide, 75, 79, 81, 109, 168–186, 218
Hypnotism, 33

Impaired therapists, 130, 137, 219
Indigenous clients, 97–98, 108, 216
Informed consent, 20–29, 36, 39–40, 41, 45, 47–50, 110, 127, 218, 219, 221
Insurance, *see* Third-party payments
Intervention, 20, 35, 38, 49, 124, 189, 194–196, 199

Justice, 44, 69, 81, 87, 103, 149, 175, 211, 215, 216

Legislation:
    and child abuse, 190–191
    and confidentiality, 78
    and dangerous clients, 169, 180, 183, 184
    and insurance benefits, 214
    and licensure, 90, 139–143, 150
    and suicide, 199
Licensure, 59, 90, 121, 135, 136, 183, 212, 215, 217

Malpractice, 21, 23, 36, 59, 106, 110, 121, 130, 136, 168, 171, 194, 196, 199–201, 218, 219
Minimal risk research, 47–49
Minority groups, *see* Ethnic and cultural minorities
Minors, *see* Adolescents; Children

Nonmaleficence, 37, 44, 51, 59, 61, 62, 68, 74, 77, 79, 81, 96, 98, 103, 105, 106, 107, 113–115, 119, 218–219

Paradoxical techniques, 35
Paraphilias, sexual, 7, 183
Paternalism, 81, 106–107, 111, 195
Practicum counselors, *see* Trainees
Privileged communication, 79–84, 177, 180, 218
Punitive damages, 161

Record keeping, 23, 48, 70, 73, 74, 77, 78, 79, 83, 84, 108–113, 149, 201, 218
    client access to, 111–113
Referral, 25, 44, 59, 61, 68, 73, 74, 75, 96, 113–114, 116, 130, 131, 162, 166
Research:
    and APA code, 129
    and Autonomy, 47–52, 218
    and client records, 108, 113
    and groups, 125, 126
    and value of crisis counseling, 195
    and value of psychotherapy, 90, 145
    and value of self-help books, 123

Self-Interest, 45, 96, 97, 110, 111, 114, 129, 148, 165–167, 168, 175, 187, 191, 196, 205
Sexual relationships, 17, 56–59, 78, 109, 123, 135–136, 146, 150, 156, 157, 163, 164, 166, 169, 181–183, 188–189, 191, 218
Subpoenas, 83–84, 111, 166, 218
Suicide, 75, 79, 93, 109, 125, 126, 165–166, 174, 190, 211, 218, 219
Supervision, 22, 25, 70, 71, 131, 139, 141, 143, 165
    by peers, 115, 131, 217, 219

Testing, 43–46, 48, 91, 108, 110, 111, 112, 146–149
Third-party payments, 59, 68, 74, 95–97, 98, 107, 109, 143, 144, 165, 212–214
Trainees, 39, 70, 114, 131, 141, 162, 216

Utilitarianism, 50

Violence, 119, 170, 172, 175, 177, 178, 179, 180, 183, 184, 219. *See also* Child abuse; Homicide; Suicide

Waiver of confidentiality, 81, 132